'The debate over land will occupy more of our time. Answers must be found, and quickly too. This is particularly so in the light of sentiments in predominantly black areas and after the recent elections. Stephen Meintjes and Michael Jacques have set out in *Our Land, Our Rent, Our Jobs* a comprehensive exploration of ways in which there can be a shift away from taxation of our labour and capital to the collection of land rentals instead, both in South Africa and elsewhere, which will stimulate growth of both small and large businesses.

'Let the ideas in this book be looked at with an open mind. They could be slotted into traditional beliefs, accepted in part, or even scrapped in their entirety.

'But they must be debated, for only in this manner can solutions to the crisis be found.'

**Dr Thami Mazwai**

* * *

'This is a well-researched book that confronts an uncomfortable yet inevitable discussion.

'Leaders across the continent have been considering policies that have had limited success in the past. A "land rent" based approach could answer some developmental questions for the continent. If Africa can quantify its immense resource potential and harness it through an effective land rental regime, underdevelopment and poverty can be effectively tackled.'

**Percy Takunda**

'Steve Meintjes with his background of being a student of history, law and investment analysis, makes a massive contribution to South Africa and potentially the world with this visionary book. Together with his friend, the late Michael Jacques, he challenges us to totally rethink the nature of taxation. They propose a radical change – but one that falls neatly in line with the Freedom Charter and the Consititution.

'Given the challenges of finding an equitable and efficient system for raising revenue, their proposals cause us to think creatively "out of the box".

'In so doing they also provide a refreshing look at how South Africa's pressing problems of job creation, rapid economic growth, revenue shortfalls, corruption, and poverty can be alleviated.

'There is a compelling logic to their argument and they present practical ways and means for this alternative system to be introduced. Their comprehensive analysis relating to various sectors of the economy is commendable. This new concept (albeit old in its origin) stimulates us mentally and is worthy of serious consideration.

'Much detail needs to be worked through and the book is intended to stimulate thoughtful contributions from Economists, Businessmen, Politicians, the Treasury, Academics, and Students – as well as all those who would like to see the South African economy lifted onto a strong growth path for all.'

**Kennedy Maxwell**

# OUR **LAND**
# OUR **RENT**
# OUR **JOBS**

# OUR **LAND**
# OUR **RENT**
# OUR **JOBS**

### Uncovering the explosive potential
### for growth via resource rentals

Stephen Meintjes | Michael Jacques

SHEPHEARD-WALWYN (PUBLISHERS) LTD

First published in 2014 by
Quickfox, Cape Town, South Africa

This edition published in 2015 by
Shepheard-Walwyn (Publishers) Ltd
107 Parkway House, Sheen Lane
London SW14 8LS
www.shepheard-walwyn.co.uk and
www.ethicaleconomics.org.uk

British Library Cataloguing in Publication Data
A catalogue record of this book
is available from the British Library

ISBN: 978-0-85683-504-9

Typeset by Alacrity,
Sandford, Somerset
Printed and bound in the United Kingdom
by Short Run Press Ltd, Exeter

# Contents

# List of Figures

# List of Tables

# Acknowledgements

IT WAS PROFESSOR Peter Rose who, in the darkness before the dawn of the new South Africa, when Michael Jacques and I were worried about the unemployment and poverty we anticipated it would suffer, said we should publish our vision of the 'broad sunlit uplands' we had in mind for our country. Contrary to his suggestions, however, we wrote[1] in a Townships dialogue format. This proved hopelessly inadequate in the face of the newly triumphant and unchallenged orthodoxy of the Washington consensus that dominated mainstream economics, let alone the euphoria, turbulence and jostling of agendas that accompanied the transition to democracy. Many years later, as our worst fears began to materialise, we returned to the drawing board with a more orthodox, and hopefully thorough, approach.

Having worked together for decades on the practical aspects of resource rental collection it was a great shock and setback when Michael Jacques died in January 2009, just when he was in full harness with lance tilted at all the ridiculous and counterproductive aspects of modern taxation. Soon afterwards, however, Jill Jacques said, 'Finish the book!' So 'we' did. Apart from the chapters specifically written by Michael – including those to do with Adam Smith, of whose work he was a perceptive admirer – his thoughts and likely responses to new questions continued to guide and inspire. We have also benefited from the work of the Economics Faculty of the School of Economic Science, under the leadership of Ian Mason, and inputs from South African Georgists such as Peter Meakin and Godfrey Dunkley.

Discussions with many economists, businessmen and political analysts have also been of invaluable help to us.

As to the originality of the ideas in this book, readers will probably gather that they are restricted mainly to some of the more detailed

---

1 Meintjes, S. and Jacques, M., *The Trial of Chaka Dlamini – An Economic Scenario for the New South Africa*, Amagi Books, Johannesburg, 1990.

aspects of the practical proposals for South Africa. The text makes it clear that these principles have long been expounded by the likes of Adam Smith, David Ricardo, Henry George, Fred Harrison and Professor Mason Gaffney, all of whom are quoted and referenced. Farmers and agricultural experts including Chris Stimie have also patiently heard us out, while Clara Msinga, a leader of the Kgautswane community near Burgersfort, helped with valuable insights into the plight of rural communities.

Thanks are due to my family and my wife Simone for their patience and support. For all errors and shortcomings, we accept full responsibility.

Finally, to all the energetic actors on the local economic stage, from the unemployed, protesting township dwellers and striking unionists to baffled bosses and battling politicians, we acknowledge your efforts to solve our problems, as we have long wished to participate in the debate. But without a full exposition of what is, in effect, a new paradigm, we have felt unable to do so. Hopefully from now on our contributions, of which this book is perhaps only the beginning, will be better understood and in addition be of some use.

# Foreword

THIS BOOK IS, in a sense, immediate and topical and in another, universal and timeless. The former refers to the ongoing debate on the nationalisation of mines and the redistribution of agricultural land. Rent arises in the consideration of the optimal and productive allocation of resources. By this common definition, rent is understood in a very limited and not entirely accurate sense as referring to returns and particularly the (super) profits accruing to owners of resources for their use by others. The crisis then is inequitable ownership of resources and the legitimacy of existing property rights. This has been the emphasis of current discourse insofar as it is applicable to land in the strict sense and its use for primary production.

Much more subtle, and often overlooked, is the sense in which rent arises in the context of the reproduction of resources in the theory of value. The Ricardian conception of economic rent qua locational advantage that should accrue to any factor of production, including land itself for its use in production, is both more relevant and general. It relates returns to factors of production to the margin of production, which is the production generated on the best available rent-free equivalent. Rent, then, is the difference between the productive capacity of a factor and its margin of production. By this definition, the usual relationship between productivity and returns is spurious because it neglects that the monopoly power of owners of resources derives from locational advantages and not from the appropriation of marginal returns. The associated returns are then much higher and so a large proportion of revenue remains uncollected for use elsewhere. By this understanding characteristic crisis is a tendency towards stagnation; the increasing, successive underutilisation of resources.

It is the adverse consequence of the misappropriation of rent by the second definition that explains the secular decline apparent in South Africa today. All actual returns have systematically diverged from potential returns. Land, labour and capital all earn lower returns than those suggested by potential returns. This book applies this observation in explaining that both urban and rural resources lie redundant. The issue is not that resources are scarce and concentrated. It is that a staggering number of existing resources are not in use at all. It is this that policy should seek to address. This book can then be understood as illustrating what might happen in the event that it does not.

**Nobantu Mbeki**

*School of Economic and Business Sciences*
*University of the Witwatersrand*

# Preface

## Collecting the resource rentals that belong to the people of South Africa

WE SEEM TO have reached some sort of consensus – at last. Poverty is the real issue. Employment, with real jobs, is the single most critical social and economic issue to be resolved in South Africa today – and this needs to be tackled with the utmost urgency. As it happens, the solution is obvious and to hand. We will argue that, at its root, the problem really stems from a failure of the taxation system – a failure to collect natural and community-created rentals. Destructive taxes on labour and consumption, such as PAYE and VAT, are not only stifling economic growth, but are the principal cause of the apparently intractable unemployment problem. Regressive taxation oppresses the poor and depresses economic activity in marginal areas, which is exactly where job creation requires stimulation. Moreover, even in prime, mostly metropolitan areas, full collection of these rentals would provide the stimulus that is distinctly lacking in the prevailing situation of gross economic underperformance. The solution: collect the rent, stimulate rapid economic growth, and finally release the grip of the dead hand of taxation on employment.

Our argument is simply that South Africa can eliminate unemployment and achieve rapid economic growth by collecting the natural and community-created rentals on land and other natural resources instead of inflicting mostly destructive taxes on labour and consumption.

The practical proposals that follow show that the collection of resource rentals in a developing economy like South Africa's can take effect in a surprisingly short time.

Right at the outset, however, we need to recognise that this situation is a part of a global phenomenon.

So what, then, has the global credit crisis, for example, got to do with our proposal that South Africans act like owners of their own land and other natural resources by charging a rental for their use, instead of taxing themselves for working and risking their capital?

Well, everything actually.

For a start, houses – the decline in prices of which sparked the sub-prime and then the global credit crises – are still, even in this era of technology, built on land! And, as we shall see, if our proposals had been adopted, the crisis simply could never have happened.

## 'We must get homes for the poor.'

The roots of the crisis lie deep indeed, but the seemingly laudable aim to extend home ownership to record levels, which motivated the Clinton Administration in 1992, is a good place to start. Clinton's Housing and Urban Development Agency took aim at the banking criteria that seemed to exclude the poor from ever owning a roof over their heads, and strong-armed the banks into granting more mortgages. Not only were practices such as redlining strictly forbidden, but lending performances were closely scrutinised for evidence of prejudice against minority groups, especially Hispanics and blacks.

After initial protests, not only did banks eventually make millions from these loans, but they thought of wheezes to turn the whole process to their advantage. Since it was recognised that loans to individuals with poor payment or employment records were indeed 'sub-prime', banks 'sliced and diced' or put them into packages with varying grades of better-quality mortgages. Lo and behold, this process of securitisation, blessed by the profligate issue of credit default swaps by the giant insurer AIG, led supposedly strict ratings agencies to give these packages investable ratings. This enabled them, together with other 'asset backed securities', to be taken off their balance sheets and sold worldwide as safe, high yielding investments suitable for pension funds, and widows and orphans. Instead of the traditional, more modest profits on mortgage loans advanced and paid back over 20 years, the banks were able to make the raising fees and on-selling profits again and again. This practice, aided and abetted by remarks from Greenspan and Bernanke to the effect that 'long-term, house prices do not decline,' helped pump up the property bubble, which, in turn, provided collateral for the mega-loans advanced by investment banks for hundreds of massive mergers and acquisitions, many of which failed to enhance economic productivity. And the rest, as they say, is the history of why we are where we are.

'Yes,' you may say, 'so land speculation lay at the heart of the global credit crisis, but how would our proposals have prevented this from happening and what was wrong with Clinton's idea in the first place?'

## The myth of ever-rising house prices

Unimproved land prices are the market's best estimate of the present value of uncollected land rentals. Had these been collected by the government, rising land prices, on which the myth of ever-rising house prices was based, would not have been available for collateral. Housing loans, therefore, would have been just that, i.e. for the bricks and mortar and not the land. With no capital payment for land, houses would have cost a lot less as well! As we shall see, failure by government to collect rising land rentals has enabled banks to default to the somnolent model of a collateral-based lending order, which has encouraged excessive consumption and deficient production. Because land values naturally increase with rising populations and increasing productivity, land prices have, in the absence of land rental collection, tended to increase accordingly. Since every man and his dog understands the long-term trend – and bankers have often been all too obliging – speculation usually drives land prices way past any reasonable estimate of the present values of uncollected rentals. Hence the long-term prevalence of cycles of boom and bust.

## So what about our jobs?

The global credit crisis might well seem worlds away both in time and causality from South Africa in 2014 amid huge anxiety around job creation. But we are following the same model and we, too, will go nowhere unless we change it! Yes, South Africa was fortunate enough to have stuck to relatively responsible fiscal and monetary policies as well as, at a crucial time, to have wisely reigned in irresponsible lending with the National Credit Act. We are also fortunate enough to have seen from a distance how the American political and financial sectors combined to pump up mainly land-based collateral, from subprime mortgages to the mega-billions in exotic securities traded on Wall Street, with disastrous economic consequences. How many of your banking friends are prepared to tell you with a straight face that our much-maligned exchange control did not play a role in preventing us from following suit? The fact of the matter, as we hope forcefully to show, is that the deeply flawed Western banking systems are a direct outcome of the fundamental failure of governments to collect land

and other natural resource rentals. Their taxation instead of economic activity is likewise hugely destructive of jobs.

## Why South Africa?

In a way this is a silly question. Yet we have to ask it because our proposals mean we have to take a lead, and so far, all we have done is timorously follow some (by now discredited) Eurocentric economic models. We will answer this question at length, but right now we can say we have much more going for us than even our optimists think! For example, until recently, we had one of the world's most successful and widely applied municipal site value rating systems (the abolition of which in Johannesburg, at any rate, has led to the proliferation of blackjack farms). Even the horrendous Anglo-Saxon land ownership model results from a Norman overlay on a relatively egalitarian society and land tenure system, with some features not far removed from the traditional African tribal model. For the most part, our Roman Dutch system of land tenure is well-suited to the higher levels of transparency in ownership that will be required to implement the necessary changes. Then again, from the most unlikely source, i.e. gold mining, we have a tried-and-proven tax system that readily lends itself as a means of collecting natural resource rentals for the mining industry as whole. But above all, South Africans, with their love of the land, are not about to fall for the accounting practices that allow land to dwindle to insignificant proportions on company balance sheets, nor will they accept economic models that treat land as 'no different from any other form of capital'. We all, without exception, understand the importance of land! Finally, the desperation with which 'new' plans are formulated for growth is directly related to the huge need for jobs. There is a limit to the efficacy of 'plans burble' in warding off mass discontent. Yes, action is required rather than proliferating red tape. But actually it's just the tax jungle that needs clearing. It's taxes that are shackling growth! It's their replacement by natural resource rental collection that will incentivise businesses and turn the former homeland sinkholes of poverty into thriving growth partners for the rest of South Africa.

## How?

So how do we propose to collect this rent, and we are sure you're also thinking, 'Would it be enough and wouldn't it be too radical for the economy and foreign investors to stomach?'

Well, the answer to this is that after a few chapters dealing with why we should collect rent, most of the remainder are about the nitty-gritty of how it should be done.

We will spell out how a rental can be collected equal to the annual market value of the permanent use of a particular piece of land or other natural resource. In principle, this will replace taxation, except on activities that the community explicitly wishes to discourage. Yes, there will be some exceptions and a phasing-in period, as well as special measures for collection of rent in various areas such as the mining and fishing industries, as well as the use of the electromagnetic spectrum. Yes, there will also be arguments about the value of particular pieces of land and other natural resources; but in contrast to the sterile debates on tax evasion and avoidance, they will be productive because they will relate to the best use of our patrimony. Tax dodging will become history, since you cannot hide South African land or park it in Bermuda!

Finally, we will show that collecting the rent is not simply another proposal for tinkering with the tax system, but is about unleashing a mighty force for economic regeneration and vitality. Here's how:

- Since they will be paying in full for it anyway, whether they use it efficiently or not, all landowners, urban as well as rural, will be incentivised to maximise production.

- Withholding land from use, or underutilising it, for speculation, won't pay any more: it will be 'use it or lose it' throughout the economy.

- Replacing all indirect taxes with natural resource rentals will be a huge boon to all sites with minimal locational advantage, such as many of our rural areas, and hence, there may be little or no resource rental to pay, so economic activity there can thrive and survive even during tough times.

- By the same token, the South African Revenue Services will no longer be the bogeyman chasing marginal businesses for VAT and PAYE and pushing them into bankruptcy.

- Effectively, this will revitalise economic activity in all the depressed rural areas that 'support' nearly half the country's population.

- Given the direct link between the quality of service delivery, land values and their income, government at all levels will have a much more powerful incentive to deliver.

- Sterile tax debates and avoidance stratagems that consume billions become instead an examination of the best use of natural resources.
- By immediately providing all people with the full value for all their land, the deep-seated and emotionally explosive attitudes around land reform will be defused.
- Ongoing programmes for a better distribution of land ownership can proceed in a much more constructive context.
- With one of the most profound causes of poverty and unemployment laid bare, labour and business will see that they are partners rather than adversaries. This, in turn, will lead to the easing of many regulations stifling business and aborting jobs.
- Mass housing – currently a big white elephant in many rural areas – will not only be cheaper, but will actually attract businesses to what will be in effect any number of 'tax-free' zones.
- Banks will be incentivised to lend more for production rather than consumption or speculation.
- With businesses in prime areas really incentivised, and with the rural areas becoming a new 'trading partner' instead of being a millstone around the neck of the economy, economic growth will accelerate so as to enable the National Development Plan to surpass its otherwise unattainable aspirations.

In short, to explain 'how' is why we are writing this book, which we hope, will be interesting; not least because it shows how we can and must do away with most taxes! Nor do we pretend that our 'how' is the last word on the subject. Far from it. But if it stimulates vigorous debate on the best ways to do it, we will have achieved our goal. We have faith in the acumen of our business folk and economists, as well as the common sense of our people to see it through. So, while the present system is battling in vain against the forces of nature, we propose to harness and unleash them so as to achieve that level of abundance which is appropriate for the dignity of all South Africans, and is their natural birth right.

**Michael Jacques and Stephen Meintjes**
**2013**

## CHAPTER I

# TAXES, PLEASE, OR ELSE!

*'To tax and to please, no more than to love and
be wise, is not given to men.'*[1]
Edmund Burke

## Why we pay our suppliers …

### A dialogue

*Question:* Why do you pay your suppliers?

*Answer:* Assuming that's a serious question, I pay my suppliers for two main reasons. First, I have a contract – sometimes verbal, but generally in writing – in the form of an order; secondly, if I don't pay them (assuming they delivered the right goods or services on time and at the agreed price), my supplies will be cut off and my business will grind to a halt.

*Question:* OK, next question: why do you pay your rent?

*Answer:* As with the first question, because I have a contract with the landlord that allows me to use premises that at present are optimal for my business; that is suitable premises in the right location for a good rent.

*Question:* Finally, why do you pay your taxes?

*Answer:* Now you're talking! Simply because if I don't, my business will be closed down and I'll probably end up in jail or bankrupt. With the other two questions there is a definite quid pro quo: arm's length transactions where I pay for what I get. If I can get a better deal elsewhere, I'm free to take it up. With taxation, I have no such choice (other than to move my business to another country) and quite

---

1 *Thoughts on the Cause of the Present Discontents*, 1770.

1

frankly, it is difficult to see what direct benefits I receive. As for the direct benefits I do get, like utilities and garbage collection, I pay for them anyway.

*Question:* So what you are saying is that while tax is a business expense like supplies and services, wages and rent, tax does not have the same relationship to your business output that the other expenses have?

*Answer:* Well, income tax does have a loose relationship with the profits I make, but one couldn't cost this into the selling price of my products or services. Then there are a myriad other taxes: some of these, like customs and excise duties can be costed into the relevant products, but many taxes are so sneaky that we hardly know they exist. The problem with this is that most businesses try to overcompensate for these taxes in their product pricing. If you can get away with it, fine, but this must be inflationary.

## ... is not for the same reason we pay tax!

Taxes have been extracted from citizens by brute force since people started living in homogenous social, religious or economic units, known as states, ruled by a governing entity that has power over its citizens.

The ancient Persian ruler, Artaxerxes (ca. 440 BCE), put it like this: 'The authority of the prince must be defended by military force; that force can only be maintained by taxes; all taxes must, at last, fall upon agriculture, and agriculture can never flourish except under the protection of justice and moderation.'[2]

So first of all, the authority of the prince (government) must be defended by 'military force' (army and police). Today we can add treaties with other countries and the nebulous concepts of patriotism, nationality and citizenship. In modern times, these matters require organs of state that go way beyond just the army and police. And these organs of state can only be maintained, as Artaxerxes puts it, by taxes.

Then he says, 'All taxes must, at last, fall upon agriculture.' Today we could say 'any wealth-producing activity'. The words, 'at last', are taken to mean 'when it can no longer be passed on to anyone else'. So regardless of how (or from whom) a state tries to collect its taxes, they can, at the end of the day, only be paid by a wealth-producing entity.

2 Gibbon, E., *The History of the Decline and Fall of the Roman Empire*, Methuen & Co., London, 1909, p.228.

Brute force apart, is there any reason for this universal, albeit reluctant, acceptance of tax?

The concept of taxation goes back in time well before that of Artaxerxes. Probably hundreds of different types of taxes have been imposed over the millennia and they all have one common feature: they were imposed by rulers who had the power to do so. So over time, taxation seems to have been built into our social and economic genetic structure, and today almost everyone accepts it as a necessary evil.

How did taxation, which is not a factor of production, come to claim such a large portion of wealth and then, in value-added financial statements, come to usurp a place as a factor of production to which wealth must be distributed? It is all very well to say that governments collect taxes because they have the power to do so, but surely there must be some historical basis for this weird system?

The question that needs to be unravelled, however, is how this universal acceptance came about over many centuries. To do this we will look – hopefully as briefly as possible – at the economic and socio-political histories of three countries: Britain, the United States of America and Brazil.

## How it came about in Britain

In Britain, the Norman Conquest of 1066 heralded a far-reaching change in the tenure of land. In Saxon times, land was held by individuals in a loose and complex system.[3] After the Conquest, land was held, to put it very simplistically, by the king. This meant that the king could hand out land to favourites and in time, powerful barons came to own large tracts of land – a situation that persists, to a large extent, to the present time.[4] As parliamentary democracy evolved over the centuries, those who controlled the land effectively controlled the parliamentary process. Even when universal franchise was introduced, an upper house of parliament, the House of Lords, comprising mainly hereditary landowners, still had the last say in the adoption of legislation passed by the House of Commons, the lower house of Parliament.

---

3 'But even in Wessex the idea still persisted that the tie of Lord and man was primarily personal, so that a free man could go from one Lord to another and transfer his land with him.' Winston Churchill, *A History of the English-Speaking Peoples*, Cassell & Co., London, 1957, vol. I, p.137.
4 This lengthy process is described by Sir Kenneth Jupp in *Stealing Our Land: Law, Rent, and Taxation*, Othila Press Ltd., London, 1997.

Adam Smith presented his great masterpiece, *An Inquiry into the Nature and Causes of the Wealth of Nations* in 1776, a time of revolution, change and upheaval. It was at the cusp of the change from a simpler, more agricultural way of life, to a more modern world of industry, commerce, finance and new socio-political dynamics. Smith alludes to this change in '*Of the Funds or Sources of Revenue which may peculiarly belong to the Sovereign or Commonwealth*', where he deals with this simpler, less sophisticated state, but ends this short part with these words: 'Public stock [capital] and public lands, therefore, the two sources of revenue which may peculiarly belong to the sovereign or common-wealth, being both improper and insufficient funds for defraying the necessary expense of any great and civilised state, it remains that this expense must, the greater part of it, be defrayed by taxes of one kind or another; the people contributing a part of their own private revenue in order to make up a public revenue to the sovereign or commonwealth.'[5]

Smith then starts his great dissertation, '*Of Taxes*', and this goes on for a further 83 pages. But it is in the words above and in his part on taxes that Adam Smith gives the modern, industrialised state 'permission' to levy taxes on its citizens. He lays out the framework of taxation in his four maxims of taxation (generally called the 'canons of taxation') and describes most of the taxes with which we are familiar today. A careful reader may note that he opposed nearly all of them!

It is interesting that a few years after the publication of *The Wealth of Nations*, William Pitt, the Prime Minister of Britain, introduced income tax for the first time to help pay for the Napoleonic Wars. Did Pitt feel that Adam Smith justified this move? Also, there was an interesting social dynamic at play here. The ruling class (even if not the political party in power) was the aristocratic landed class that dominated the House of Lords, and was not to be confused with the wealthy merchants and bankers. By the middle of the eighteenth century, taxation comprised mainly a land tax, or, as Adam Smith called it, 'Taxes upon the Rent of Land', as well as various customs and excise taxes. The land tax was, of course, paid by the (rural) landed classes. Churchill, referring to the political situation in the mid-eighteenth century, alludes briefly to this: 'Taxation was low; the land tax, which was anxiously watched by the Tory squires, was reduced by

5 Smith, A., *An Inquiry into the Nature and Causes of the Wealth of Nations*, The Modern Library, New York, 1994, Book V, Ch. 2, Part I, p.879.

economy to one shilling.'[6] So an income tax on the merchants and bankers would not be politically difficult, especially if this meant an even further reduction of the land tax.

So while Adam Smith may have outlined our present tax systems and given modern economists justification for their tax theories, he certainly did not start the change from simpler agricultural taxes to more complex income and consumption-type taxes. There were far greater dynamics at play. First, the state was getting larger and more expensive to run and warfare was technologically more advanced, lasted longer and was becoming extremely costly to prosecute. Secondly, there was a far subtler dynamic that stretched back to times when human beings started living in organised communities with a hierarchical ruling structure. It was as simple as this: those who controlled the land controlled the community and the wealth it created. There is nothing good or bad about this: it is just the way things are and always have been. Socialists who don't like this system and who have had the chance to overthrow it, usually create a new class of rulers who are generally more dictatorial and less democratic than the previous lot (but still control the land and the wealth produced).

The point is that as countries adopted the tax systems that we are familiar with today, one could see the hand of the land-owning classes guiding taxes away from anything that would harm land values and on to taxes that *they* considered to be 'fair and equitable' (like VAT). What they really mean to do is introduce taxes that will increase the value of prime land. In Britain, as mentioned above, the land-owning aristocracy was the real power behind any elected political party, and they showed their hand when David Lloyd George, Chancellor of the Exchequer in the Liberal government, introduced a land tax in his 1909 budget. This was immediately rejected by the House of Lords. While this started a diminution of the powers of the House of Lords, it ended Britain's first real chance to introduce a truly equitable tax.

## And in America, despite war about 'no taxation without representation'...

In America, the start of the Republic after the War of Independence was dominated by two opposing forces represented by Alexander Hamilton, the Federalist from New York and Thomas Jefferson, the

---

6 Churchill, W., *A History of the English-Speaking Peoples*, Cassell & Co., London, 1957, vol. III, p.97.

Virginian democrat. Churchill describes this battle in detail in his *A History of the English-Speaking Peoples*.[7] It should be remembered that at the end of the War of Independence in 1783, the thirteen states that had signed the Declaration of Independence were joined together by a loose confederation with George Washington as the president. Congress was weak and its proposals subject to veto by any of the states. The post-war dangers (political, economic and international) threatened this arrangement and the stability of the individual states. To address these threats, a convention of the thirteen states met in Philadelphia in 1787. From this convention a new constitution was drawn up, envisaging a stronger, more centralised form of federalist government. But in spite of the dangers facing the newly independent states, the proposals for a more cohesive republic faced fierce opposition.

'To the leaders of agrarian democracy, the backwoodsmen, the small farmers,' wrote Churchill, 'the project seemed a betrayal of the Revolution. They had thrown off the English executive. They had gained their freedom. They were now asked to create another instrument no less powerful and coercive. They had been told they were fighting for the Rights of Man and the equality of the individual. They saw in the Constitution an engine for the defence of property against equality. They felt in their daily life the heavy hand of powerful interests behind the contracts and debts which oppressed them ... But the party of Hamilton and Morris, with its brilliant propaganda ... carried the day ... On April 30, 1789, in the recently opened Federal Hall in New York, George Washington was solemnly inaugurated as the first President of the United States. A week later the French States-General met at Versailles. Another great revolution was about to burst upon a bewildered world. The flimsy, untested fabric of American unity and order had been erected only just in time.'

One of the issues behind the conflict between the agrarian democrats and financiers of New York, was a proposal by Hamilton for the new government to take over the bonds and certificates issued by the thirteen states to fund the War of Independence. According to Churchill, 'The moneyed interest was overjoyed by this programme, but there was bitter opposition from those who realised that the new government was using its taxing powers to pay interest to the speculative holders of state debts now assumed by Congress ... In Virginia there was fierce revolt against Hamilton's scheme. The planters distrusted the whole idea of public finance.'

7 *Ibid.*, vol. III, pp.212-216.

Thomas Jefferson was not present at the Philadelphia Convention; at the time, he was the Confederation's ambassador to France, but returned to become the first Secretary of State of the new Federal government (Hamilton was in charge of the Treasury). Churchill describes Jefferson as 'In touch with fashionable Left-Wing circles of political philosophy in Europe, and, like the French school of economists who went by the name of Physiocrats, he believed in a yeoman-farmer society. He feared an industrial proletariat as much as he disliked the principle of aristocracy. Industrial and capitalist development appalled him. He despised and distrusted the whole machinery of banks, tariffs, credit manipulation, and all the agencies of capitalism which the New Yorker Hamilton was skilfully introducing into the United States.'

What we see in the formation of the United States is the culmination of the spirit of independence that had inspired the early settlers. They left England to free themselves from the stifling constrictions of English political, social, economic and religious hegemony. Nevertheless, they took with them their inbred sense of English justice and equity. These qualities shine through in their early struggles, their fight against British political domination and taxation, and in the formation of the United States of America. While there were strongly opposing factions, it was always a meeting of equals getting together to forge a common destiny. The agrarian democrats may well have seen their cause as the equality of the people against the moneyed interests of the few, but they were just as wedded to the concept of property as the Hamilton-led financiers of New York. And they cherished not only property in land, but in houses, farms, equipment, and, in the South, in people as well. The ownership of slaves, although abolished in most countries in the Western world in the early part of the nineteenth century, was to continue for almost another hundred years after the formation of the United States. It also took a long, bloody and destructive civil war to free the slaves.

Nevertheless, the 'Jefferson-democrats' may well have had a moderating influence on the rapacity of the New York financiers: the US tax system (at least on a federal basis) has steadfastly rejected the inclusion of consumer taxes in the tax code. This has partially been the reason why America still has thousands of relatively prosperous towns and villages spread across this vast land. It has also avoided the agglomeration of huge slums around its major cities.

This, as we shall see, is in direct contrast to the situation in Brazil.

# Brazil

Brazil was 'discovered' by the Portuguese almost in error. Following Vasco da Gama's discovery in 1498 of a route to the East around the Cape of Good Hope, a large armada of ships was sent to exploit this route. To avoid the calms around the Gulf of Guinea, the ships veered to the west, and in April 1500, they landed on the coast of Brazil and promptly claimed the land in the name of Portugal.

Initially only the east coast of Brazil was developed by early Portuguese settlers, but the lure of the rich hinterland to the west was too much to resist. The brunt of 'the march to the west' was borne by the Paulistas, the settlers of Sao Paulo who organised great expeditions into the interior, known as bandeiras, to capture Indian slaves and to find gold and precious stones.

An important factor in the unification of the people of Brazil was the heritage of Portugal; the Portuguese language formed a common bond between plantation residents, cattlemen, miners, slaves and city dwellers and the expanded patriarchal family structure, also derived from Portugal, was nearly uniform throughout Brazil. Power was exercised by the heads of those families that controlled the land, slaves, cattle and mines that produced the wealth of the colony.

Unlike the American colonies, Brazil attained its independence relatively easily. The Portuguese king, John VI had taken refuge in Brazil in 1807 to escape Napoleon and when he returned to Portugal in 1821, he left his son, Dom Pedro, as regent. However, Dom Pedro, supported by a majority of Brazilians, declared independence from Portugal and was crowned Emperor in December 1822. The Brazilian monarchy continued until 1889 when Dom Pedro II abdicated after a revolt by army officers and was banished to Portugal.

Brazil as a republic was initially run by the military, and the first civilian president was installed only in 1894. The military influence in politics continued strongly for most of the 20th century and probably even continues to this day. They, in turn, were backed initially by the powerful rural landholders, and later, also by a wealthy and largely urban-based middle class.[8]

Quiet and benign as this alliance may seem, it has been the real power behind all the democratically-elected governments. One of their most enduring legacies has been the tax system. Brazil, along with

---

8 Based on *History of Brazil*, Encyclopaedia Britannica, Macropaedia, 1978, vol. III, pp.144-151.

many other South American countries, has had one of the world's most extensive indirect tax systems for almost the past fifty years.

According to Organisation for Economic Cooperation and Development (OECD) statistics, Brazil collects about a third of GDP in taxes, which is slightly less than the OECD average.[9] Commenting on this, *The Economist*[10] was heavily critical of the huge burden on the development of Brazil, and showed how taxes as a percentage of GDP are considerably less in Latin America on average (19.4%) as well as in other developing countries such as South Korea and China (the OECD average is raised by developed countries with extensive – and expensive – social welfare systems).

*The Economist* shows how, in the case of Brazil, such large tax revenues, in the hands of relatively weak governments, can be wasteful and inefficient. Also, where a large portion of tax revenue derives from indirect taxes, this causes a greater divide between rich and poor. It goes on to say: 'Because most revenue comes from consumption taxes, a Brazilian earning less than twice the minimum wage pays out nearly half his income in tax, whereas someone on 30 times the minimum wage pays only about a quarter in tax. Such benefits as pensions and free tuition at public universities flow disproportionately to the well-off.' Not only are poor people paying a large portion of their incomes in (mainly indirect) taxes, but indirect taxes have a constricting effect on rural development, especially where many rural dwellers are poor and illiterate.

## South Africa

What then of South Africa? Like Brazil, it is a developing country, also has a huge proportion of under-educated and unemployed poor, and its major cities, like Brazil's Rio de Janeiro and Sao Paulo, gather huge shanty-towns and slums. It is no coincidence that South Africa has, in the last sixteen years, introduced a large number of indirect taxes.

In South Africa today, government revenue is approximately 28% of GDP. While the social and political landscape in South Africa has undergone enormous change since the election of 1994 – mainly for the better – the tax system remains doggedly Western. The only real

9 OECD/ECLAC/CIAT (2012), *Revenue Statistics in Latin America*, OECD Publishing. Statlink: http://dx.doi.org/10.1787/888932691194
10 Special report: Brazil, April 14, 2007.

change is that it has become considerably more efficient and has cast its net ever wider. When Trevor Manuel (a left-leaning firebrand of the old United Democratic Front and one of the main destroyers of apartheid) became Minister of Finance in 1996, his predecessor, Chris Liebenberg, took him on a tour of Western financial capitals. Liebenberg was a highly respected banker with impeccable credentials in global financial circles. Manuel came to meet all the right people in international finance and soon came to learn how the global financial system works. His earlier sarcastic comments about the 'amorphous markets' were quickly forgotten; and Manuel soon adopted the economic imperatives of the Washington Consensus,[11] even though he may hotly deny this. During his long tenure as Minister of Finance he became the darling of South Africa's business and financial community, guiding South Africa's economic revival. At the same time, however, he also saw a steady increase in the wealth gap between rich and poor. So, while South Africa may not have had powerful capitalist interests nudging tax laws in their direction, the politicians of the socialist-leaning government have, perhaps unwittingly, done the capitalists' bidding.

What is wrong with the present system of taxation? After all, the basic principles of modern taxation, which were started in the late seventeenth century in Britain and Europe, have been exported to almost every other country in the world. Even if not greatly loved, taxation is accepted as a necessary evil. While there have been attempts to introduce more equitable systems, these have lasted for a while, but in most cases were overturned by powerful vested interests.[12]

But the tax system is generally accepted because, as we have theorised above, it seems to be ingrained in our economic and social genetic make-up. It's not that people don't want to change the system – every year, just before budget-time, the South African Minister of Finance's e-mail was clogged with citizens giving their 'Tips for Trevor' – but that they are all trying to fix a system that is fundamentally flawed. Also, most 'tips' are really requests to change something that will favour their own personal or business finances.

---

11 Washington Consensus: this comprised a series of policy prescriptions formulated in the early 1990's by the likes of the IMF, World Bank and US Treasury for crisis-ridden developing economies but, after nearly two decades of assiduous application, including in countries like Zimbabwe, it had largely lost its lustre.

12 For example, Denmark 1957 to 1960: Tholstrup, K., *Economic Liberalism*, 1 Vester Farings Gade, DK 1648, Copenhagen V, Denmark.

## Essence of the problem: taxes can come only from earnings of land, labour or capital

The problem, basically, is this: taxes can only come from the earnings of the three factors of production, land, labour and capital, or, as Adam Smith put it, 'Rent, Profit and Wages. Every tax must finally be paid from some one or other of those three different sorts of revenue.'[13] As we have attempted to illustrate above, landowners have always represented a powerful political entity. Today they are no longer only the descendants of 'robber barons', but comprise a large block of any population: ordinary house-holders, farmers, owners of residential and commercial property, and shareholders of property companies. There are also huge emotional issues regarding the ownership and occupation of land. For these and other reasons, the taxation of land is strongly resisted and the bulk of taxes tend to fall either on labour or capital. The arguments against the taxation of land, or to be more precise, the rent of land, are also clouded by emotion: it is tantamount to the nationalisation of land; it is not based on 'ability to pay'; it is difficult to assess; and taxes will not be spread equitably among all classes of society (code for 'the poor will pay almost nothing').

There are also strong arguments against the taxation of labour and capital. Taxes on wages, as Adam Smith pointed out, are really paid by the employer and are a cause of inflation (although he did not use those words). He also pointed out that taxes on consumption (especially the necessities of life) are again paid by the employer. In the case of countries like South Africa and Brazil, consumption taxes have a devastating effect on the unemployed and unskilled poor, many of whom (in South Africa) live on social grants, a goodly portion being clawed back by the government in the form of VAT. Taxes on capital are criticised as being a drag on production and enterprise, and discouraging foreign investment.

However, for all the reasons given above, governments prefer the long and complicated route of taxing labour and capital in spite of the social and economic problems this causes. In the next chapter we will give an analysis of what Adam Smith really said about taxation, without the flim-flam of modern interpretations. In Chapter 3 we will show how the taxation of labour and capital, without considering the real ability to pay, destroys production at the margin, causes unemployment and drives down wages.

13 *Op. cit.*, *Of Taxes*, Book V, Ch. 2, Part II.

11

## CHAPTER 2

# ADAM SMITH, GODFATHER OF MODERN TAXATION

*'All taxes upon consumable commodities … tend to
reduce the quantity of productive labour …'*
Adam Smith[1]

## Today's tax bubble

WHY, YOU MAY ASK, do we have this obsession with tax? And what is it with Adam Smith, that doddery, absent-minded professor who lived over 200 years ago, and who wrote an almost incomprehensible book on Economics? Modern tax theory has moved well beyond Adam Smith and his theories must now surely be obsolete.

Our obsession with tax is that tax practitioners – both those who devise the rules and those who advise taxpayers – live in a hermetically-sealed bubble with the walls created by legislated tax laws. The walls change from time to time and tax commentators excitedly examine the changes to see what effect they will have on specific classes of tax-payers, such as companies, shareholders, consumers, and households and so on. Those who devise the tax laws look first at optimising the tax take, and secondly at increasing efficiency, i.e. getting more tax revenue at lower cost and less effort. Or, as Jean-Baptiste Colbert (1619-1683) is reputed to have said, 'The art of taxation consists in so plucking the goose as to obtain the largest amount of feathers with the least possible amount of hissing.'

---

1 *The Wealth of Nations*, Modern Library, New York, 1994, p.970. Highlighted for the authors in O'Rourke, P.J., *On the Wealth of Nations*, Atlantic Books, 2007, p.145.

Tax legislators like to think that they build the tax system within the parameters of the ruling party's economic and social policy, but in many countries, South Africa included, poverty seems to increase with increasing wealth and increasing tax revenues. Much of this tax revenue is then spent attempting to alleviate the poverty.

Jeremy Cronin (a Red gone Green),[2] deputy secretary-general of the SA Communist Party, in a critical analysis of an ANC discussion document, *Economic Transformation for a National Democratic Society*, says 'The ANC document nowhere analyses (or even recognises) the profoundly contradictory character of the world economy. It admires its breathtaking technological advances, but fails to notice its simultaneous destruction of the environment, the headlong depletion of critical non-renewable resources and the immiseration of huge parts of humanity.'[3]

## Derived from Smith?

Cronin despairs at the disconnection between economic planning and economic reality. This is exactly our view of tax policy; it is built seemingly without any consideration of its likely effect on social, economic or ecological consequences. Nobody questions the tax system because it is believed to have been built on a rock-solid foundation. And many people think that foundation came from Adam Smith.

Adam Smith wrote *The Wealth of Nations* at a time when tax systems were rudimentary and haphazard even in the then-developed world. He first argued the need for greater tax revenue in a developed political state. He said that the revenue currently coming from the land and capital belonging to 'the sovereign or commonwealth' was both improper and insufficient, and the people must start contributing from their own private revenue.[4] He then set out the fundamental maxims for a good tax system, and described in detail the pros and cons of taxing revenue from the three factors of production: land, labour and capital.

Adam Smith set out his proposals for a tax on the rent of houses (a footnote in the edition of *The Wealth of Nations* used by the authors

---

2 Considering the Soviet Union's cavalier disregard for the environment, Cronin's views are welcome.
3 'Polokwane Briefing, The dangers of two-faced development', in *Mail & Guardian Online*, 3 June 2007.
4 *Op. cit.*, Book V, Ch.2, Part I, p.879.

states that 'Since the first publication of this book, a tax nearly upon the above principles has been imposed'). Smith describes the ludicrous methods that had been attempted over the centuries, such as the hearth (fireplace) tax. This involved the tax-gatherer entering every room to count the number of hearths. 'This odious visit,' says Smith, 'rendered the tax odious.' Some reports state that tax-gatherers were at times assaulted by the home-owners. This tax was replaced by a tax on houses inhabited, with more being paid by houses with more than ten windows. This tax itself was replaced by a simple window tax 'over and above the duty of three shillings upon every house, plus a duty upon every window, which augments from two pence to two shillings upon houses with twenty five or more windows'.[5] English tour guides love pointing out bricked-up windows as a quaint method of tax avoidance.

Britain, some twenty years after publication of *The Wealth of Nations*, was one of the first countries to introduce an income tax. Although this was supposed to be a temporary tax, by the early 19th century, the foundations of the British tax system had been established. We have postulated that Adam Smith set the modern tax system in motion and tax theorists have quoted him as the basis for our tax systems. In fact he is quoted almost as 'holy writ', but tax theorists, like many religious fundamentalists, quote him selectively, ignoring the contradictions that a closer reading would bring out.

As we have tried to illustrate in Chapter 1, the taxation of labour and capital as the main targets of government revenue, are now almost built into our genetic make-up. Benjamin Franklin's throw-away line about 'death and taxes'[6] is quoted ad nauseam as if it were a statement of absolute truth. This is why we believe it is necessary to go back to Adam Smith's description of the various forms of taxation. He did not invent taxation, or any particular taxes, but set out the taxes on the three factors of production that could be imposed without infringing any of his four maxims. He also described any such taxes that were prevalent at the time, together with his critique of these taxes.

5 *Op. cit.*, *Taxes upon the rent of Houses*, Book V, Ch.2, Part II, p.911.
6 'But in this world nothing can be said to be certain, except death and taxes' written in a letter to Jean Baptiste Le Roy in 1789, a few months before his death and not long after the end of the American War of Independence in 1783, caused largely by the imposition of taxes on the American colonies by its imperial power, Britain.

## Back to Smith's maxims

Adam Smith's originality is his critique of each type of tax and his four maxims of taxation.[7] These are (in abbreviated form):

1   The subjects of every state ought to contribute towards the support of the government … in proportion to their respective abilities; that is, in proportion to the revenue which they respectively enjoy under the protection of the state (Smith usually refers to this as 'equity', but today it is referred to as 'Ability to pay').

2   The tax that each individual is required to pay ought to be certain, and not arbitrary ('Certainty').

3   Every tax ought to be levied at the time … in which it is most … convenient for the contributor to pay ('Convenience').

4   Every tax ought to … take out … of the pockets of the people as little as possible over and above what it brings into the public treasury of the state ('Efficiency'). In other words, the tax should cost as little as possible to collect. Adam Smith has quite a bit to say about this; in his day, a major tax was customs duties and smuggling taxable goods into the country was a well-established 'industry'. Smith points out how the law 'first creates the temptation, and then punishes those who yield to it'. Customs and excise duties continue with increasing force to this very day, but whether the cost of police and customs officers used to combat smuggling is counted against the tax collected, is doubtful.

Governments with taxing powers like to think they adhere to these maxims. Each separate tax needs to be judged against these benchmarks, some with greater success than others. With some taxes, they are ignored altogether, government deeming the tax to be more important than some rules drawn up by a long-dead economist. In the first maxim, the concept of 'equity' often means, in modern terms, that taxes must be spread to as many people as possible. For example, consumption taxes, such as valued-added tax, are said to be equitable (i.e. paid by everyone) and conform to the maxims of certainty (the percentage tax on the purchase price is known – even if most of us have completely forgotten that there is a tax of 14% on the packet of biscuits we have just bought); convenience (the tax is paid when you buy the product; if you can't afford it, you don't buy it and avoid the

---

7 *Op. cit.*, *Of Taxes*, Book V, Ch.2, Part II, pp.880-890.

tax); and efficient (most of the cost of administration is borne by the organisations that buy and sell goods and services). The fact that it actually offends the first maxim – ability to pay – is almost completely ignored. Eventually, do-gooders complain that poor people with almost no income are being taxed on the necessities of life. Then what started off as a nice, clean, simple tax, becomes complicated with zero-rated, exempt items and, in some countries, different rates of the tax. But it still offends the first maxim.

As noted previously, Smith said that the 'private revenue of individuals ... arises ultimately from three different sources: rent, profit and wages. Every tax must finally be paid from some one or other of these three different sorts of revenue.'[8] Today he may have called these three sources of revenue, land, labour and capital, or the three factors of production. After dealing with the four maxims of taxation, he then goes on to deal with taxes on the three sorts of revenue.

## Smith on land tax

In Adam Smith's day, land was held by the crown, the church, and a small band of wealthy landowners. Ordinary people rented land or buildings in terms of leases of varying length. Therefore, when dealing with taxes on land or buildings, Smith always deals with taxes on the rent of land or buildings. In the late 18th century the primary industry was farming and Smith spends a large part of the section on *Taxes upon Rent of Land*[9] dealing with the taxation of farm land. Although one may think this is of little interest today, it is here that is hidden Adam Smith's thoughts on the structure of an equitable tax system. Some later commentators (especially Henry George and some of his modern followers) have chided Adam Smith for tip-toeing around the question of a land tax, being, in their opinion, the only tax necessary. This, they assert, was due to his so-called deference to wealthy landowners, especially Charles Townshend who paid him a handsome living for tutoring his sons and accompanying them on a grand tour of Europe. However, a close reading of this Article shows that Smith did no such thing.

First he explains (somewhat obviously) that a land-tax can be assessed either on a fixed valuation (i.e. based on a certain rent at a point in time), or a variable valuation based on the real rent as it

---

8 *Ibid.*, pp.887-888
9 *Ibid.*, Book V, Ch. II, Part II, Article I, p.891

changes over time. He goes on to explain that the first method, which was the method used in England during the late 18th century, 'should be equal at the time of its first establishment, (but) becomes unequal in the process of time'.[10] At the time Smith was writing *The Wealth of Nations* 'the valuations according to which the different counties and parishes were assessed to the land-tax by the 4th of William and Mary (the fourth year of their reign – 1693), was very unequal even at its first establishment … It therefore offends against the first of the four maxims (equity/ability to pay), (but is) agreeable to the other three.'[11]

Smith then spends another three or so pages explaining the theory of a land tax based on a variable valuation, and ends with these words: 'In all the variations of the state of the society, in the improvement and in the declension of agriculture, … a tax of this kind would, of its own accord and without any attention of government, readily suit itself to the actual situation of things, and would be equally just and equitable in all those different changes. It would, therefore, be much more proper to be established as a perpetual and unalterable regulation, than any tax which was always to be levied according to a certain valuation.'[12]

Smith then deals briefly with a type of land tax that is proportioned, not to the rent, but to the produce of the land. In England this seems to have been a tythe [*sic*] on church lands rented to farmers. He also cites a number of other countries (mainly in the East) where this system has been used. In general however, he rejects this type of tax as being 'very unequal'.

## Other property tax

Smith's section on the taxation of 'houses' (i.e. all property other than farm land), is of considerably more interest to us today, and continues his support for a tax based on a variable valuation of the land. Smith states that the rent of a house consists of two parts: the rent of the land and the rent of the building, even though the tenant may pay one sum of money as rent for the property.[13] The building rent is based

10 *Ibid.*, p.891
11 *Ibid.*
12 *Ibid.*, p.897
13 This may sound obvious, but is not always considered by those in the property market, who speak only of 'house prices' that are either increasing, in a bubble, or in recession. Also, the ground rent is completely in step with the value of the land; the building rent is tied to the value of the building, but in some cases may be nil. For example, a run-down cottage on a valuable site may be worthless if it is to be demolished; in this case the 'house price' is simply the price of the land. This may sometimes be of less consequence when buying and selling property, but is of utmost importance when determining taxes on property.

on the same principles as the rent of any other depreciable asset: the rate of interest, the expected life of the asset and expected sums to be paid for repairs and maintenance (if this has to be paid for by the landlord). Any sum paid in excess of this putative amount paid for the building rent will be rent for the land (what Smith calls 'ground rent').

It is in this section on taxes on the rent of houses that we see rare glimpses of Adam Smith's philosophy on taxation and also the origins of modern systems of property taxation. In many countries around the world, especially those countries that were originally colonised by Britain, municipal rates (local property taxes) are generally based on a valuation of the property.[14] This valuation could be either the property considered as a whole (building plus ground), or on separate valuations of building and ground, or on a valuation of the ground only (site value rating).

Where the tax is based on the whole rent or value (building plus ground),[15] Smith maintains that this will force prospective renters/ buyers to look for a cheaper property so that they are able to afford the rent (or repayments) plus the tax. Whether this is so in practice is difficult to determine, as Smith seems to deal with this topic on a theoretical basis. Later in this section he states that in Great Britain the rent of houses is subject to a land tax, which 'falls more lightly upon the rent of houses [presumably the building rent] than upon that of land'.[16]

Nevertheless, the property rates in Britain today are based on his earlier suggestion, i.e. on the whole rent of the property. If the house is occupied by the owner, (the majority of cases today) then the tax is assessed on a putative rent. He also stated that if a house is unoccupied, no tax should be payable and that is still the case today. This has led to anomalies such as that of Centre Point, an early London skyscraper built in the mid-1960s. The developer, Harry Hyams, wanted only one tenant for the whole building and kept it vacant for about nine years before achieving this aim. No rates were payable during this time, but the capital value increased enormously.[17]

---

14 Land in the colonies was more freely available, with ownership based on freehold title rather than leasehold as in Britain. Property rates were therefore based more on valuation rather than rent.

15 Adam Smith only deals with taxes on the rent of houses; insertions regarding the purchase of property on freehold title are the authors'.

16 *Op. cit.*, p.910.

17 *The Property Masters – a History of the British Commercial Property Sector*, Scott P. Taylor & Francis, Abingdon, Oxon, 1996.

## Ground rent a more proper subject ...

When Adam Smith comes to the subject of a tax on ground rent (site value), he goes into philosophical mode even though he cannot cite any examples where it had been implemented.[18]

> Ground-rents are a still more proper subject of taxation than the rent of houses. [Or, to put it another way, site values are a more proper subject of taxation than the total value of properties.] A tax upon ground-rents [site values] would not raise the rents [value] of houses. It would fall altogether upon the owner of the ground-rent, who acts always as a monopolist, and exacts the greatest rent which can be got for the use of his ground.
>
> Both ground-rents and the ordinary rent of land are a species of revenue which the owner, in many cases, enjoys without any care or attention of his own. Though a part of this revenue should be taken from him in order to defray the expenses of the state, no discouragement will thereby be given to any sort of industry.
>
> Ground-rents, so far as they exceed the ordinary rent of land, are altogether owing to the good government of the sovereign ... Nothing can be more reasonable than that a fund which owes its existence to the good government of the state should be taxed peculiarly, or should contribute something more than the greater part of other funds, towards the support of the government.[19]

Henry George, who wrote his major work, *Progress and Poverty*, a hundred years after Adam Smith, based his entire proposition on a similar philosophy. But while George believed that a single tax on the value of land was the only tax needed, Smith argues that some taxes on other forms of revenue are necessary. One of the purposes of this book is to carry forward both Henry George and Adam Smith's thinking into a modern economy where monopoly rents arise not only from ownership of land, but ownership of other natural resources that belong in the public domain. To this end, we will now look at Adam Smith's comments on taxes on capital, labour, capitation taxes and taxes upon consumable commodities.

---

18 If he had been able to live for another 150 years or so, he would have seen its successful implementation in cities like San Francisco and Johannesburg.
19 *Op. cit.*, p.909.

## Capital

Adam Smith titles Article II (of Book V, Chapter 2, and Part II) *Taxes upon Profit, or upon the Revenue arising from Stock*. In the 18th century, capital was known as 'stock' or 'capital stock'. This was divided between fixed stock (or what accountants today call fixed or non-current assets) and current assets such as cash, debtors and inventories (sometimes known confusingly as stock). The total value of all assets is represented by the owner's capital plus borrowed money.

Adam Smith recognises this distinction as regards the capital employed which 'naturally divides itself into two parts; that which pays the interest and which belongs to the owner of the stock [i.e. the lender], and that surplus part which is over and above what is necessary for paying the interest [i.e. the profit]'.[20] Now comes an interesting observation that appears to have been misunderstood by many who design tax systems. Smith contends that profit is 'a subject not taxable directly'.[21] Why not? Because, says Smith, the employer of capital must receive compensation 'for the risk and trouble of employing the stock'.[22] If he is taxed on his profit, he must pass it on, in the case of a farmer to his landlord as a reduction of rent, or if a manufacturer or merchant, to the consumers of his products as an increase in the price of the goods.

Smith then makes the observation that perhaps interest on money could be taxed as directly as the rent of land and gives reasons why interest on money is similar to the rent of land, such as that a tax on rent cannot raise rents, so a tax on interest cannot raise the rate of interest; and the quantity of money, like the quantity of land, remains the same after the tax as before it.

Nevertheless, there are good reasons why interest is 'a much less proper subject of direct taxation than the rent of land'.[23] First, the quantity and value of land can be ascertained exactly, but this is not so with the quantity of money possessed by an individual at any particular time. Secondly, 'land is a subject which cannot be removed; whereas stock [capital] easily may. The proprietor of land is necessarily a citizen of the particular country in which his estate lies. The proprietor of stock is properly a citizen of the world ... He would be apt

---

20 *Ibid.*, Article II, p.912.
21 *Ibid.*
22 *Ibid.*
23 *Ibid.*, Article II, p.914.

to abandon the country in which he was exposed to a vexatious inquisition, in order to be assessed to a burdensome tax, and would remove his stock to some other country where he could either carry on his business, or enjoy his fortune more at his ease.'[24]

Smith then spends some time on what he calls *Taxes upon the Profit of particular Employments*. In modern terms this is similar to a licence to operate say a public bar, or butchery. While such licences may be necessary to control the operations of such businesses, specific taxes on the profits are the same as taxes on the profits of any business: they are ultimately paid by the consumers. Smith gives examples of various such taxes imposed by different countries in Europe, but all this does is illustrate the lengths to which tax gatherers go in order to find new ways to collect tax revenue. All of them have one thing in common: the tax is always borne by someone else and often with additional economic distortions.

Adam Smith then makes a slight detour to deal with *Taxes upon the Capital Value of Land, Houses, and Stock*.[25] Today we would call these wealth taxes such as transfer duties, estate taxes, donations tax and capital gains tax. Included in these taxes are stamp duties on the registration of certain documents. These duties were common throughout Europe at the time and probably continue to be so. Smith's only comment was: 'There is no art which one government sooner learns of another than that of draining money from the pockets of the people.'[26]

On taxes on the transference of property, his opinion was that so far as they diminish the value of the property, they tend to diminish the funds available for the maintenance of productive labour; i.e. they can cause unemployment.

## Labour

Article III is entitled *Taxes upon the Wages of Labour*, and here Adam Smith has some very strong opinions. Like taxes on profits, which are not paid by the owner of capital, taxes on wages cannot be paid by the employee but by the employer, who must pass it on in higher prices to his customers. 'In all cases,' says Smith, 'a direct tax upon the wages of labour must … occasion both a greater reduction in the rent of

24 *Ibid.*
25 *Ibid.*, Appendix to Articles I and II.
26 *Ibid.*, p.929.

land, and a greater rise in the price of manufactured goods, than would have followed from the proper assessment of a sum equal to the produce of the tax partly upon the rent of land, and partly upon consumable commodities. Absurd and destructive as such taxes are, however, they take place in many countries.'[27]

Britain did not have such a tax in 1776 other than a 'tax of five shillings and sixpence in the pound upon the salaries of offices which exceeded a hundred pounds a year.'[28] Adam Smith agreed that senior civil servants deserved to have their salaries taxed. 'The persons who have the administration of government [are] generally disposed to reward themselves and their immediate dependants rather more than enough. The emoluments of offices, therefore, can in most cases very well bear to be taxed.'[29]

Finally, in Article IV, Adam Smith describes two taxes which he states 'should fall indifferently upon every different species of revenue' (i.e. the tax could come from rent, capital or wages).

## Capitation taxes

These are otherwise known as poll taxes and Adam Smith gives them very short shrift. He says they are arbitrary and uncertain and generally unequal. It is surprising that Margaret Thatcher, prime minister of Britain from 1979 to 1990, attempted to replace Adam Smith's local property tax with a poll tax. Her proposal did not succeed and was probably a major cause of her eviction from office by her own party. Did she not study Adam Smith? While her proposed tax was neither arbitrary nor uncertain, it was very unequal. Four poor people living in the same house would pay four times as much as a wealthy widow living alone in a large mansion. More to the point, had she not heard of Wat Tyler? 'A graduated and disappointing poll-tax had been levied in 1379; in 1380 a most unjust and level poll-tax of three groats[30] a head, oppressive to the poor, was laboriously exacted, and this set the pile of discontents ablaze.'[31] The leader of this rebellion was Wat Tyler, an ex-soldier. 'Tyler with a band broke into

---

27 *Ibid.*, Article III, p.933.
28 *Ibid.*, p.935.
29 *Ibid.*, p.934.
30 A silver coin worth four old pence, *Pocket Oxford Dictionary*, 1960.
31 Previté-Orton, C.W., *The Shorter Cambridge Medieval History*, Cambridge University Press, Cambridge, 1953, p.987.

the Tower unresisted, and summarily beheaded the archbishop.'[32] Margaret Thatcher was lucky merely to have been evicted as prime minister!

## Taxes upon consumable commodities

Adam Smith spends 39 pages on this topic of taxation, far more than any other, and he seems to feel that in many cases such a tax is necessary. In his criticism of taxes on wages he says that taxes (i.e. all taxation) should be partly on the rent of land and partly on consumable commodities. But, 'the state, not knowing how to tax, directly and proportionably, the revenue of its subjects, endeavours to tax it indirectly by taxing their expense, which, it is supposed will in most cases be nearly in proportion to their revenue. Their expense is taxed by taxing the consumable commodities upon which it is laid out'[33]

To cut a very long story short, consumable commodities are divided between necessities and luxuries. Necessities should not be taxed, but luxuries should. This much is obvious and probably every country that imposes an indirect tax on consumables thinks that they have the right balance between not taxing necessities, and having a simple, inexpensive tax that brings in lots of revenue.

Adam Smith's long article on this subject brings out only two things that are of real interest to a modern reader. First, 'a tax upon the necessaries of life operates exactly in the same manner as a direct tax upon the wages of labour'.[34] In other words it will increase wages requiring the employer to raise the price of goods and if these in turn are taxed, will perpetuate the cycle of inflation or increase the level of poverty. Secondly, he shows how difficult it is to differentiate between necessities and luxuries. Everyone seems to know what's best for the general population, especially 'nanny-state' politicians. Even the vegetarian, Adam Smith, has strong views on the taxation of 'butchers' meat' (which he considers to be a luxury, therefore taxable). The authors themselves will argue in a later chapter that value-added tax (VAT) has patently added to poverty in South Africa.

32 *Ibid.*, p.988.
33 *Ibid.*, Article IV, p.938.
34 *Ibid.*, p.940.

## Smith would be shocked at most of our taxes

What we have tried to illustrate here is that, while Adam Smith laid the foundations of modern tax systems, tax theorists, like religious fundamentalists, read into it that which suits their own political and economic policies. He would be shocked at the odiousness and intrusion of most taxes and would tell us that he had pointed out how two of our main taxes, taxes on the profits of companies and taxes on labour, would have a detrimental effect on the economy. We can go back to Adam Smith now for help, and a re-reading of his work will illustrate the glaring obnoxiousness of our tax systems. It is no use being proud of how much the revenue service has collected and how much more it can squeeze out of a complacent population when we are surrounded by a sea of ever-increasing poverty.

## CHAPTER 3

# THE MAGIC OF RENTAL COLLECTION AND TYRANNY OF TAXATION

'... *every improvement in the circumstances of the society tends either directly or indirectly to raise the real rent of the land, to increase the real wealth of the landlord, his power of purchasing the labour, or the produce of the labour of other people.*'
Adam Smith[1]

B EFORE EXPOUNDING on the 'how' of rental collection, however, we need, in this and the following chapter, to say more about the magical way in which it encourages production everywhere. This is as opposed to taxation, which is not only a burden to economic activity, but positively obliterates it in marginal locations such as the poorer South African rural areas.

## Locational advantage: the high ground and the low ground

To do this we will use a model that looks at the effect of locational advantage i.e. shows that when the same effort and capital are used on similar-sized stands in a particular industry, the value added varies purely due to location. While we have worked on this model for many years and have attempted to tune it to South African conditions, we cannot claim authorship. It was originally based on a story the American author, Henry George, used in his book *Progress and Poverty*,[2]

---

1 Smith, A., *An Inquiry into the Nature and Causes of the Wealth of Nations*, The Modern Library, New York,1994, Book 1, Ch. XI, Part 3, 'Rent of Land: Conclusion'.
2 Edited and abridged by Bob Drake, Robert Schalkenbach Foundation, New York, 2006, p.131.

to illustrate how wealth increased with the growth of a new community on the American prairies in the 19th century. From this story the model was developed by the School of Economic Science, London, using eight stands or sites on which the same form of economic activity occurs – for example, farming, mining, manufacturing, or retailing – so as to demonstrate the differing rental values of each site. Each bar, representing a site, shows the value added (or net wealth produced) on an equal measure of land, a hectare perhaps in the case of farming, a square metre in the case of a retail store. Also, it assumes the application of equal labour and capital, that is, an equal piece of land on which is applied equal effort and skill.

As to the type of activity compared, we could take a series of, say, maize farms, furniture or clothing factories, or even hairdressers. If, however, we take a retail chain with stores in various locations from, say, Sandton to Springbok, it would be reasonable to assume that management trains its people in a particular way and uses standardised buying and credit granting criteria, inventory controls, computer software and hardware and so on. So one could go into any Shoprite, Woolworths or Pep Stores and expect the same type of store layout and service. Per square metre of store, one could assume that the company's labour and capital costs would be almost identical wherever the store was located.

Despite this, some stores have far better returns (per square metre) than others. In its 2013 report Capitec Bank, which has branches in the remotest rural areas as well prime shopping centres, and prides itself on the training all its staff get from its academy at Stellenbosch said, 'At our smaller branches seven employees perform on average 14,000 transactions per branch per month. Our larger branches are staffed by 16 employees that perform on average 82,000 transactions per branch per month.' Assuming a similar area used per employee, the larger branches, with 5,125 transactions per employee, would be more than twice as productive as the smaller branches with 2,000 transactions per employee. We would also assume that the larger branches were on more valuable sites.

In some places a chain store would not open a shop because the returns would be too low for the capital invested. Such a location would be sub-marginal (for that chain). The difference in returns in different locations is likely to be in line with property values in different places. Land values do, of course, vary very much more than the 80-150 range shown here, the numbers of which are chosen purely for illustration.

Figure 3.1 shows the value added per hectare or other unit of space achieved by similar businesses operating on seven sites (A to G) ranging from prime to marginal. The eighth site, H, is sub-marginal as far as these similar business entities are concerned. Value added is simply the difference between sales revenue and input costs (i.e. the cost of goods and services bought in from outside the business). This value added, which is the result of applying labour and capital on land, therefore comprises 'rent', labour costs, and returns to capital; i.e. the returns to the three factors of production. These concepts will be dealt with more fully as the figure is developed.

**Figure 3.1: The value added obtainable on differing sites with equal area and equal inputs of labour and capital**

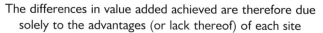

The differences in value added achieved are therefore due solely to the advantages (or lack thereof) of each site

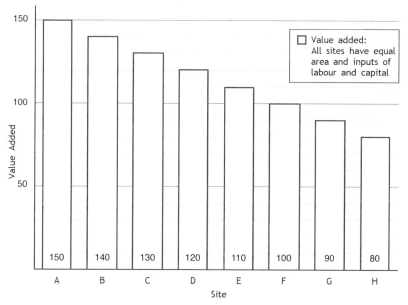

**Source:** Authors' development of model used by School of Economic Science, London, in turn based on Henry George's description of a new community in *Progress and Poverty*, Robert Schalkenbach Foundation, New York, 1992, Book IV, Ch. I, p.235.

The numbers on each site illustrate a different assumed value added per similar unit of land (hectare, square metre, and so on). We now need to divide the value added on each site between the three factors of production.

# The emergence of rent

Starting with labour and capital, we assume that the returns to these factors of production on all seven sites will be 90, the value added on site G in Figure 3.2. We have shown site G at the margin of production because 90, which is the assumed minimum return required by labour and capital together, is achieved there; this is not so on site H which is therefore sub-marginal and remains out of production. So, after deducting these minimum required returns to capital and labour, we are left with a surplus, i.e. the 'land-rent,' on sites A to F. Figure 3.2 shows the locational advantage enjoyed by the owners in respect of the unimproved value of the land. In this example it is assumed to vary from 60 (or 40% of the total) on the most productive stand A, to 10 (or 10%) on stand F. There is no rent on G because it has no locational advantage. It is the least productive site in production which is, however, sustainable because it achieves the minimum return required by labour and capital together. This, as we shall see, is of enormous importance.

**Figure 3.2: The locational advantage or rent as difference between production on site G (the margin) and sites A to F**

At site G, minimum required returns on labour and capital are obtainable. H remains out of production, as minimum required returns to labour and capital cannot be obtained there. G yields no rent but production is viable. Land is assumed to be freely available at the margin.

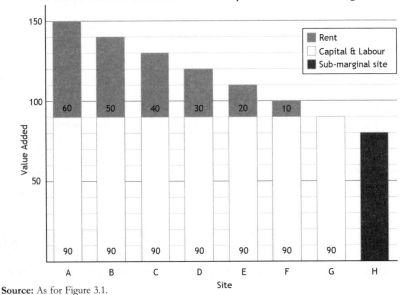

**Source:** As for Figure 3.1.

28

In passing we should note that, as regards residential land, completely different criteria will apply compared to properties such as mines, offices, retail shops, services and manufacturing industries. Our figures only relate to business enterprises. The concepts of value added, returns on capital employed and labour costs do not necessarily apply to residential property. Nevertheless, the concept of land rent, which applies to all land, is well illustrated by the relative land values of residential properties. This is a universally understood phenomenon albeit with the need for a reminder that a major factor behind 'house price' variances at any given time is their location i.e. land value.

## Returns to capital and labour

The returns to capital and labour in Figure 3.3 on page 30 are assumed to be the same for sites A to G. As regards capital, this is because the suppliers thereof need to attain a minimum risk-adjusted return on capital regardless of where that capital is employed. Thus BHP Billiton, which prides itself on its focus on Tier 1 assets (prime deposits in countries with reliable and predictable mining jurisdictions) would normally avoid mediocre deposits, especially in countries like, say, Somalia, the DRC, Central African Republic and so on. However, were it to decide to go there, it would certainly require a much higher return to compensate for the extra risk. So, while in practice operators in high risk areas would expect much higher returns, we are, for the purposes of illustration, showing them as being equal on a risk-adjusted basis.

In addition, as regards labour, we have, as in the case of George's Prairie, assumed free land available at the margin. It is this, therefore, that determines the level of wages; since labour will not accept less than it can obtain by working for itself out there.

Figure 3.3 shows the division between returns to the three factors, land, capital and labour, on seven business sites performing similar economic functions and applying equal capital and labour. Rent could therefore be said to be the difference between the value added (net production) on the marginal site (G) and all others, given equal inputs of labour and capital. It has, however, also been referred to as economic or natural rent,[3] and has been described as 'a measure of market

---

3 As stated in the definition of economic rent, this is the relative return to any factor of production. In respect of land, we prefer to use the term 'natural' rent. This refers to the relative return to a piece of land due to its real or perceived superiority: for example, superior agricultural attributes, or its location.

power: the difference between what a factor of production is paid and how much it would need to be paid to remain in its current use.'[4] The *Pocket Economist* also says that under conditions of perfect competition, economic rent would disappear as other players entered the market. This may be true in respect of capital and possibly in the case of labour, but we are talking about land, the supply of which is finite, especially as regards suitable sites.

### Figure 3.3: The division of value added between rent, return on capital and earnings of labour

Capital will be deployed wherever it can achieve the minimum risk-adjusted hurdle rate return. Riskier sites require higher returns; it is only on a risk-adjusted basis that they will be equal (as shown here for the purposes of illustration). Since land is available at the margin, labour will not accept less than what can be produced there, after meeting the minimum return on capital.

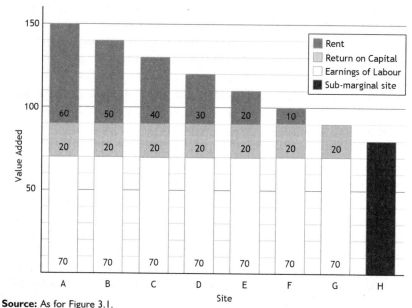

**Source:** As for Figure 3.1.

In Figure 3.3 we have, by the way, arrived at potential economic Nirvana! All we have to do now is recognise that all the benefits, or lack thereof, arising from the community or its proxy (the government)

4 Bishop, M., *Pocket Economist*, The Economist in association with Profile Books Ltd., London, 2000.

are reflected in land values. The rents arise naturally from the benefits of land enclosure conferred by the community and are therefore the natural source of revenue for the community. So all it needs to do is collect the value it creates and not tax the value created by labour and capital!

Now why should we be so excited about yet another apparently boring old economics figure?

Well, as we have said, production continues to thrive on 'site G' which, in South Africa, would equate to poorer rural areas housing over 40% of the entire population, quite apart from any other depressed or marginal areas you can think of. Just think for a moment what a difference it would make if, instead of these rural areas over-burdening urban facilities with their ever-growing influx into informal urban settlements (as they have increasingly done since transition), they were instead to become thriving partners in economic growth. It would be a bit like 19th-century America when ordinary folk headed from the settled areas into what was then (in economic terms) the marginal western interior. Was the first thing the US Government did to tax the Wild West? Not much (as any cowboy movie will indicate), apart from making the land freely available. What did the eastern states do? They traded with the hinterland; bought its beef and maize and sold it clothes, wagons and other goods. No doubt the eastern states, as they grew more prosperous, yielded more tax revenues, but the bottom line is that the US Government did not tax the West out of existence before it had even got going.

This innocent-looking Figure 3.3 hides an equally momentous phe-nomenon. By now you have probably wondered what would be so exciting for investors in new businesses, since they all appear to be restricted to exactly the same modest rates of return: 20 out of a total of 90 on the marginal stand G, and 20 out of the total of 150 pro-duced on the prime site A.

Do not forget, however, the two little assumptions we had to make for the purpose of illustration, namely the same effort (labour, includ-ing skill) and capital applied. In reality, of course, some businesses invest too much too soon and others too little too late while some management teams are brilliant and others incompetent. So the value they add, or wealth they create, will vary enormously in practice. Land values, however, are readily ascertainable and established by a reason-ably efficient market. In other words, the rental shown on the figure will not change if the value added doubles, but will still correctly reflect the value of the community's (government's) contribution to wealth created. The value added totals produced on different stands will, however, vary according to the quality of effort and capital applied. In practice, it is notable that more efficient and successful firms, like modern gladiators, do not shy away from top rentals in top sites.

If the business on the site G was doubly efficient and produced 180 instead of 90, the extra 90 would increase the return on capital from the standard 20 assumed in the figure to 110. What's more, the 'marginal tax rate' would be zero! In other words, the entire extra would go to return on capital. Capital would therefore be attracted back to the margin or, in South Africa, the poor rural areas. Bear in mind, however, that if management on site A was also doubly efficient and produced 300 instead of 150, the return on capital would be raised from 20 to 170, or more than eight fold. We therefore have a system that is enormously incentivising wherever production takes place. The contribution of the community, or government, to value added is established objectively by the marketplace and if the business cannot afford to pay that rental it will have to sell the site to someone who can. Critics, in particular, who point to the disincentivising effects of 'taxing away all the rents' need to note that, where the rentals are objectively fixed by the market, the incentivising effect of a zero marginal 'tax rate' can be powerful indeed.

It does not require a stretch of the imagination to believe that this will lead to the creation of many more jobs. This increase in employment will also lead to rising wage levels. Over time, generally rising levels of prosperity and opportunity will lead to increased demand for land and so the rentals, or government's share, would in due course rise in recognition of its having contributed to (or at least not having got in the way of) economic growth.

## Returns to capital dissected

So, Figure 3.4 is exactly the same as Figure 3.3 but we have just shown the division of the wealth created between the three factors of production in accounting terms: rent to land, profit to capital and wages to labour. As previously mentioned, the numbers chosen are purely for the purposes of illustration. Although returns to labour, capital and rent/government on the diagram, if added up, might bear some relationship to their share of GDP at some time or other, this is not meant to be a statement as to what share we think each should have right now. As regards the apportionment of return on capital between dividends, interest and depreciation, this is purely notional and not to recommend any particular ratios, as these would obviously depend on factors such as the level of capital intensity of the individual business, its gearing and dividend policies. It does, however, reflect the fact that many companies, in their value added statements, give a similar break-down except that 'reinvested in the business' is sometimes shown instead of depreciation. This vision of Eldorado, or things as they naturally are, is not as unattainable as you may think, especially if we use it to understand how we have arrived at the mess we're in. And when we say 'we', we are not just thinking of our own pre-and post-transition history in South Africa, but of everywhere in the world where land is privately owned with taxation imposed instead of natural rental collection.

### Figure 3.4: Return on capital disaggregated and rent collected in lieu of taxation

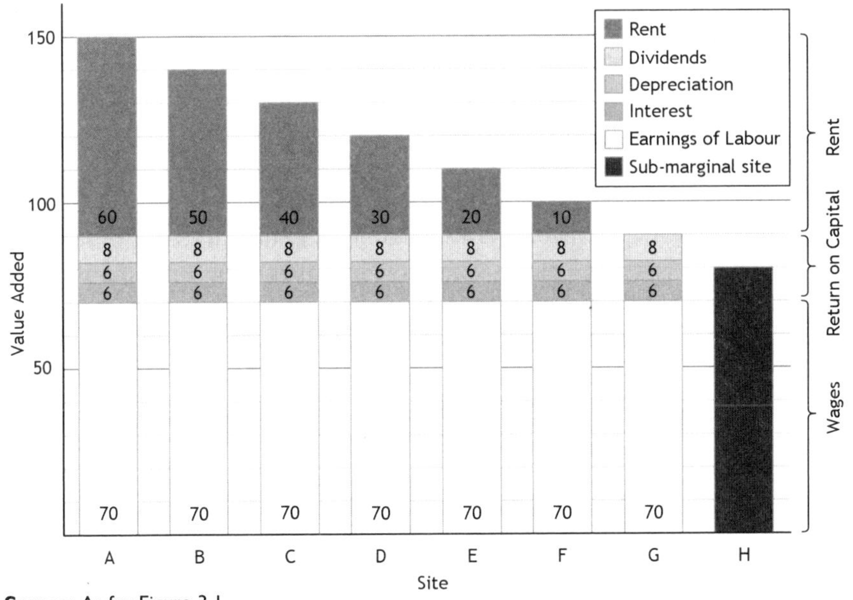

**Source:** As for Figure 3.1.

## The initial distortions of taxation: marginal sites close down; landlord's claim emerges

So let us look at how taxation distorts the natural state of affairs. To begin with, tax authorities try to tax everything that generates cash: profits, wages, sales, donations, capital gains, deceased estates and rent (but only the rent received for leasing goods, letting space in a building or for the use of land). But as Adam Smith pointed out, most of these tax targets are 'subject(s) not taxable directly'.[5] In the case of profits, the owners of capital must get their required return or they will put their money into a more profitable venture, or simply invest it in other assets that will give an acceptable return. In the case of taxes on wages, workers will demand a 'living wage' and, if taxes take this threshold below this level, they will resort to various means to get it back there. A similar problem will occur in the case of the taxation of necessities.

Figure 3.5 shows what effect taxation would begin to have on the returns to land, capital and labour. While prime sites would certainly bear the largest brunt of tax in absolute terms, the marginal sites will bear the largest amount relative to their ability to bear tax. Figure 3.5 shows first that site G (the erstwhile marginal site) has gone out of production because taxation (i.e. all taxes paid from the value added created by the company: income tax, PAYE, VAT, customs and excise duties, fuel taxes and so on) has eaten into the return on capital to such an extent that it is no longer viable to stay in business. Tax has also pushed the returns to capital on sites F and E below the accepted norm, but they may be able to continue in business for a while, although they are unlikely to make any fresh investments.

Furthermore, because taxation does not collect all of natural rent on the better sites, the balance stays with landlords. This uncollected economic rent (the 'landlord's claim' on the diagram), or the market's best estimate of the present value thereof, is the basis for land prices and the conventional rental the owner, say a farmer, would get in respect of the unimproved bare land value of his property if he let it out instead of operating himself. Moreover, as shown in Figure 3.5, the relative share of uncollected rent is much greater on prime sites than near the margin. For example, on site A it is $\frac{19}{150}$ (or 12.7%) of total value added as compared with $\frac{1}{100}$ (or 1%) on Site F.

Given that Site G contributed 90 out of the original total value added of 920 (diagrams 3.1 to 3.4), this would indicate a decline of nearly 10% in our notional 'GDP', but again, this is a notional number purely for illustration.

---

5 Smith, A., *Op. cit.*, p.329.

**Figure 3.5: Initial effect of taxation puts site G out of production and reduces returns on capital below required minimum on near marginal sites F and E**

Taxation bombs dividends and depreciation, making operations non-viable. Rent uncollected by government shows up as Landlord's Claim.

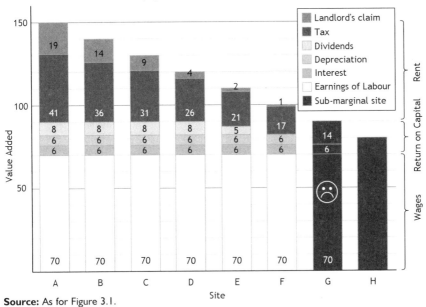

**Source:** As for Figure 3.1.

# The secondary distortions of taxation: the paradox of wages dropping and returns to capital restored on semi-marginal sites E and F

The next stage in the distortion caused by taxation is shown on Figure 3.6 where the effect of site G going out of production is shown to lead to rising unemployment which forces wages down to 60. This restores the minimum required return on capital on sites E and F, but the landlord's claim on sites A to F goes up. Remember that old song about the rich getting richer and the poor getting poorer? Well, now we know why! But we also know now that it doesn't have to be that way.

For Site G in South Africa, read all non-prime mining and agricultural land outside the metropolitan areas, in other words, some 70% of the surface area of the country with over 40% of the population. The importance of restoring viability to economic activity at this 'margin' cannot be overemphasised and is one of the most compelling reasons why collection of natural resource rentals will boost economic growth dramatically.

**Figure 3.6: Secondary effects of taxation: landlord's claim increases; profit recovers on sites E and F as unemployment depresses wages**

This effect is best seen where, for site G to recover, wages must fall even further to 56 units or less.

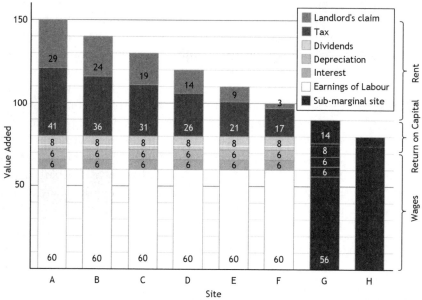

## Why stop at 60? The least men will accept, and inflation

For the purposes of illustration, we assumed wages dropped to 60 which, of course, begs the question, why not 65, 55 or even 50? Well, a little earlier on we said Adam Smith remarked that most of these tax targets were 'subject(s) not taxable directly' and that, as regards taxes on wages, workers will demand a 'living wage' so if taxes take the threshold below this level, they will resort to various means to get it back there. The first thing to note about this 'living wage' (or 'decent work' as mooted by trade unions in South Africa in 2013), is that it is a far cry from the level of wages where 'men and land are free' as pertained to some extent in the mid-19th century in America, i.e. employers had to pay what men could earn for themselves on the best land freely available at the margin. The second thing to note is that, bereft of the powerful leverage of land freely available at the margin, the position of labour is inherently weaker. So what 'means' are available to labour 'to get it back there'? Clearly, in an oligarchical semi-democracy (as in mid-19th century England) not much. If anything, the margin was emigration to the New World or the colonies. But with advent of universal franchise and access to means of influencing public opinion, let alone enjoying spells of worker governments in power, there was a considerable improvement in bargaining power. In addition, if we take legislated improvements in working conditions as part of real wages, there were obviously great advances. This 'living wage', therefore, would vary from time to time depending on social, political and economic circumstances as well as cultural and other established customs. In South Africa in mid-2013, platinum miners were vociferous in demanding much higher wages despite big increases in 2012. The stage was set for a clash between 'the least workers would accept' and the minimum returns required by shareholders for further investment. In Greece, on the other hand, there was no bargaining power and wages remained way below pre-crisis levels, despite massive protests. So, to return to the question, what are the 'means' available to labour? Well, the short answer is: where persuasion fails, the industrial version of mutually assured destruction is a strike. In our view, the fundamental cause of this endless confrontation and tension is that the economy (as shown in our rudimentary model in Figures 3.5 and 3.6) is being assailed by massive demands on it for no equivalent input by a fourth claimant. For, in addition to the three factors (if we take government as having the natural right to claim rent), we now have the landlords' claim. Moreover, the government, while collecting some of the rental, is under-collecting on prime sites and destroying production by attempting to collect on sites where there are no rents (locational advantages). This is a fundamental contributor to inflation and explains why Smith said most of these tax targets are 'subject(s) not taxable directly'.

## Discussion of a progressive formula tax in relation to the taxation of economic rent and resource rentals

The ultimate aim of any business is to add value. In other words, to manufacture and sell a product, to on-sell products, or to provide a service where the selling price is more than the cost of such goods or services. This added value is then distributed to the three factors of production: to labour (all the people employed in the business), in the form of wages; to the providers of capital (owners and lenders), in the form of dividends and interest; and to 'land', represented by the government as the custodians and administrators of the country's resources (land, mineral resources, water, air space, coastal waters and the electromagnetic spectrum). The government currently collects taxes as its share of the value added, instead of (as we believe would be infinitely preferable) collecting a rental specifically on the unimproved value of resources.

These three 'partners' in every business enterprise from a street hawker to a multi-billion company like Sasol, provide their unique contributions to the success of every business and no business can operate without all three factors of production.

Profit comes out of value added and is a concept that is important to the providers of capital. In terms of the capitalist paradigm, the providers of equity capital own and control the business; labour is merely a cost of production and taxation is considered to be an arbitrary and predatory impost that only has weight and force because of various acts of parliament. While the government is expected to provide various services to the businesses and citizens of a country, no-one directly relates such services to the tax they pay. In fact, taxation is seen by many as simply an exercise in wealth-distribution.

But these are only ideas and opinions; in the same way that socialist, communist, fascist, or any economic theory are only ideas and opinions. A large amount of time is wasted in futile arguments about which system is right or wrong, or better or worse.

All of these theories are imposed on the reality that business adds value using the contributions and services of the three factors of production. If a business has insufficient capital, under-skilled, lazy or corrupt staff, or the government is unable to provide an environment that is conducive to its business operations, it may struggle to optimise its added value and the distributions to the three factors of production. Here, the providers of equity capital always seem to hold the short straw: lenders want their interest, workers their wages and the government its taxes, regardless of the difficulties the business may be experiencing. But workers can be retrenched or fired and smart consultants can work out ways to reduce the tax liability, leaving the share due to the providers of equity capital more or less intact.

Taxation is universally despised because, as stated previously, it is seen as arbitrary and predatory, and not adding any direct value to the business. While most business people accept the need for taxation, they do not correlate any direct or indirect benefits for the amounts paid. Taxation on a company's profits is generally recognised as the company's sole tax liability. However, as mentioned in the previous section, these taxes are certainly not the only taxes that a company pays. While income statements are only obliged to show company tax and, until 2012, the Secondary Tax on Companies (STC), many companies are showing the full extent of taxation in a statement of monetary exchanges with government. In the income statement, most of the other taxes (such as employees' tax, property taxes and unre-covered VAT input taxes) are included in the relevant expenses and therefore not readily discernible.

Businesses and individuals use the resources that make up the patrimony of a country with the implicit blessing of the people of the country, represented by the government of the day. It is our vision that a way can be found to charge a rental on the use of such resources, in other words, a 'resource rental' ultimately to replace taxation.

Hence our proposals to that end in this book.

## CHAPTER 4

# PROBLEMS AND PRECEDENTS

*'The thing that hath been, it is that which shall be;*
*and there is no new thing under the sun.'*
Ecclesiastes 1:9

N OW, YOU MAY SAY, these proposals we are making in this book are all very well, but are there not some counter arguments and examples of its application for us to consider?

## Counter arguments

A wide range of objections, mostly dealt with elsewhere in the text but briefly answered here as well, were proffered by Dr Richard Grant.[1]

He begins by quoting Ludwig von Mises:

> Ricardo calls the powers of the soil 'original and indestructible'. However, modern economics must stress the point that valuation and appraisement do not differentiate between original and produced factors of production and that the cosmological indestructibility of mass and energy … does not enjoin upon land utilisation a character radically different from other branches of production.[2]

It is true that current accounting conventions do not pay much attention to the difference between land on the one hand and plant and machinery on the other. The remarkable changes wrought so swiftly

---

1 Grant, R.J., *Nationalisation: How Governments Control You*, Free Market Foundation, Sandton, 1994, Ch.6, p.51. See also Fred Harrison's vigorous rebuttal of these arguments in *The Corruption of Economics*, Shepheard-Walwyn, London, 1994, pp.242-257. Many of Dr Grant's comments relate to our earlier publication: *The Trial of Chaka Dlamini – an Economic Scenario for the New South Africa*, Amagi Books, Johannesburg, 1990.
2 *Ibid.*

this century by International Financial Reporting Standards (IFRS) do, however, show how much change accountants can manage if they have to. Modern economics does not necessarily have to follow accounting conventions: if needs be, it should be the other way around! As regards the cosmological indestructibility of mass and energy, this points very obviously to the difference between Earth and man-made objects even if, millennia hence, many of them will have returned to dust. Finally, with respect to the famous economist, are there *any* branches of production that do not utilise land?

> Although the distinction between land and capital is important in some contexts, it is irrelevant when discussing intervention and taxation: the consequences will be the same for any asset .... The constantly repeated argument that the single tax on land would force idle land into use is simply not true. The tax would lower the returns on all land that is used.[3]

The first part of this argument seems, once again, to rely on legalistic grounds as well as current accounting conventions. As for the argument that resource rental collection would not force idle land into use, it completely ignores the fact that this is designed to be introduced at the same time as moving away from current taxes. As we argued elsewhere, the proportion of marginal land in South Africa is unusually high and, therefore, in many instances 'costs' i.e. tax/rental payments would be much less. Even on prime sites, those operations with above average efficiency could well find themselves paying less. Studies in America[4] and South Africa[5] have shown that, even at the local government level, a switch from rating on improvements or composite rating, to rating on site value only (or even a change in weighting from the former to the latter), has measurably beneficial effects.

> [T]he single tax on land rent is unjust and confiscatory; compels arbitrariness in assessments, inviting collusion and corruption in government.[6]

Resource rental collection requires landowners benefiting from exogenous or community-caused improvements in land value to pay accordingly; and, with equal justice, requires less of them in the converse case.

---

3 *Ibid.*
4 See Ch.7 of *Land Value Taxation Around the World*, 2nd edition, ed. Robert V. Andelson, Robert Schalkenbach Foundation, New York, 1997. See also Mason Gaffney, 'What's the Matter with Michigan? The Rise and Collapse of an Economic Wonder' in 'Insight' column of *Groundswell*, Nov/Dec 2008.
5 *Op. cit.*, Ch. 13.
6 *Op. cit.*, p.58.

While all taxes are, in a sense, confiscatory, a tax change to resource rental collection compensates the landowner by removing taxes on the product of his labour and capital. The undoubted success of site value rating in Johannesburg and elsewhere in South Africa throughout much of the 20th century refutes the allegation of arbitrariness in assessments, never mind the success of local authority land value tax assessments in Australia, New Zealand amongst others. In the 1970s when the Chief City Valuer, John McCulloch, attended international municipal property valuation conferences, he was routinely greeted with incredulity when he said Johannesburg had a system of site value rating only. Until then, his international peers had simply believed it to be impossible. Meanwhile, his staff were successfully updating land values from the many 'buy, implode and rebuild' deals at the time and, in other cases, routinely updating land values as residuals from property transactions not involving demolition. In contrast to the confidentiality of tax matters as between SARS and individuals or companies, we propose that all resource rentals be published precisely so that justice can not only be done, but can be seen to be done. Nor is Greece the only country where corruption in taxation prevails.

> Rent is a general phenomenon that applies to all assets not only land. Within a particular category of assets, some are better suited to their particular uses than others. The benefit or return that accrues to an asset reflects this, and the economic rent is the difference between the return to one asset and a return to the poorest asset being used for the same purpose.[7]

So what if the rent of a crane hire company's new machine is the difference between its return and that on its oldest item? That information would be relevant to the company's management, and its accountants would have to record both land and plant and machinery as assets. Moreover, they would have to provide for depreciation on the latter so as to be able to keep providing their customers with the best available cranes. How often does one hear of accountants providing for depreciation on land, as distinct from impairments on ill-judged purchases or speculation? So the expansion of the definition of rent from its Ricardian or Adam Smithsonian roots, while not necessarily incorrect, is not particularly helpful except as yet another attempt to pretend that there is no need for the Treasury to treat man-made assets differently from the gift of nature.

7 *Ibid.*, p.52.

The suitability of various plots of land for various uses is reflected in the land value and the rent paid on that land ... to ignore these differences in productivity and attempt to tax away all the rent would, as in the case of state ownership of the land, leave no differential rent for the purposes of economic calculation. This would subject land use to the same difficulties associated with the Socialist calculation problem: market information is not properly disseminated. The tax would be capitalised so as to make the price of land the same everywhere, regardless of location or quality. With this artificial levelling of relative prices, the property market would thus be 'blinded' with respect to quality. Poor land would have the same price as good land.[8]

Apart from the irony of our being lectured about land prices reflecting differences in suitability for various uses from this source, we note that this comment steadfastly ignores our proposal that this asset would be priced continuously on its current rental value. Estate agents, property developers and the media in general would ensure that all rental values were constantly published and updated. Changing land values would be highlighted, *inter alia*, by the differences between transaction prices and replacement values of improvements on the properties concerned. Needless to say, life would go on with, if anything, a livelier market. Transaction prices for properties where the improvements were demolished would, as always, provide a reliable indicator of current land values. Wherever necessary, especially in the case of larger properties, use could be made of auction mechanisms to settle disputes. So, although full collection of resource rental will result in property changing hands at improvement values (since current capital values of land comprise the market's best estimate of the present value of uncollected rent), it is not true to say that there will therefore be no basis for discriminating between different sites because they have zero capital value.

As a tax rate approaches 100% of any tax base, revenues will approach zero in the long run. This tax on rent is not compatible with a market economy, and leads inevitably to socialism.[9]

Dr Grant asserts that, because full rental collection would eliminate capital values of land, there would be no basis for market determination of relative values. This is not so because as we have explained, in implementing rental collection, the existing nationwide matrix of relative land market values would be used to begin with. The next step

8 *Ibid.*, p.52.
9 *Ibid.*, p.60.

would be to take note of ongoing property transactions as regards the extent to which prices exceed (or fall short of) improvement values, which, in turn, would indicate the extent to which the rentals would need to be adjusted. This would be enough for the majority of cases but, as we have also explained, provision would be made for the use of auction mechanisms, especially perhaps with bigger properties, to ensure rental values continue to reflect the market.

Dr Grant then leaped to the conclusion that the absence of relative (capital) land values would necessitate arbitrary rental estimates by officials and, quoting Professor Knight, 'to collect such rent, the government would in practice have to compel the owner actually to use the land in the best way, hence to prescribe its use in some detail.' Since we have shown that rentals will indeed be market based, this assertion is without foundation. Nevertheless, it is then used for repeated assertions that full collection of rent will lead to socialism. Whatever Henry George may have said (and Dr Knight digs up some quotes in this regard), readers of this book, and especially socialists, will note that we have made no reference whatsoever to the need for intervention in the economy by government. On the contrary; we believe that the renaissance of business, freed from the shackles of indiscriminate taxation, will rapidly reduce what is becoming an unsustainable welfare burden for the state.

> [A]ny benefits that a landowner derives from land that is better than the worst land in use is to be taxed away. ... What good are title deeds if the government takes all the net income? How long would you want to hold an asset from which all the income is expropriated?[10]

This objection is a complete misreading of the fact that, whereas resource rentals on a site are objectively determined by market values without regard to the efficiency or lack thereof of the owner, it is precisely the present tax system that ratchets up its take in line with his productivity or profitability.

> [Land speculation is risky and expensive; speculators do not, on average, earn undue profits.] Moreover, if society proposes to confiscate the gains of the winners, it ought to compensate the losses of the losers – not only to meet the demands of justice, but also to preserve entrepreneurial incentives.[11]

Not only is this automatically effected by higher or lower resource

10 *Ibid.*, pp.52-53.
11 *Ibid.*, p.53 (quoting Professor Frank Knight with permission).

rentals, but the lower business start-up costs (no capital outlay for land), would undoubtedly whet entrepreneurial appetites.

> The Georgists have apparently forgotten that we are no longer a hunter gatherer society ... even though all land may once have been common 'property', this does not give to every newborn today a share in everyone else's property. The whole meaning, and practical virtue, of private property is that it is privately owned and controlled ... the collective farms of the old Soviet Union prove this ... a drive through the tribal land of (the now former) Lebowa is very instructive on the issue of common property ... the grass has been overgrazed and the trees are steadily disappearing ... it is in these regions where property rights are suppressed or undeveloped that no one laughs at Malthus.[12]

It requires a huge leap of the imagination to confuse acknowledgement of the fact that rent is community created with advocacy of Soviet-style state ownership of land or, worse still, the corruption of traditional tribal systems of land tenure, the results of which were apparent in late-stage apartheid Homelands. On the contrary; resource rental collection will free up the land market, increase supply, improve access for individuals and incentivise efficient management. Moreover, as far as the former Homelands are concerned, we have strongly recommended that steps be taken to ensure security of tenure as a first step towards rental collection.

> Lacking a clear understanding of what economists call 'positive externalities', some Georgists honestly believe that they would not be taxing labour and capital. Positive externalities are those benefits that a person bestows on others while working on his own behalf. For example, if your neighbour takes extra care to make his property aesthetically pleasing, you will also benefit (whether he intended it or not) and your property value will be commensurately higher. Symmetrically, if you also take extra care of your property, your neighbour will benefit. But it must be emphasised that these benefits result, not from the existence of some abstract 'community', but from the efforts of real individuals. The Georgists, thus, stumble into a fallacy of composition. By attempting to tax only the 'site value' of a property, they claim not to be taxing the labour and capital used on their property. But whenever they tax one person's property, they are in fact taxing everyone else's labour and capital that have contributed to its value.[13]

Anyone doubting the existence of 'community' in South Africa need

12 *Ibid.*, pp.55-56.
13 *Ibid.*, p.56.

only note the numerous, and regrettably often violent, protests by township communities against lack of service delivery, inclusion into the 'wrong' municipality or other real or perceived grievances. The town councillors and law enforcement authorities on the receiving end would laugh bitterly at the suggestion that they were perpetrated by 'abstract entities'. Moreover, it is far more than the neighbours' care (or lack thereof) of their properties that determines site value, but the entire spectrum of other amenities with sparse or highly developed infrastructure as the case may be. The chain of causality would extend, not only to the far corners of the country, but back to the making of the constitution, which has created the framework within which property owners can enjoy security of tenure. The relative stability that makes this possible is, of course, in stark contrast to that of some countries in the Middle East, which are still undergoing sectarian strife. Finally, rejection of the principle of resource rental collection at the local government level (i.e. site value rating) is by default to support rating of improvements, which is undoubtedly a tax on all labour and capital that contributed to value. If, however, it were to make the objectors happier, we would gladly restate our proposition to the effect that owners of individual properties should 'pay back' (via resource rentals) to the millions of (other) 'real individuals' who contributed to the value of their land. Thus, the latter would have the satisfaction of knowing that their efforts were resulting in the beneficiaries paying them back.

> It is ridiculous to assert that any income accrued through land ownership is unknown. The normal way of acquiring land ownership is to pay for it. The market price already has capitalised into it the expectations of future income accruals.[14]

This is true enough and will also apply to buyers of property when resource rentals are collected, as they will also have to turn their minds to likely developments. Needless to say, these are often unforeseen and this applies to windfall gains (such as those accruing to property owners in the vicinity of the Gautrain stations) or unexpected losses occurring when a particular local authority becomes dysfunctional (as, sadly, has occurred often enough). Resource rental collection will naturally increase or reduce rentals from owners accordingly. Yet again, of course, we have to remind objectors that property owners will benefit, to a greater or lesser extent, depending on the value of their properties, from the switch away from taxation.

14 *Ibid.*, p.57.

[S]ome supporters of the single tax now propose to collect only 80%
of the rent (Harrison 1983, Dunkley 1990). Without fanfare they are in
retreat. ... This is a move in the right direction and is to be welcomed
... As the rate falls, the tax on land rent comes to approximate a tax on
property values – at the limit.[15]

A move to collect 80% rent would be great progress and, indeed, our
proposals provide for incremental collection thereof. Collection of full
rental, however, probably remains first prize. It is also strange that an
avowed protagonist of free markets should be so distrustful of the
ability of free markets to value the land rental on an annual, instead
of capitalised, basis. Maybe the jury is still out; but we are betting that
markets will do it.

> Thus, the 'user charge' has no claim to elevated moral status. Indeed, it
> is not a land user charge at all, but merely a tax that goes to the govern-
> ment, thereby lowering returns to all capital and labour [that] are used
> on that property.[16]

We have, at times, used 'user charge' as synonymous with rental collection because it carries the clear connotation of a payment for value
received, in this case the economic rent or locational advantage. To
most taxpayers, the very word 'tax' connotes burden and is very rarely
seen as related to a specific benefit received in return. This applies even
in respect of the most basic function of the state – i.e. law and order
– the general provision of which is often sadly lacking. As regards
the lowering of all returns, we have already explained that, with rental
collection replacing taxation, operators on marginal sites will enjoy
enormous relief, efficient operators may well come out square while
inefficient operators on prime sites will certainly be incentivised to do
better or sell up and relocate.

In a somewhat different vein, the Land Tax Subcommittee of the
Katz Commission of Enquiry into A Rural Land Value Tax[17] noted
that the agricultural sector pointed out that, in provinces where alternative uses affected land values (such as in Gauteng), market value-
based land taxes could render land used for farming uneconomic.
Hence, it was seen as distortionary. For this reason, the commission
recommended that local authorities be given legal aid to apply use value
instead of market value. Generally speaking, of course, we were not
in favour of the tax because of its limited application (just another tax)

15 *Ibid.*, p.62.
16 *Ibid.*, p.58.
17 See discussion in the ensuing subsection.

and the likelihood that it would simply bring the principle of resource rental collection into disrepute.

Interestingly enough, however, one of the motivations for recommending its implementation was the principle of equity, since much of urban land was at the time subject to site value rating.

## Precedents

In this book we certainly claim no originality and, in answer to the question 'Has this been done before?' we can cite many examples, although none of them have been as comprehensive as what we propose. Nevertheless, and without attempting a full history of resource rental collection since the dawn of civilisation,[18] we can certainly provide food for thought.

### Ancient

To begin with, it is worth noting that the Biblical system of returning lands to their former owners in the Jubilee year, while by no means an example of rental collection, would, to the extent that it might have been applied, have prevented over-concentration of lands in the hands of the few.[19] As regards Byzantium, 'in spite of trading wealth the main source of the imperial revenue continued to be the land tax, and this was intimately bound up with the existence of free peasant proprietors who supplied recruits for the army.'[20]

### England

In England, the original feudal obligation of landholders in respect of military service was gradually commuted over the centuries to money payment. In 1198, under Richard I, one of the first attempts failed. Hubert Walter, who governed in Richard's absence 'attempted the revision of taxation and of the system of military service [and] arranged a new assessment by ploughlands, estimated at 100 acres each and demanded three shillings per ploughland,' but this failed and 'the old method of a mixture of personal service and scutage (money payments later permitted instead of knight or personal service) survived.'[21] Eventually, however, scutum fell into disuse rendering freehold 'scot-free'. Nevertheless, land tax played an important role in the reign of

18  For perspective in this regard see Ch.1 of *Land Value Taxation Around the World*, 2nd edition, ed. Robert V. Andelson, Robert Schalkenbach Foundation, New York, 1997.
19  Leviticus 25:10, 23-24.
20  Previté-Orton, C.W., *The Shorter Cambridge Medieval History*, Cambridge University Press, 1953, vol.1, p.271.
21  *Ibid.*, pp.718-19.

Queen Anne (1702-1714) which according to Churchill was one of the greatest reigns in English history 'rendered glorious by Marlborough's victories and guidance'.[22] The latter, of course, came at a cost and the Tories 'declared that the country gentlemen were being mulcted while the City of London, its bankers and merchants, established an ever-growing mortgage upon the landed estates.' Later, 'with a businessman at the head of affairs the atmosphere of national politics became increasingly materialistic.' Under Sir Robert Walpole who, by an entente with France and by rigid non-intervention in European politics avoided another war, 'taxation was low; the land tax, which was anxiously watched by the Tory squires, was reduced by economy to one shilling.'[23]

## South Africa

The first land tax in South Africa was the annual rent or recognition (*recognitie*) imposed in 1714 at the rate of £2-10s on the loan places (*leenings plaatsen*). These were farms or 'great cattle runs of 3,000 morgen held on loan from the [Dutch East India] Company first for six months and then for a year at a time. Until then the loan place was to all intents and purposes a free grant of land for which the government made no charge at all.'[24] The *recognitie* continued to be payable in the Cape of Good Hope, Orange Free State, Natal and the Zuid-Afrikaansche Republiek throughout the 19th century and was only finally abolished during the Great Depression of the 1930s. Two years after the Voortrekker republic of Natalia was founded in 1839, a land tax of 12 rix-dollars was imposed on farms of between 1,000 and 3,000 morgen. A farm exceeding 4,000 morgen was regarded as a double farm and the tax doubled.[25]

During the 20th century, in addition to the successful variants of resource rental collection via municipal site value rating and the gold mines formula tax discussed elsewhere, there was considerable interest in rural land tax, and a conference was held in Pretoria in 1992 on the topic.[26] Despite its narrow focus, it yielded a wealth of useful detailed examination and data not only as regards advantages and

---

22 Churchill, W., *A History of the English-Speaking Peoples*, Cassell & Co., London, 1957, vol. III, p.37.
23 *Ibid.*, pp.96-7.
24 Walker, E., *A History of Southern Africa*, Longmans, Green and Company, Limited, London, 1957.
25 *The Impact of Property Rates on Agricultural Land*, Elsenburg, June 2006, focusing on the KwaZulu-Natal PROVIDE decision-making enabling project, www.Elsenburg.com.
26 Franzsen, R.C.D. and Heyns, C H. (eds.), *A Land Tax for the New South Africa?* The Centre for Human Rights, University of Pretoria, Pretoria, 1992.

disadvantages, but also as regards valuation methods and its potential in the context of evolving African systems of land tenure. In 1995 the Commission of Enquiry into Certain Aspects of the Tax Structure of South Africa (Katz Commission) appointed a sub commission under the chairmanship of Dennis Davis which, in 1998, reported back on The Implications of Introducing a Land Tax in South Africa. Its detailed recommendations, based on extensive research, were broadly in favour of the introduction of a rural land tax subject to numerous caveats and exceptions, including tribal land where the relevant authorities lacked the capacity and the land had not been surveyed. Further useful research was conducted in 2006 on the impact of property rates on agricultural land in KwaZulu-Natal following the Local Government Property Rates Act 2004, as amended. Whereas at the time of the 1990s Land Tax investigations many South African cities had site value rating only, and so a rural land tax would at least have recognised the principle of equity as between rural and urban taxation, this act stipulated rating on both land and improvements with the result that talk of a rural land tax as such subsided. By 2013 the system was still undergoing many teething problems and valuation inconsistencies as regards implementation by the various municipalities.

## Asia

Land tax played a crucial role in the industrialisation of Japan following the Meiji restoration in 1872 as well as that of Taiwan in 1949. An account of this process is included in Robert Andelson's *Land Value Taxation Around the World*[27] and includes a description of how, after initially providing an indispensable boost to the process, vested interests and a general lack of understanding of the underlying principles, led to gradual disuse. Andelson has also assembled accounts of limited application in Korea, China and, with particularly useful effect at local government level, Australia and New Zealand.

Singapore and Hong Kong are interesting in as much as, despite their both being former British colonies, the Crown retained ownership of all land in Hong Kong and, in Singapore, over four-fifths is owned by the government. According to Andelson 'the inefficiencies that could have resulted from state ownership have been minimised through the creation of markets for state land and property leases. Unlike the socialist city where the absence of land markets had very negative impacts on efficiency, productivity, and environmental quality,

27 *Op. cit.*, ch. 15 & 17.

property markets are active in Hong Kong and Singapore and transmit important information to both users and urban planners.' Although neither government distinguishes between land and improvements it is apparent that both have, to a large extent, over many decades, succeeded in capturing a substantial proportion of land rent for the benefit of all. In both cases this has much to do with their famously low tax rates and bustling economies. It could well be, that owing to the extreme shortage of land on both states, owners are in any case incentivised towards optimal use of their properties.

In any event Singapore, in particular, to judge by the 2013 Budget estimates, still enjoys substantial capture of land rent. Of the total revenue forecast of SGD78.32bn some SGD15.9bn, or 19.9%, came from 'land sales' (we assume this means sale of land/property leases). Another 5.2% came from property rentals pushing the total to 25.1%. Neither should one ignore another 1.4% of 'rentals' elsewhere in the budget nor the 9.8% from investment income which, we suspect, is a result of judicious investment, over time, of land rent surpluses. The property tax, 10% on Annual Value for all properties (the majority of Singaporeans live in state-owned housing), kicks in at 4% on Annual Values over SGD55,000 and reaches 6% on properties with an Annual Value over SGD70,000. More than 55% of people in employment do not pay any income tax and, indeed, some 30% of the workforce actually receives 'workfare' payments. Personal income tax, accordingly, comprises a mere 9.7% of the 2013 budget revenue estimates. The corporate tax rate is 17% but, judging by all the tax breaks in the 2013 budget, the effective rate is significantly lower. Dividends are tax free and there are numerous incentives for business start-ups. The statement of Assets and Liabilities (31 March 2012) also makes for interesting reading with cash comprising SGD150bn of total assets of SGD765bn. Investments comprise SGD615bn and include SGD118bn of government stock. Quoted investments comprise SGD299bn and unquoted SGD197bn. Liabilities include 'Funds Set Aside for Special Purposes' of SGD537bn which, in turn, includes SGD206bn for Development as well as SGD390bn in respect of Government Securities. According to the Minister of Finance, Singapore has no debt and this is borne out by the nearly SGD500bn of net assets in its nest egg.

From its commencement in 1841, the British Government of Hong Kong generally leased land for 75 years either by selling at public auctions or by granting directly for the payment of an annual rent. There was no site value rating as such, and owners of income-yielding land or buildings were charged at a standard rate of 15% on the annual income of their properties. Rates were levied on land and property (whether income yielding or not) and were 5.5% of the estimated annual rental value. According to Andelson,[28] a study showed that the Hong Kong Government was able to capture 39% of land value increments occurring between 1970 and 1991 from land leased in the 1970s. Land revenue from the initial auctions, rather than from modifications and renewals, was the most important source of land revenue. Between 1970 and 1991, land revenue averaged 21% of total revenue and peaked at 35% in 1982. According to the 2013 estimates, land revenue is estimated at HK$69bn or 15.9% of total revenue of HK$435bn. It is still high, but we get the impression that rental capture is not as efficient in the post-colonial era and there have been suggestions that governance as regards the awarding of leases is somewhat lacking.

## Denmark

Denmark had for a long time valued land separately from improvements as well as implemented variants of land tax at local government level when, in 1957, the small Justice Party came to power in a coalition with the Socialists. When the so-called Ground Duty Government announced its intention to introduce a land tax, real estate speculators, anticipating lower land prices, switched to real investment and, for three years, Denmark prospered with low inflation, rising production and major improvements to its endemic foreign trade deficits. The fact that it lost all its seats in 1960 was due to a complex array of factors described in detail in Andelson's chapter on that country.[29] In 2007, land and property taxes comprised 8% of local government income.[30]

## Elsewhere

Detailed accounts in other countries by different writers in *Land Value Taxation around the World* of various forms of land value taxation, practised to a greater or lesser degree in the past, include Classical Antiquity and European feudalism, Argentina, Canada, Chile, Jamaica, Sunderland, Germany, Hungary, East Africa and Korea. To the extent that a partial collection of natural rent was thereby effected, the results

---

28 *Ibid.*, p. 235.
29 *Ibid.*, ch 8, p.135.
30 *The Danish Local Government System* Produced by Local Government Denmark (LGDK), February 2009, http://www.kl.dk/ImageVault/Images/id_38221/ImageVaultHandler.aspx. Date accessed 25 May 2014.

were beneficial. Finally, following numerous instances of valuable rights to oil, gas, mineral and other resources being given to government cronies for a song, governments are increasingly beginning, as suggested here, to auction them to suitably qualified bidders instead.

CHAPTER 5

# THE TANGLED TENTACLES
# OF TYRANNY REVEALED:
# UNPACKING THE TAX BURDEN

*'We, the people of South Africa ... Believe that South Africa belongs
to all who live in it, united in our diversity.'*[1]

W E BELIEVE THAT the stirring words above, taken from the
Freedom Charter and incorporated in the preamble to
the Constitution of South Africa, are not merely rhetoric,
but point the way to the large-scale replacement of existing taxes by
natural resource rentals that alone can put South Africa on the higher
growth path so vitally needed for job creation.

For, twenty years after the transition to a fully-fledged democracy,
it is common cause that much more remains to be done to achieve the
government's target of 6% in GDP growth and even if it were to be
attained, unemployment would remain at unacceptably high levels. And
yet, this is despite an era of increasing prosperity and, up to 2007, a
global economic boom. In South Africa, democracy and a newfound
social mobility have produced a constantly growing black middle class,
and this has fuelled a booming housing market and retail sector.
Together with a global boom in commodity prices, the Johannesburg
Stock Exchange (JSE) was propelled to all time highs in 2008, and
again in 2013, but the under-classes of the urban townships and shanty
towns, and the rural poor, remain mired in poverty and poor service
delivery. In addition to this, they bear the brunt of diseases such as

1 *The Constitution of the Republic of South Africa*, Act 108 of 1996, as adopted on 8 May 1996
and amended on 11 October 1996 by the Constituent Assembly.

HIV/Aids, tuberculosis, cholera and malaria. Unemployment, heavily concentrated among these classes, is variously estimated to be between 23% and 40%, and idle young men become cannon fodder for crime gangs and syndicates.

## Why all this poverty despite progress?

Why is this? Is it the fault of government? And if so, how is it that the country has prospered, relatively speaking, under its watch? Prior to the power-supply problems in early 2008 and the global credit crisis, levels of economic growth appeared to be robust and sustainable and were at their highest levels for decades. Although the government has put in place a wide range of benefits for the poor, it is widely credited for resisting pressure to adopt populist measures and has instead adopted responsible fiscal and monetary policies.

Nevertheless the question remains, why is there such a high rate of unemployment, and why is poverty increasing in step with increasing prosperity? At this juncture, the familiar refrain from government critics is that the economy cannot reach its potential because of rigid labour policies, lack of delivery from parastatal monopolies and government, over-regulation generally and, of course, crime and corruption.

## Not the usual suspect! It's the taxes stupid!

Surprisingly enough, while not absolving government of its responsibilities in these areas, we tend to regard these issues more as symptoms than causes. Our focus of concern – the tax system – may seem a strange one. Nevertheless, we believe it is the tax system that is debilitating for economic growth and hence motivates the government to be hyperactive in other areas. Most will contend that there is nothing wrong with our tax system; it is fully aligned with systems used in developed, industrialised countries around the world and is administered by an extraordinarily efficient government agency. That is indeed so, which is why the system is also extraordinarily complex. We have income tax on corporations and individuals; indirect taxes such as value-added tax (VAT), excise and customs duties; wealth taxes such as donations tax, estate duty, and capital gains tax; about 17 so-called 'green taxes'; 'sin taxes' on alcohol and tobacco; local property rates, and a myriad of sundry levies such as the petrol levy to finance the Road Accident Fund, the Unemployment Insurance Fund (UIF) and Skills Development.

Our real concern however, is that the burden of these taxes falls disproportionately on the poor, especially the rural poor, and on economic activity at the margin.[2] This distorts the economy and wreaks havoc on growth and social cohesion. This effect of the tax system is almost completely ignored and, in our opinion, is the reason why the Mbeki and Zuma governments had so little success dealing with the unemployed, the rural poor and their own allies in the trade union movement and the Communist Party.

## Taxes built into the cost of goods and services hit tax-exempt organisations and VAT-free foods

Below we give a glimpse of the horrendous complexity of the tax system and show how most taxes paid by business entities are built into costs (and therefore the prices) of goods and services. We also give a theoretical model of how built-in taxes plus VAT on the final selling price puts inflationary pressures on the prices of even VAT-free foods. These models also show that many so-called tax-exempt organisations are required to pay property, payroll and some indirect taxes, besides suffering the built-in taxes on the goods and services they purchase. This places funding pressures on them and may be restricting the useful work they carry out for society.

We outline below the principles that the tax system could follow in order to collect what naturally belongs to the citizens of the country, while allowing people to retain what belongs to them as individuals or business entities.

To put it very simply, if the state collects where it and the community as a collective have created value, instead of trying to collect where they have not, and thereby obliterating economic activity at the margin, we will prosper profusely.

It is possible for the government to collect the revenue it needs and at the same time lift the burden of taxation from the poor and middle classes, as well as from businesses at the margin in the vast areas of our country that have no locational advantage.

The first thing we need to do is establish what we should be taxing and what we should not be taxing. This is really quite simple: we should tax that revenue which arises from the establishment of good governance, justice, the rule of law and freedom, and we should not tax that

2 As shown in Chapter 3; the 'margin' and other key terms are defined in the Glossary.

which arises from individual and private effort and investment. At present we do exactly the opposite: we allow the natural wealth, the 'common property' of the citizens of the country to be appropriated as 'private property', and then attempt to extract taxes from the investment, work, consumption and savings of individuals and corporations. This leads to an enormously complex and ever-evolving tax system that pits the state against private citizens and corporations (who jealously guard what they believe is theirs) in a constant and costly battle of wits.

First, let us explain what we mean by the term 'common property'. As indicated earlier, we take our standpoint from the preamble to the Constitution, which states: *'South Africa belongs to all who live in it ...'*

South Africa, insofar as it is a physical entity, comprises its land, water, forest and mineral resources, its airspace, its coastal waters and the electromagnetic spectrum. These are the natural resources[3] that are common to all countries and pre-exist human occupation of the land. Land, water and air are the first factors necessary for humans to continue living in a particular area, and the others may help determine their relative prosperity. But the one common feature of these resources is that once an area becomes an identifiable political entity, these resources should become the common property of the people of that country.

But what is the reality? Most of these resources have been allowed to become private property, so that the resource rentals from the relative locational advantages, natural fertility or abundance of specific units of these resources, accrue to private owners, not to its constitutional owners, the totality of the citizens of that nation. There is a conundrum here: obviously, for reasons of good order and governance, individuals or corporations must have security of tenure in respect of such resources. Therefore, the owners of such resources would argue, they are also the legal beneficiaries of such resource rentals, even though these rentals are not due to any efforts on their part, but rather to the presence of a well-governed community, investments in infrastructure by the various levels of government, or the natural fertility or abundance of a specific unit of land. These individual owners or corporations may also argue that such unearned benefits arise from the concept of private property, and that any assault on such benefits is an assault on the concept of private property itself.

3 See Glossary.

We will argue, however, that such conflation of private property and a perceived corresponding right to any unearned benefits (arising from such property) has no foundation in natural law and is totally unnecessary. In our view, an unquestioning acceptance of such a right causes tax law to become not only unnecessarily complex, but results in taxation reaching into the pockets of those who palpably have no taxable capacity.[4] This includes people living on subsistence agriculture or social grants, but who still have to pay VAT on goods whose prices have already been inflated by various duties and taxes and levies included in the cost of transporting such goods. These taxes also obliterate meaningful economic activity in marginal areas, which could otherwise sustain economically active people, weaning them off dependence on social grants.

## Natural resource rental collection

To begin clearing these major distortions of economic activity, we must begin with the replacement of a large portion of existing taxes with the collection of what we have called 'resource rentals', while retaining a few special taxes. The revenue to be collected would comprise a number of elements:

- Resource rentals based on the unimproved value[5] of all land sites registered in the names of individuals, corporations and government agencies;
- Annual market-determined rentals for licences granted
  - to use the electromagnetic spectrum;
  - for fishing rights; and
  - for rights to operate sea- and airports, and to operate toll routes and specific rail routes;
- A special resource rental on mines that would take into account, *inter alia*, the depth and grade of ore, international commodity prices, distance from markets and the availability of public infrastructure and community facilities. This rental should adjust automatically as these factors change and would be similar to the profit/revenue ratio tax imposed on gold mines;
- An income tax on individuals earning over a high threshold, e.g. R2m per annum;

4 See Glossary.
5 See Glossary.

- A special tax regime for legacy rentiers such as banks; and
- Taxes on high-value luxury items, alcohol and tobacco products, carbon emissions and other environmentally negative activities.

In subsequent chapters we will detail the rationale and possible modus operandi for collection of each of the above elements.

A main feature of this proposal is that collection of all of these resource rentals and taxes would, unlike the present tax system, have much less (and in the case of marginal sites, zero) effect on the cost of goods and services provided by business entities. Furthermore, governments (at all levels) would largely cease to be major tax payers although they would become liable for land rentals. This would nevertheless reduce government budgets by up to 14%, and simplify government accounting. The Public Works Department (PWD) would immediately assume much greater importance both as a bigger cost centre as well as an opportunity for the public sector to use land optimally. Consideration could therefore be given to outsourcing its activities to the property industry or, at any rate, establishing industry norms and benchmarks for measuring its efficiency.

The vast cost and effort required to administer the present tax system by taxpayers, their advisors, and the South African Revenue Services (SARS) would be reduced considerably, thus freeing up a large number of highly skilled people to perform more productive work including more accurate and comprehensive resource rental evaluations.

(The cost of operating the SARS office is approximately R10bn per annum. On top of this, there is the cost of some 2,000 tax consultants registered with SARS, charging their clients at least R1bn per year. A further inestimable cost is incurred by other institutions and people who deal with tax matters in their daily work, for example, the courts that hear tax cases; the tax and other lawyers involved in such cases and in arranging their clients' tax affairs; financial consultants advising clients on investments that will minimise their tax liabilities; and the army of accountants, bookkeepers, paymasters and accounting and payroll system providers employed to account for and ensure the regular payment of PAYE, VAT, company tax and other taxes and levies. All of this is 'dead money', and yet is counted in the country's GDP.)

We envisage that the following taxes would, over a number of years, disappear:

- Income tax on individuals, except for those on a high-threshold income as suggested above;
- Company tax, except as envisaged in point 5 above;
- Value-added tax (except on certain high-value luxury items and alcohol and tobacco products);
- Most excise taxes and fuel levies; and
- Transfer and stamp duties.

We recommend that the Road Accident Fund be placed again under the control of the private short-term insurance industry, and that motor vehicle owners be obliged by law to purchase third-party cover on an annual basis.

Finally, we believe that the above proposals will provide a fiscal system that is not only pro-productivity (and therefore pro-business), but would also assist the government's pro-poor policies by expanding the spatial and other margins of productivity, removing the fiscal disincentives to fuller employment, and assisting individuals to earn a better living rather than relying on social grants.

## The strange phenomenon of government taxing itself

In South Africa, the national government collects the vast majority of taxes; provincial governments collect small amounts of taxes, mainly in the form of motor vehicle licences. The metropolitan local governments and some of the larger local municipalities are partially self-funding through the collection of property rates, but do receive some 'grants and subsidies' from central government. Johannesburg, for example, showed in its Medium Term Budget for 2013/14 that it would receive R5.2bn for operating expenses and R3.0bn for capital expenditure as compared with R6.5bn from its own property rates. The other metropolitan councils and large municipalities are supported likewise. Smaller municipalities (210 out of 245) are funded mainly by grants and subsidies from national government.[6] An amount of about R467bn was allocated for transfer to municipalities (R78bn) and the provincial governments (R389bn) for the 2012/13 financial year. This represented 48.1% of the total of R971bn in the medium-term expenditure estimates in the 2012/13 Budget.[7]

6 Makgetla, N., 'Local government budgets and development: a tale of two towns', in *State of the Nation: South Africa 2007*, HSRC Press, Cape Town, 2007.
7 *2013 National Budget Review, Estimates of National Expenditure 2013*, Table 4. p.xv, www.treasury.gov.za.

**Table 5.1: Consolidated government expenditure 2012/13: breakdown to facilitate estimates of taxes on salaries paid and goods and services purchased**

| Economic Classification | Rbn | % |
|---|---|---|
| **Current Payments** | | |
| Compensation of employees | 106 | 10.9 |
| Goods and services | 56 | 5.8 |
| Interest and rent on land | 89 | 9.2 |
| | 251 | 25.9 |
| **Transfers and Subsidies** | | |
| Provinces | 389 | 40.1 |
| Municipalities | 78 | 8.0 |
| Departmental agencies and accounts | 74 | 7.6 |
| Universities and technikons | 21 | 2.2 |
| Public corporations and private enterprises | 25 | 2.6 |
| Non-profit institutions | 2 | 0.2 |
| Households | 115 | 11.8 |
| | 704 | 72.5 |
| **Payments for Capital Assets** | | |
| Building and other fixed structures | 10 | 1.0 |
| Machinery and equipment | 4 | 0.4 |
| Software, intangible and financial assets | 2 | 0.2 |
| Land and subsoil assets | | 0.0 |
| | 16 | 1.6 |
| **Total** | **971** | **100.0** |

**Source:** 2013 National Budget Review.

Table 5.1 shows a breakdown of the national budget for the 2012/13 financial year divided between actual expenditure incurred to run the 34 government departments, and transfers made by these departments to provincial and municipal governments, departmental agencies (e.g. SARS), public and private corporations and non-governmental organisations (NGOs) that work with the various departments, foreign governments and corporations, and social grants paid to individuals and households. Actual expenditure to run these departments is broken down between salaries and wages, goods and services purchased, and capital expenditure on assets such as equipment and buildings. Also included in this category are interest on the national debt (R89bn) and, ironically, some small amounts paid for 'land rent'.

Unpacking the taxes on this expenditure requires some assumptions and rough estimates. For the salaries and wages paid to government employees (from the president to a janitor in a state school), payroll taxes are required to be deducted from employees' salaries and paid back to the government. These include PAYE, the employer's share of UIF contributions and the Skills Development Levy (assuming the government is required to pay this levy). These amounts have been estimated at 20% of the total salaries and wages expense of R106bn (called 'compensation of employees' in the printed appropriations) i.e. R21bn.

For expenditure on Goods & Services, Machinery & Equipment and Other Assets (usually referred to as 'Software and other intangible assets'), it has been assumed that the full amounts are all subject to VAT. These amounts have been calculated on the formula (VAT = $i$ x $^{14}/_{114}$) where $i$ = the VAT inclusive price paid; this VAT will be paid to SARS by the vendors of these goods and services. On these bases, government 'gets back' about R6.9bn on its expenditure of R56bn, or about 12.3% of this expenditure. However, included in the purchase price of goods and services, machinery and equipment, and other assets, would be fuel levies on petrol and diesel purchased by government departments, plus customs and excise duties on various items purchased, such as motor vehicles and computer equipment. With the limited information available, it would be impossible to even estimate how much this would come to. But all of these taxes and levies (PAYE, VAT, fuel levies and customs and excise duties) flow back to the government as revenue.

In respect of transfers and subsidies paid to other levels of government, government agencies, companies, NGOs and households, some of the money spent by these entities will also flow back to government in the form of taxes, levies and duties.

For the provinces, municipalities and the various government agencies, it has been assumed that these transfers (R541bn) constitute almost 100% of their revenue and that this money is spent in a similar fashion to that of the main government departments, i.e. on salaries and wages, and the purchase of various goods and services. For PAYE and VAT, this has been estimated at 17.1% of expenditure, about R93bn.

So, for PAYE and VAT paid by government and its agencies alone, nearly R121bn is returned to government coffers. If fuel levies (R41bn) and customs and excise duties (R28bn) were also included, would it be unreasonable to assume some 10% of this (R7bn) was paid by government, and therefore to estimate the total tax paid by government at over R128bn for the financial year 2012/13 i.e. over 13% of the total expenditure?

In respect of the transfers and subsidies paid to the other entities (universities and technikons, public and private corporations, NGOs and households) it can be assumed that they also spend this money on salaries and wages, and goods and services that include taxes and levies. As all these entities have other sources of income, it would be almost impossible to calculate how much of their government subsidies is returned to government in the form of taxes and levies.

The amounts paid to 'households' (R115bn) represent mainly social grants paid to the poorest of the poor: the unemployed, people with disabilities, child support and old-age pensions. Around 15 million people now receive grants, and in spite of administrative shenanigans, and despite the fact that the poverty it alleviates is largely caused by government failure to collect natural rent in the first place, this money is, in the circumstances, well spent. Nevertheless, rough surveys carried out by the authors and others show that at least 10% of these grants is returned in the form of VAT included in the price of goods and services purchased by grantees. In addition, in rural areas, these prices are further inflated by the cost of getting goods to these areas and other taxes such as fuel levies and customs and excise duties. We deal with this further in the final paragraph of this chapter.

Taking the other entities (R48bn) at 10% would return another R5bn and push the total tax recovered to not far short of R145bn or nearly 15% of the total expenditure in Table 5.1.

The main point, however, is that if taxes such as PAYE, VAT, fuel levies and some customs and excise duties are replaced by the collection of resource rentals, we could do away with this costly and complex roundabout of taxes that inflates government revenue and expenditure. Some may argue that this doesn't matter, as the ins and outs will neutralise each other. That is not entirely true; this 'give and take' requires the services of thousands of skilled people and their computer systems to account for this money. In spite of this, billions of Rand will be lost and misappropriated in the process. In addition, these taxes inflate the price of goods and services in the rural areas where people can least afford them. This is the greatest iniquity of all and it is one of the reasons why the rural areas are kept in poverty.

## What companies really pay in tax

A number of companies listed on the JSE present a value added statement in their annual financial report. Together with this statement, some also show a 'Statement of Monetary Exchanges with

Government'. This statement lists the taxes paid to government and any subsidies received.

From this information, and the information supplied in the audited financial statements, it is possible to strip out taxes that are included in the companies' costs, such as customs and excise duties, PAYE and other payroll related taxes and levies, property taxes and unrecoverable VAT, and arrive at a new operating profit or EBITDA (earnings before interest, taxation, depreciation and amortisation). However, this information is not required by statute or accepted accounting standards and it is difficult for an individual to obtain sufficient data to come to a meaningful conclusion on the total taxes borne by companies.

In a report[8] on the total tax contribution of companies, based on a survey of 50 of South Africa's largest companies, Pricewaterhouse-Coopers (PwC), an international accounting services firm, reported that South African companies are subject to 21 taxes divided between profit, property, employment, indirect, environmental and other taxes.

PwC categorise taxes as either taxes borne or taxes collected. Taxes borne, it states, 'are the company's immediate cost and will impact their results. They are charged to the company's profit and loss account and passed on to customers, employees and shareholders.'

Taxes collected, on the other hand, 'are not the company's own costs, but collected on behalf of government'.

The PwC report is important in that it sheds light on the large number of taxes that companies have to deal with and the implied costs associated with accounting for these taxes. However, we believe their distinction between 'taxes borne' and 'taxes collected' is not wholly accurate. We suggest that three categories of taxes would better reflect the state of corporate taxation in South Africa today.

The first category comprises taxes borne by the company, paid to the revenue authorities and not passed on in the cost of their goods or services. Following the phasing out of the STC, the only tax in this category is company tax. Such taxes are, of course, passed on indirectly to shareholders in the form of lower dividends.

The second category comprises taxes collected on behalf of government but which are not costed into their goods or services. At present only VAT falls into this category, i.e. output VAT on sales less allowed input VAT on goods and services purchased.

All the remaining taxes are costed into the price of the company's goods and services. Not all these taxes are paid by the company to

8 'Total Tax Contribution: How Much Tax Do Large South African Companies Really Pay?'

Revenue: the excise tax on fuel, the fuel levies and the Road Accident Fund levy, for example, are paid by the oil companies to Revenue and passed on to the end users in the price of fuel. For other companies purchasing this fuel for their vehicles, these taxes are included in their costs and passed on to their own customers.

Some taxes in this category are paid to Revenue, for example PAYE deducted from employees' salaries and wages. PwC state that these taxes are not borne by the company, but are merely deducted from the salaries and passed on to Revenue. In our opinion, this is not strictly correct. If an employee receives a salary of R10,000, this full amount is treated as a cost; the fact that some gets paid to the employee and some to Revenue, is immaterial.

The point being made, however, is that the wealth created/value added by companies bears considerably more taxation than simply company tax. Company tax is the only tax that appears in the income statement; most other taxes are hidden in various expenses, and, of course, allowed as deductible expenses in the calculation of company tax. But these 'other' taxes are costed into the price of goods and services, to which, in turn, VAT is added. The PwC report makes a huge contribution towards highlighting these facts; our regret is that it does not emphasise the volume of taxation that is buried into business costs and passed on to end consumers.

In our opinion, all this involves huge complication, is unnecessarily expensive, and above all, is inflationary.

## Individuals: bearing the final brunt of taxation

We have pointed out that while business entities themselves actually pay some of the taxes imposed on them, many taxes such as customs and excise duties, payroll taxes, *ad valorem* duties on capital items, and fuel taxes and levies are costed into the price of goods and services. If these supplies are purchased by another business, they are costed into the price of their goods and services, and these taxes, together with the additional mark-ups settle as a kind of sediment into the prices finally paid by the end consumer. The hardest hit by this build-up of taxes are the rural poor. The further goods have to be transported to their destination, the greater the amount of taxes that accumulates into the cost of these goods. To this final cost is added the retailer's margin, then finally VAT of 14%. One has to accept that small retailers operating at a distance from their suppliers will always pay a higher price for goods because of their inability to negotiate bulk purchasing deals, and the additional transport costs. But to apply additional taxes and levies on top is to add insult to injury.

To calculate the exact amount of tax in any product would be difficult without details of the precise costing of a particular product and the amount of tax in each component of these costs. The price of a simple staple such as a loaf of bread has emotional resonance in a country with a large population of poor people, but the tax component of the price (other than the VAT) is glossed over. The *Financial Mail*[9] gave a glimpse of the costing of a white (brown bread is zero-rated) loaf of bread and *Business Day*[10] reported on a tentative probe into the effect of taxation on the price of white bread. However, only VAT and the import duty on wheat were considered. A real debate will start when it is possible to consider other taxes that are costed into the price of bread, and of course, into all goods and services. In spite of the difficulty in calculating the extent of these taxes embedded into the price of manufactured goods, an attempt is made to do so here in the case of a loaf of white bread, based on information that is available.

The starting point is the retail price of a standard white loaf at R9.40.[11] From this is deducted VAT of R1.15 to arrive at an exclusive price of R8.25. According to a report in *Business Day*, this exclusive price is shared between the producer, infrastructure, miller, baker and retailer and varying percentages calculated by the National Agricultural Marketing Council.[12] The breakdown of the share of the retail price between these providers and government is shown in Table 5.2.

Each of the five providers has input costs (both direct and indirect) and a profit margin, on which income tax is levied. Input costs comprise raw materials and other direct costs such as electricity and water, fuel and packaging; salaries and wages (both direct and indirect); marketing, distribution and administration costs; depreciation and amortisation; and interest on loans. All of these costs (other than interest) have various taxes embedded in them, some of which are paid by the entity, and some that are included in the cost of the inputs, i.e. are paid by the original provider. The major taxes included in these costs are set out in Table 5.3.

Survey: September 2008.
9 *Financial Mail*, 8 February 2008.
10 *Business Day*, 20 February 2008.
11 Average price of a white loaf at a Johannesburg northern suburbs Spar, June 2008.
12 Source: *Business Day*, 'Pioneer aims to reduce shelf prices', June 19, 2008.

### Table 5.2: A loaf of white bread: contributors' slices[13]

|  | R | % |
| --- | --- | --- |
| **Inclusive Price** | **9.40** | **100.0** |
| Government (VAT only)* | 1.15 | 12.2 |
| Producer | 1.68 | 17.9 |
| Infrastructure | 0.41 | 4.4 |
| Miller | 0.92 | 9.8 |
| Baker | 4.13 | 43.9 |
| Retailer | 1.11 | 11.8 |
| **Total** | **9.40** | **100.0** |

*VAT is 14% of the exclusive price of R8.25

### Table 5.3: Major taxes built into the cost of goods and services[14]

| SA Main Budget Revenue 2012/13 | Rbn |
| --- | --- |
| **Taxes on goods & services** |  |
| VAT | 217.0 |
| Specific excise duties | 28.4 |
| *Ad valorem* excise duties | 2.2 |
| Fuel levies | 40.5 |
| Electricity levy, etc. | 10.9 |
| Customs duties | 37.6 |
| **Total** | **366.6** |
| **Total tax revenue** | **810.0** |

These 'hidden' taxes are not inconsiderable; the estimated revenue from these taxes for the 2012/13 tax year of R367bn[15] was about 45% of the estimated total tax revenue.[16] All of these taxes are borne by end consumers, most of whom (such as low-paid workers, informal workers, the rural poor and the unemployed) have no taxable capacity.

So, getting back to our loaf of bread, what's the bottom line? Well, if we had to take a wild guess at the pre-tax margins of the providers from producers through to retailers (and this is often a subject of acrimonious debate among them) as being, say, 5% of the remaining

13 *Ibid.*
14 Source: SA Budget 2013/14: www.treasury.gov.za.
15 Some of these taxes are borne by individuals and are not directly built into the cost of goods and services.
16 The total tax revenues of R810bn do not include local property rates estimated by the authors at R24bn for 2012/13. A large portion is borne by individual home owners; only the portion by business entities will be built into the cost of goods and services.

87.8% after VAT this would amount to 4.39% of which the government, assuming average tax at 28%, would get 1.23%. Again, taking another wild guess at fuel comprising 10% of the players' 87.8% then, based on our estimates in Chapter 11 of fuel levies (and so on) comprising 28.5% of the retail price, the fuel levy (etc.) would comprise 2.85%. These two items would therefore comprise another 4.1%, taking the government's take to 16.3%. As regards other hidden taxes such as customs duties on plant and machinery used, even we would hesitate to guess but we are sure no one would begrudge us rounding the government's take up to 16.5% for what we feel detailed research would show to have been a conservative estimate. Of the then price of R9.40 for a loaf of white bread therefore, the government would have got R1.55. The fact of the matter, of course, is that whatever contribution the government made to the production of this loaf of bread would have been reflected in the providers' site values. So it is there that it should have collected its dues rather interposing itself between the product of labour and capital on the one hand and the bread buyer on the other.

For the rural poor, the problem is compounded by the additional costs and taxes to get these goods to the rural areas. Seen in this light, it is hardly surprising that there is a continual flight of rural poor to the metropolitan areas. Ironically, this flight is in itself a testimony to the success of our government, as is the case with many the world over, in extracting taxes from the people via intermediaries. The flip-side of this, of course, is the resultant urban shanty towns. We believe these taxes are not only regressive in the sense of oppressing the poor, but also in terms of depressing economic activity in remote rural and other less favourable locations. Merely shifting this burden would, we believe, go a long way towards restoring normal economic activity in these blighted areas.

## CHAPTER 6

# RENTAL COLLECTION: GENERAL

*'There is a sense in which all taxes are antagonistic to free enterprise …*
*In my opinion the least bad tax is the property tax on the unimproved*
*value of land, proposed by Henry George long ago.'*
Milton Friedman[1]

## Our land

SOUTH AFRICA'S land mass is about 1.2 million square kilometres. Of this, 68% is used for grazing land, 15% is arable, and 10% is used for nature conservation. The balance of 7% is termed 'other' i.e. urban or mining land.[2] While this 7% is obviously South Africa's most valuable resource in terms of straight land value, all of the land, together with the other resources we have previously listed (mineral wealth, water, the electromagnetic spectrum, and the littoral space around its coast), is the 'South Africa' which, we maintain, 'belongs to all who live in it'. These are the resources that are used by all inhabitants, both citizens and non-citizens, to live, play and earn a living in, and the rental for the right to use these resources is the country's patrimony.

Of South Africa's estimated population of nearly 52 million in 2011, around 32 million lived in urban areas and 20 million in rural areas.[3] However, *South Africa at a Glance* states that the agricultural sector employs about 1 million people which means that most of the rest are subsistence farmers or are retired, unemployed, or children living in

1 November 1978 (http://www.wealthandwant.com/themes/Friedman.html).
2 Dept of Agriculture, *South Africa at a Glance 2007-8*, Editors Inc, Johannesburg.
3 Statistics SA: 2011 Census and Statistics SA.

rural areas. This conjures up a picture of poverty and deprivation which, by comparison, makes the urban areas attractive, even though they comprise only 7% of the total land area of South Africa.

Most of the 'rural area' on which 20 million people live, is what is described as 'grazing land', but large portions on the eastern seaboard have good soil and considerably better rainfall than the western half of the country. Much of this land is arable, but not well-developed as commercial farmland for historical, social and cultural reasons. For this and many other reasons, there is an enormous difference between the value of the poorest grazing land and the prime areas of the large cities. For example, a hectare of the poorest grazing land (in a commercial farming area) can be bought for about R450, but prime residential land on the Atlantic Seaboard of Cape Town can fetch up to R40 000 per square metre (R400 million per hectare).

This vast range in the value of land reflects absolutely the differential demand-productivity and locational advantages of the various sites. Yet those who live and work on the poorest land are subject to the same indirect taxes such as VAT, and in fact are penalised with escalating fuel taxes the further they live and operate from their markets and sources of supply. Viewed in this light, the poverty in rural areas and the overwhelming desire of many who live there to escape to the cities can be better understood.[4]

It is this cruel anomaly that provides the background against which we have based our proposals for the collection of resource rentals, and on which many before us, going back to Adam Smith and Henry George, have based their 'land-value taxation' ideas. While poverty-alleviating programmes are commendably high in South Africa, they will always hit the brick wall of poverty-creating taxes imposed on the marginal areas. Removing these taxes will not necessarily remove the need for these programmes, but will certainly make them far more effective.

## Proposals

As discussed in Chapter 5, the proposed policy aim is to collect the annual rental value of all land, excluding the value of improvements thereon. We now set out below the broad steps that would be necessary to achieve this.

4 The problem of individuals bearing the brunt of taxation is developed further in Chapter 14.

## 1 Establish a nationwide database

The first step to this end would be to build up a nationwide database of unimproved site values early on in the planning stages for a transition to a resource rental collection system. South Africa is fortunate in that it already has an advanced system of land registrations and, except for communal and tribal-held land, all registered sites are properly surveyed and demarcated. In most cases, the current owners of such sites are also known.

## 2 Change the municipal rating system to one of site value rating

The change to a system of total value rating in the Local Government Municipal Property Rates Act of 2004[5] was regrettable in that the majority of municipalities had been on site value rating for many years (Johannesburg since 1918) and the system was well-established and understood. In addition, it is easier to value land on its own, as most sites in a particular area (such as a suburb) have similar values per square metre and Computer-Assisted Mass Appraisal (CAMA) techniques can be used. Moreover, in surveys[6] conducted in the 1980s it was shown, not only that there had been a steady swing away from rating improvements towards rating land values only, but that towns and cities using the site value rating only grew about twice as fast as the others in the 10-year period to 1984. In the 48 largest towns and cities, the discrepancy was even more marked with those on site value growing 413% as compared with 282% for those on composite (separate rates for land and improvements) and 189% for those on flat rating (a single rate on the combined value of land and improvements).

But most importantly, a change in the local property rating act needs to be made to allow the establishment of a national land value database well before any fundamental change in the tax system.

## 3 Set up a special SARS unit

In order to ensure uniform valuation criteria, it is proposed that SARS set up a special unit to liaise with local authorities to this end. Many municipalities, especially the smaller ones, are in any event struggling to implement the new total value rating system.

5 Act no. 6 of 2004.
6 Dunkley, G., *That All May Live*, A. Whyte Publishers, 1990, Ch. 14.

## 4 Phasing-in proposals

It is important to remember at the outset that existing taxes do collect a good proportion of natural rent, albeit inadequately and in a distorting fashion. Current land prices therefore only reflect the market's best estimate of future uncollected resource rentals.

It follows, therefore, that as existing taxes are reduced, the proportion of uncollected resource rentals will increase. In other words, were the Treasury not about to collect resource rentals on an annual basis, land prices would increase! The full annual revenue potential of resource rental collection is therefore far greater than would be indicated by the estimated annual value (say 5%) of total current land valuations. These should nevertheless provide an invaluable matrix of relative values throughout the spectrum from remote rural to central urban land, and this database will be an essential tool for establishing initial annual resource rentals payable to the Treasury on all sites.

The initial phasing-in programme will be all-important from a political and fiscal point of view; however, it may be necessary to signal a change in fiscal direction without it being so momentous that it causes damage to the national revenue. A suggestion is that once the national land-value database has been established, a national land-value rental be levied at a low percentage on all land values over a certain threshold. Depending on the level of revenue that would be raised, it could be used to reduce VAT to, say, 10%. While this is a fairly simplistic example of what could be done, it balances a payment by landowners and tenants (the land rental would generally be passed on to tenants), against benefits for everyone in a reduction in VAT.

This sort of initiative would signal two fundamental changes to fiscal policy without causing a major fiscal earthquake. First, it signals a move (over a number of years) to a site value land rental on a national basis; and secondly, a gradual phase-out of VAT and PAYE.

While the initial step in this programme would cause a small reduction in land prices, it would not be sufficient to cause a problem for home owners with large mortgage bonds. Besides, there would be a reduction in prices as VAT was phased out, enabling home-owners to accelerate mortgage repayments.

As the national land value rental scheme is phased in, land *resale* prices will tend to zero. This does not mean that the *initial relative capital value database* for the purpose of calculating the national land-value rental will change; the only time it will change is when there are locational changes, making the site less or more desirable, that is, reducing or increasing the relative value of the site. This will necessitate an ongoing programme to update land values with provision for objections by land owners as well as auction mechanisms to establish market related land rentals if necessary. In the latter event, the value of improvements would be independently established up front together with proof of ability to pay from the buyers so as to prevent frivolous or mischievous bids.

## 5 Commercial farms

The aforementioned proposals apply as a generic model for all land, urban or rural. However, we believe that special attention needs to be paid to agricultural land due to South Africa's erratic weather patterns and the often harsh physical land conditions as well as the need to ensure the country's food security.

With many municipalities battling to cope with urban valuations and revaluations, it would be unrealistic to expect them to address the farm valuations falling nominally within their areas of jurisdiction.

We therefore propose that:

- SARS set up a dedicated unit for this purpose with responsibility, as in urban valuations, for overall coordination and oversight of appropriate benchmarks;
- Regional valuation review boards be established with equal representation from SARS, the Department of Agriculture and Land Affairs on the one hand, and organised agriculture and rural real estate practitioners on the other hand;
- Valuations be conducted by teams appointed by the review boards comprising both suitably qualified officials and private sector practitioners;[7]
- Valuations be based initially on the matrix of nationwide land values for farms established on the same basis as for urban valuations;
- Valuation teams be directed to base their valuations primarily on actual transactions; and
- ALL improvements be excluded, i.e. fences, dams, roads, and buildings as well as standing crops, orchards, cane plants and so on.

7 There would be nothing new in this, as Adam Smith, when discussing the levying of a land tax, suggested the landlord be allowed 'to ascertain, in conjunction with the officers of revenue, the actual value of his lands, according to the equitable arbitration of a certain number of landlords and farmers in the neighbourhood, equally chosen by both parties.' (from *An Inquiry into the Nature and Causes of the Wealth of Nations*, The Modern Library, New York, 1994, Book V, Ch. 2, Part II, p.896).

The practical implications of this approach for the commercial sector are explored in more detail in Chapter 11.

## 6 Redistributed farms

Although the obligation to keep the 'people's land in good condition and pay the people's rent' rests on the shoulders of these owners as much as anyone else, allowance needs to be made for certain handicaps such as a possible lack of expertise, training and so on.

It is therefore proposed that:

- The same valuation procedures as for commercial farms be adopted;
- Where necessary, a phase-in period of, say, five years, be allowed;
- In the event of continued inability to pay the rent after the phase-in period, the Department of Agriculture should determine whether there is a reasonable prospect of the owner being able to do so within the ensuing five-year period and, if so, under what conditions (including training or obligation to adhere to systems/programmes recommended by the Department) to grant a further phase in period; and
- In the event of continued failure to pay the resource rental the owner, or Department of Agricultural Affairs, would be obliged to sell the farm to another suitably qualified farmer.

## 7 Communally held land

While it would be necessary to value all land, including communally held land, we have suggested that the 2014 income tax threshold of R67,000 per annum for individuals be made applicable to individuals for rental collection as well. In many cases, land held by individuals in communal areas would fall below this threshold. This would in effect represent marginal land enjoying little or none of the locational advantage or rent, which we believe is the primary basis of payment to the Treasury. Nevertheless, we discuss on the following page some important principles relating to this type of land.

- Security of tenure – Regardless of whether the former Homelands move to full congruence with the system of land tenure in use in the rest of the country or not, the prime requirements both for efficient fiscal purposes as well as normal economic activity remain security of tenure and transparency of transfer and valuation procedures.
- Valuation – In the event that communal title remains in place, security of tenure would probably best be achieved by a system of

leasehold, in which case annual rental valuations and the regular (triennial) revaluation would most effectively be achieved by auction.

- Traditional leaders – Traditional leaders would need to play an important part in ensuring the transition to a modern efficient economy, based on efficient use and equitable allocation of the natural resources in their areas.

- Community representation – Several speakers at the Land Value Tax for the New South Africa conference in 1992 stressed that community involvement in the valuation process was vitally necessary.

- Existing resource-based income – Rural authorities, such as the Royal Bafokeng, who succeeded in leveraging their ownership or control of natural resources into royalty income, are to be commended for their wisdom and ingenuity. Likewise, the Royal Bafokeng's success in persuading Impala Platinum to commute the royalties into a Black Economic Empowerment (BEE) shareholding was an intelligent move that avoided a possibly awkward conflict of interest between its right to a royalty from Impala and the latter's obligation, under the recent royalty legislation, to pay royalties to the Treasury.

- Roll-out potential of Royal Bafokeng model – Under the constitutionally provided for (S.219) allocation of centrally collected land resource rentals, local authorities, especially in the rural areas, would be entitled to considerably higher *per capita* allocations for infrastructure development than before. In principle, it should be noted that all rural people of South Africa are entitled to as healthy a share in natural resource-based revenues as those currently enjoyed by the Bafokeng. According to *Finweek* (24 March 2007), Royal Bafokeng Holdings, owned by the Royal Bafokeng Nation, had assets of about R25bn and dividend income of between R750m and R1bn per annum. Of this sum, R400m/year is spent on social infrastructure programmes under the Bafokeng's Vision 2020 (a plan to ensure the Bafokeng become economically self-sustained by 2020). There are about 300,000 Bafokeng who live mainly in the Phokeng area, but these upliftment plans benefit all those who live there, comprising about 50% non-Bafokeng. For some reason, it appears the Bafokeng setup is corruption-free which, if so, is all the more reason for it to be taken seriously as a role model.

Additional implications for, and background to, the implementation of these proposals for traditional agriculture are given in Chapter 12.

## 8 Phasing in period

Any scheme such as that outlined above, which will in fact diminish the *price* of property, needs to be treated with the utmost caution, and may have to be introduced over a lengthy period even up to ten years. (Markets may however, anticipate this very quickly and demand certainty, in which case the pace could be accelerated accordingly.) This will give time to ameliorate any financial difficulties that may be experienced by some people during the change-over as well as to appreciate the advantages of this dispensation.

## 9 Transparency

Finally, it is of the utmost importance that all the people of South Africa, from a pensioner to the CEO of MTN, can find out at any time what the going rental is on any of our natural resources. It would probably be necessary, therefore, for a government to allocate more resources to the provision of up-to-date information; but at the same time, we envisage that the private sector would also compete to provide the best data as is the case already with banks and estate agents. We envisage also that the results of major rental settings, whether by auction, negotiation or official determination, be regularly published on news bulletins since they will be, after all, as important (if not more important) than stock exchange prices. In time, as we move closer to collecting the full rent instead of taxation, the auction mechanism will become more important especially as regards larger transactions.

Resource rental collection meets Adam Smith's maxims of taxation:

- Ability to pay (equity) – Since land rentals are directly related to the productive potential or locational advantage of land, efficient use thereof will cover the rent (see also our proposals to facilitate the necessary provision of credit in Chapter 16).
- Certainty – The abundance of market information on prevailing rentals that we envisage will guide owners as to the likely outcome of the next triennial valuations
- Convenience – For the vast majority of landowners, monthly payments would meet this criterion, but provision would be necessary for primary producers if this income occurred, say, annually, after harvest time.
- Efficiency – Some speakers at the land tax conference in 1992 doubted whether the valuation costs were justified in view of the small amounts realisable by rural land taxes. This should be seen in the context of the limited approach at that conference of

implementing a rural land tax only, whereas we are talking about land rental collection on all land. Moreover, with a clear-cut system of land title in South Africa, there is no doubt as to who is liable for the tax. Landowners would indeed, where applicable, recover land rents from their tenants. In most cases they would be doing so at the same time as recovering rentals for improvements. From a collection point of view, it would be simple.

## Benefits flowing from these proposals

These may be summarised as follows:

- In natural law land can only 'belong' to the nation established on that land. Individuals can use parcels of land, and are granted security of tenure under certain conditions such as: they pay the rent for that land and keep it in good condition. This levels the economic playing field and allows everyone to have a place of their own.
- To the extent that inefficient owners are encouraged to sell, this generally makes more land available for production.
- A much more obvious connection between benefits received from (and payments to) the community will lead to better 'tax morality'.
- In contrast to the present system, which often encourages withholding of land from use, optimal use will be encouraged, somewhat akin to the 'use it or lose it' mineral rights regime.
- It will re-awaken normal economic activity in rural areas, turning backwaters into hives of prosperity.
- It will elevate the keeping of land in good condition to a fundamental obligation of land ownership, as opposed to ad hoc recognition in various statutes and areas of the common law, and ensure that the new-found incentives to use resources efficiently do not conflict with the environmental requirements of sustainable growth
- Land speculation will be kept to a minimum, and will only be possible where the resource rental is too low. This will prevent landowners from withholding land from use, but will not stop developers from selling or letting out buildings on their land.
- The tax system will be enormously simplified; for the vast majority of the population it will simply not exist.

Incentives will be aligned more rationally; the private sector, corporations and individuals alike, will be better motivated by the realisation that, after payment of the rent, 100% of all additional value added is theirs i.e. the marginal tax rate = zero! The public sector, on the other hand, will be much more clearly motivated to fulfil its obligations to maintain law and order and infrastructure because of the direct link between its doing so and increased rentals. However, the changeover from the present system will have to be handled extremely carefully to allow for the variety of circumstances in which property owners (especially homeowners) find themselves.

## Land reform

Rental collection will immediately restore ongoing legitimacy to land ownership insofar as it will immediately be apparent to all the people that from now on they are receiving full value for their land on an ongoing basis. Although it will tend to make land more available for production, it will not in itself, however, immediately correct the legacy of a racially skewed distribution of land ownership. For that, proactive programmes and targets, such as those already legislated, are necessary. What these proposals do highlight, however, is the need to redouble efforts to ensure that recipients of redistributed land are able to pay the rent. Otherwise the people lose out not only from not getting full rental value for their land but also, possibly, suffering higher prices from aggravated food shortages. Fortunately there are signs that land reform may move from the earlier phase of mutual recriminations between established farmers and the authorities responsible towards greater realism. Many farmers, for example, are keen to act as mentors of the new entrants while the Department of Land Affairs (DLA) seems to have a better understanding of the land market, including the fact that there is plenty of land to be had from it. This realism will need to extend to appreciate that, while the lower farm prices (which should eventually comprise payment for improvements only) will save some capital outlay, all of the savings and more will be required for training and mentorship of the new entrants. To the extent that capacity is lacking for this in the DLA, provision should be made for approval and support of private sector initiatives to achieve these aims on a regional basis. The most important aspect of our proposals in this regard, however, is that they have the potential for depoliticising an issue which could otherwise easily undermine the entire economy. By highlighting the true and fundamental obligations of land ownership as well as the real work required to address the legacy of skewed ownership distribution, it will make it easier to distinguish between political posturing and positive practical proposals. Above all else, all the actors in this theatre of the economy – established farmers, DLA and new entrants alike – will know that their performance is being watched with great interest and full understanding in the light of these principles by all the ultimate owners of this land!

## New vision for land ownership

Land is an emotional issue in South Africa. Many black people, even though they may have a 'Western-type' lifestyle in the cities, often repair to what they consider to be their ancestral homes at specific times of the year. Much of what is known as tribal or communally held land is not held by individuals or corporations under freehold tenure. No first nations held such notions, even though they allowed security of tenure under certain conditions. Ownership of land does, in fact, go back many millennia because powerful men knew that ownership of land equated with control of the people. It was the Anglo-Saxons and the Normans after their conquest of England who gentrified the ownership of land with written title deeds.

This practice spread to countries colonised by the English, and in South Africa it has been the major cause of conflict between Africans and European colonists and their descendants. The system of registered title deeds is considered very civilised (and does have practical advantages), but in its present guise is a means of shutting out and controlling those who do not have land.

Any scheme, therefore, that will diminish the value of an individual's property is greeted with howls of angry indignation and protest. This is especially so in the case of homeowners, and their first line of attack against any scheme such as a new highway, a block of flats or offices near their home is: 'It will reduce the value of my property.' Yet the bursting of a house-price bubble or increases in interest rates are considered to be in the same league as an act of God. As insurance companies are loath to cover 'Acts of God', they certainly would not cover a decline in property prices due to an economic downturn.

An important aspect of these proposals is that there is a fundamental change from a multi-pronged tax system that targets all sections of the population regardless of whether they have the capacity to bear such taxes, to a system that is focused on the value people and corporations receive from their use of resources that 'belong to the people of South Africa'.

So for example, a person owning a large property in a prime residential area may pay R50,000 or more per month as a resource rental on that land. While this may sound like a large sum of money (R600,000 per annum), it should be remembered that someone in this wealth bracket will pay easily this amount in income tax, VAT, fuel taxes and levies, local property taxes and so on. Most of these taxes should hopefully fall away. Also, people in this bracket pay large sums of money to tax consultants and financial planners in attempts to avoid as much tax as possible and there should be savings here as well.[8]

These proposals are in no way a method of 'targeting' the wealthy. We have no problem with people living in mansions on large pieces of land. But it can be seen why wealthy people have strenuously resisted schemes like this in the past: for example, David Lloyd George's 'Peoples' Budget' in Britain in 1909, a further attempt in Britain in 1930, and even the introduction of site value rating in Johannesburg in 1918. (Site value rating was eventually adopted by the majority of municipalities in South Africa and became a well-known and accepted method of municipal rating. This is one of the reasons why we believe the system we are advocating here has a better chance of succeeding in South Africa than almost any other country.)

However, a 'land tax' type of revenue collection would not collect all resource rentals and would therefore not be sufficient on its own to provide our modern economy with the revenue it needs. This is especially true in South Africa with its need to sustain a large portion of the population that historically has been under-serviced in areas such as health, education, and housing. In addition, there are other resources that belong to the people of South Africa such as the electromagnetic spectrum, fishing rights and strategic sites embedded in the country's infrastructure; collection of the appropriate rentals of which is dealt with in the following chapter.

8 See also examples in Chapter 15.

## CHAPTER 7

# RENTAL COLLECTION: SPECIAL CASES

*'Rent is that portion of the produce of the earth
which is paid to the landlord for the use of the original
and indestructible powers of the soil.'*
David Ricardo[1]

## Use of the electromagnetic spectrum (EMS)

RICARDO'S DEFINITION is sometimes used to show how irrelevant rent is in an industrial age, but with a broader understanding of 'earth' and 'soil', here we go!

The full electromagnetic spectrum ranges from radio waves to gamma rays, but for practical purposes, we need only deal with the 'broadcast' or radio frequency, which ranges from extremely low frequencies (3 Hz to 30 Hz) to extremely high frequencies (30 GHz to 300 GHz).

Most sovereign countries control the allocation of the spectrum for use by radio and television broadcasters, and telecommunication operators (both fixed-line and mobile). This instils some order in the allocation of spectrum, allows governments a degree of control over their use, and is also an opportunity for earning revenue. However, while some countries earn large sums from the auctioning of licences for mobile phones and broadcasting rights, South Africa, until mid-2010, did not follow this trend. The estimates of revenue for the 2013/14 fiscal year put out by the National Treasury did not appear to show any revenue from the licensing of broadcast and telecommunication

---

1 Ricardo, D., *The Principles of Political Economy and Taxation*, Dent, 1969, Ch.2, p.33.

operators. So any revenue received from these companies presumably would have been included in company taxes and VAT, or dividends where the government is a shareholder in the company.

Up to 1986, South Africa had only one broadcaster; the government-owned South African Broadcasting Corporation (SABC). In that year, a consortium of media owners led by Naspers started a subscription TV service, Electronic Media Network, known as M-Net. There was also only one telecommunication service, Telkom, wholly owned at the time by the government. In 1993 Vodacom (50% owned by Telkom and 50% by Vodafone UK) started a mobile telephone service. This was followed in 1994 by MTN, another mobile telephone company. The licensing conditions for these companies – and for subsequent telecommunications and broadcasting companies – especially in respect of licensing fees, are unclear. The Independent Communications Authority of South Africa (ICASA) is responsible for issuing licences to such operators and one of its objectives is 'to ensure that spectrum licence fees correspond to the value/demand of the spectrum and value chain in the licensing process'.[2] ICASA is also aware that spectrum is a national asset for which users should pay a royalty, or what we have called a resource rental.

Since 1994, South African communications have been partially liberalised, and while Telkom and the SABC still dominate the telecommunications and broadcasting industries, there are now two fixed-line telephone operators, four mobile telephone operators, three television operators (with three more subscription services having been licensed, but not yet in operation), and a large number of independent radio stations. One important condition is the composition of the ownership of the company and ICASA is mandated to ensure that 'previously disadvantaged persons' are adequately represented in the ownership structure. Licences were, however, not auctioned, but in mid-2010 ICASA announced plans to auction highly profitable spectrum in the 2.6 GHz and 3.5 GHz bands which was definitely a step in the right direction. In ICASA's 2012 Annual Report the CEO reported that 'The introduction of new spectrum Fee Regulations means that some Bulk Licensees would pay significantly more. It is expected that they will rationalise their spectrum usage and return unneeded spectrum in the near future. Indeed, this is already happening. While this means that their contribution in fees will be lower, the spectrum will become available for use by others, who will in time

2 ICASA Business Plan 2007-2008, www.ICASA.org.za – accessed 29 Feb 2008.

pay equivalent fees. Overall, we will achieve more efficient spectrum usage.' While ICASA had nearly completed its framework for market-related or auction-based fees in certain cases,[3] by early 2013 no detail as to the auctions or licensees had been published. We look forward to news in this regard as well as ICASA collecting really meaningful revenues for Treasury in future.

In the USA, the Federal Communications Commission (FCC) allocates commercial spectrum after an auction of the spectrum available. Refinements of the process are ongoing, 'Incentive auctions are a voluntary, market-based means of repurposing spectrum by encouraging licensees to voluntarily relinquish spectrum usage rights in exchange for a share of the proceeds from an auction of new licenses to use the repurposed spectrum.'[4]

In the UK, the notorious 3G[5] bids for spectrum brought in £22.5bn for the treasury from five mobile phone bidders. The average bid was £4.5bn, with Vodafone topping the bids at £5.96bn. This auction proved disastrous, not only for the bidders, but for the telecoms industry in general, and later for the government itself. With the huge cash injection required for the licences, there was little money available for research and development, and this (plus high prices for consumers) restricted the take-up of 3G technology generally. In addition, broadband internet access via landlines became widely available relatively cheaply, compared with the more expensive access via 3G mobile technology. In order to protect their profits, operators retrenched large numbers of staff and the government was hit with reduced taxes from reduced profits and the social costs of the retrenchments. A similar problem occurred in Germany at about the same time. The UK 3G licences are issued for a term of 20 years from the date of issue in 2001. In 2001 Australia also held auctions for 3G licences. A news report at the time speculated that the government would raise about A$2.6bn from six bidders. These licences are for 15 years. Although South Africa missed out on a potential revenue bonanza at the time, ICASA's approach did have the merit of enabling Vodacom and MTN to invest billions in building their 3G networks. Most South Africans, however, have the perception that they were gouged by both the fixed

3 ICASA Strategic Plan 2013-2017, p.42.
4 Epstein Gary M, Americas Spectrum Management Conference 24 October 2014 www.fcc.gov/page/incentive-auctions-americas-spectrum-management-conference-speech. Accessed 24 May 2014.
5 3G: Third generation mobile technology, allowing Internet access in addition to voice and data transmission.

line and mobile operators during the limited competition era of the 1990s and early 'noughties'. With hindsight, the right approach would probably have been to auction entry rights so as to have had a few more competitors in each area without going as far as the Indian government did in 2010, which aggressively expanded the number of players – resulting in a potentially ruinous price war.

While these auctions are akin to selling land to the highest bidder for use in perpetuity (or a limited number of years with a good possibility of renewal) with few ongoing obligations, countries that do auction spectrum do recognise that it is an asset that, at least initially, belongs to the nation. This contrasts with the apparent South African system which for many years seemed to 'give away' spectrum allocations more on the basis that the really big players (Telkom, SABC, Vodacom and MTN) were awarded their licences well before the vogue of auctioning spectrum, and presumably dealt with new entrants on the same basis. Nevertheless, all these licences are awarded with a time limit and licensees need to reapply at the end of each term.

## Proposal for electromagnetic spectrum

In our view, spectrum and associated licences should indeed be auctioned and awarded to the highest bidder that also meets the other criteria laid down by ICASA. Bidding, however, should be on the basis of a once-off initial payment, plus an annual (escalating) rental. Licences should be granted for a limited number of years (say, 10 to 15), after which the licence agreement and the performance of the operator can be scrutinised publicly before the licence is re-auctioned. Prior to such auctions, the state should conduct independent valuations of the plant and physical infrastructure in which vast sums of money may have been invested. Successful bidders (other than the incumbent) would be obliged to recompense the latter accordingly. Remember, in principle, the auction lease payments tax would replace company tax.

## Intellectual property

Intellectual property may seem as ethereal as the EMS but, unlike the users thereof, the generators of intellectual property, to the extent that they have used any South African community generated values, will have paid for them by land rentals. In principle, therefore, we see no justification for taxation and, if this means South Africa suddenly becomes a global Mecca for research and development, so be it! This is a classic illustration of the lack of justification for taxation of the product of (intellectual or any other) labour and capital. There is, however, a case to be made for some kind of a user charge or fee for the protection enjoyed pending expiry of South African patents, say, 5% of turnover.

## Fishing rights

South Africa's exclusive economic zone extends for 200 nautical miles from the territorial sea, which is 12 nautical miles from the coastline. This is acknowledged by international treaty, and is thus part of 'South Africa' as envisaged in our invocation of the preamble to the Constitution. In our view, therefore, it is a resource that belongs to the people of South Africa. This view is confirmed in the general policy on the allocation and management of long term commercial fishing rights issued by the Department of Environmental Affairs and Tourism (DEAT)[6] in 2005: '[An] important purpose of the MLRA[7] is ... to provide for the exercise of control over the marine living resources in a fair and equitable manner to the benefit of all the citizens of South Africa.'

In the same way that we have proposed that individuals and corporations could be granted the right to use or own a piece of land in return for a changing, but market-related, rental, so individuals or corporations should be granted the right to exploit the resources of this littoral space.

While use of this space could be for the exploration and extraction of oil and other minerals from the sea bed, covered in the discussion on liquid fuels in Chapter 8, this chapter covers only the granting of rights for the exploitation of marine living resources as envisaged in the MLRA and how these rights could be subject to a market-related resource rent.

## Present practice

Commercial fishing in South Africa comprises two main groups: large corporations, which own fleets of modern fishing vessels capable of venturing far out to sea (even beyond the 200 nautical mile limit) and providing the bulk of South Africa's marine products for food and other uses; and individuals or groups of individuals who own one or more vessels that are smaller than those used by the larger corporations,

---

6 From April 2010, all fishing management responsibilities, including research and compliance, were transferred to the Department of Agriculture, Forestry and Fisheries (DAFF).
7 Marine Living Resources Act 18 of 1998.

and which generally return to port at the end of the day. Their catches are smaller and are normally sold in local markets or to agents of food processors or caterers. Part of the catch may be used for personal consumption by the owner and crew. Our information is that often agents of large-scale buyers wait for vessels to return to shore and immediately buy the catch for cash, transporting it to their principals in refrigerated trucks for almost immediate consumption in restaurants and hotels, including export (by air) for such purposes. Some such transactions may escape regulations such as those governing the sale of endangered or prohibited species, and safe and hygienic handling and transporting requirements. Often they may be completely unrecorded, thus escaping VAT and income tax regulations. While some may think that evading VAT and income tax on this scale is fairly harmless, this can extrapolate into highly illegal activities such as the harvesting and prohibited export of protected species such as abalone.

The general policy referred to above, states that there are four 'clusters' (A, B, C and D), each covering different species of marine living resources (some species appear in more than one cluster). Large ocean-going fishing vessels mainly operate in cluster A, but may venture into cluster B if they wish to fish for species not covered by cluster A. Smaller fishing vessels operate in clusters B to D. Clusters C and D cover species found only off specific areas of the coastline, for example, KwaZulu-Natal.

Rights are allocated to owners of fishing vessels based on a number of criteria: one important criterion is the need to transform the fishing industry in terms of both ownership and employment equity. Technical criteria cover areas such as the cluster in which the vessel will operate and the 'total applied effort' (TAE), which is determined by factors such as the size and capacity of the vessel, size of the crew, and sophistication of equipment. The TAE will in turn (together with scientific research covering matters such as depletion rates of each species) determine the total allowable catch (TAC).

Successful applicants are awarded rights within their cluster and based on their TAC. These factors (among others) determine the amount to be paid for the rights, which can be for up to 15 years. The MLRA and general policy are at pains to emphasise that fishing rights are not property rights as is the case in some other countries. The withdrawal of a right, therefore, for some or other illegal activity (or the declaration of species as prohibited during the term of a right) does not constitute expropriation of property in terms of the Constitution. In principle, however, there is no reason why these rights to the use of this natural resource should differ in their security of tenure from any other – the potential danger of expropriation upon a technicality is hardly a recipe for healthy investment. In fairness, however, we should note that, according to industry sources, bureaucratic discretion has thus far been exercised responsibly.

We should note here that the important recreational and subsistence sectors, which are included in the MLRA, as well as the 'artisanal sector' not explicitly included are now the subject of a long outstanding policy determination for the 'subsistence and small-scale fisheries' which is now being taken forward as a small-scale fisheries policy. Although this policy is in draft form, aspects of it are being used to guide implementation. Unfortunately, the commercial and small-scale commercial long-term rights allocations were completed long before the needs of the sector could be adequately addressed, and commercial companies will be reluctant to give up quota. The recreational fishery also includes both rich and poor and thus finding a fair fee for an annual recreational permit may be difficult. They are, however, arguably just as valuable as the biggest fisheries when all the associated tourism benefits and other knock-on effects are included. Our proposals are therefore addressed mainly to the commercial sector in the belief that, although the basic principle should be applied throughout, we should endeavour to avoid bureaucratic overkill in this area. As regards traditional subsistence and small scale fishers, a simplified version of TAE and licence free thresholds could be considered.

## Proposal for fishing rights

If South Africa moves towards a system of collecting resource rentals in place of taxation as envisaged in this book, fishing rights, as set out by the MLRA and the general policy, can become property rights subject to a rental.[8] This would be no different from other property rights as set out here. In other words, existing rights holders could move to a 'new order' rights regime where the rights could continue in perpetuity subject to payment of an annual resource rental. This rental would be subject to, say, a triennial review which could include auction mechanisms to ensure market-related value for the Treasury.

This new order rental regime could either become operative only when most other taxes such as income tax, VAT, PAYE, etc. had fallen

8 For an interesting discussion of the attributes of the Individual Transferable Quotas for the fishing industry in New Zealand see http://www.oecd.org/tad/fisheries/2349219.pdf.

away; alternatively, the rentals could be imposed gradually in tandem with these other taxes falling away. Rights holders would be governed by all the existing rules in the MLRA such as transformation and employment equity, permitted species within their cluster, TAE and TAC.

Rights holders could sell their assets (one of which would be their existing rights) at any time, subject to permission from the Minister to ensure that the prospective new owner fulfils all the requirements of the MLRA. If the annual rental is set correctly, the right should theoretically have no value; if set too low it should have a premium, and if too high, a discount.

If rights holders feel aggrieved at new triennial rentals, they would be able to object. If it rejects an objection, the Department should be obliged to call for an auction where holders could put in a bid for the rental they feel would conform to their own TAE and TAC and the state of fishing within their own cluster at that time. Prior to such auctions, independent valuations of the incumbent's other assets should be obtained with perhaps the right to 'put' them to the successful bidder so as to prevent excessive bids based on getting the assets at knockdown prices. New entrants could apply at any time for a fishing right, but the easiest route would be to purchase the fishing right and other assets of an existing holder. Because purchasers would have to obtain the permission of the Minister, the Department could closely monitor the state of the market, and this would inform the determination of new rentals.

Rights holders would still be subject to site value rental on their land holdings, for example, land on which warehouses, processing plants, boat sheds, and private dwellings are built. Fishing vessels would still be subject to harbour dues imposed by harbour operators.

Current levels of implementation need to be improved and need always to be seen as fair so as to ensure better compliance by persons involved in fishing. This applies to offshore compliance activities, which took a knock with vessels for this function out of operation throughout 2012.

## Marine aquaculture

With the exception of abalone, this sector is, relatively speaking, still in its infancy. According to the Department of Agriculture, Forestry and Fisheries[9] it contributed only 0.029% to GDP in 2010. Globally,

9 Marine Aquaculture 2011 Annual Report, p.18.

however, it is growing whereas the wild-capture industry is tending towards ex-growth. Over time, the sites used (both onshore and off-shore) are likely to become more valuable so that the pricing of the permits can be based on the principles outlined above.

## Sea- and airports, and the national road and rail networks

South Africa's eight major commercial seaports are owned and operated by the National Ports Authority, a division of Transnet, a government-owned transport parastatal. There are, in addition, a number of small fishing harbours. These are generally owned by the local authority, but controlled by designated Marine and Coastal Management officials of the Department of Environmental Affairs and Tourism. In this chapter we consider only the eight commercial seaports.

Airports Company South Africa Ltd (ACSA) owns and operates nine of South Africa's international and regional airports and operates the Pilanesberg Airport under a 30-year concession. Lanseria International Airport in Johannesburg is privately owned. There are a large number of small airports and landing strips that are owned either privately or by the local authority. In this chapter we consider only the international and regional airports.

South Africa's road networks have traditionally been owned and operated by the provincial governments or the South African National Roads Agency Ltd (SANRAL), a government agency for the major trunk routes. In the last 25 years, a number of national roads (or rather, portions of these roads) have been in effect privatised. The concessionaires are permitted to charge toll fees in return for maintaining the road, and in some cases, building new sections of the road. At the time of writing (2014) some 16%, or 3,120km, of the 19,500km of SANRAL roads, are tolled. SANRAL's responsibility is likely to be expanded to some 35,000km including further toll roads.

The rail network is owned and operated by Transnet, a government parastatal. Over the past ten years or so, private rail operators (mainly in the luxury rail travel sector) have been allowed to use portions of the rail network, presumably for a fee. Because of the strategic importance of these facilities, the need for full government control has been a widely-held belief worldwide. However, many countries lately have seen the benefit of allowing private companies to operate the facilities under limited-time concessions, while retaining ownership of the land, and in some cases, the infrastructure. Governments nearly always retain responsibility for the safety and security of people and property, for inspection of goods to ensure collection of taxes and duties, and to prevent the movement of contraband and illegal immigrants.

In addition, these facilities are unique geographically and cannot simply be replicated anywhere. For this reason it may not be feasible to impose a simple resource rental on the value of the land on which they are located. This chapter explores the various possibilities that could be applied and that approximate a reasonable rental a willing buyer or operator would pay.

## Airports

As mentioned above, ACSA (a government majority-owned company) owns and operates the nine largest international and regional airports in South Africa: OR Tambo (Johannesburg), Cape Town, Durban, Port Elizabeth, East London, Bloemfontein, Kimberley, George and Upington. It operates the Pilanesberg airport under a 30-year concession. ACSA is a public company registered under the Companies Act. Its website states that in the five years to 31 March 2007, it paid over R2bn in dividends and R1.3bn in taxes.

When ACSA was formed in 1993, it was wholly owned by the government; two years later, the government sold 25.4% to Aeroporto di Roma (AdR), who assumed some operational responsibilities, and there was speculation that ACSA would soon be privatised and listed on a stock exchange. However, this did not happen, and AdR sold its holding back to the government in 1999. At this point, government 'warehoused' 20% with the Public Investment Corporation and sold the balance (5.4%) to various empowerment companies.

Thus, the government effectively owns the land and property of the nine airports mentioned above through its proxy, ACSA. Even though ACSA has raised loan capital for expansion of its airports' infrastructure, these loans are effectively the responsibility of government. ACSA also has operational control of these airports. With hindsight, it may have been better to have split ACSA into a property-owning company (wholly owned by government), and an operating company with a variety of shareholders. We deal further with this possibility in our proposals. The performance of ACSA in delivering expanded efficient and modern airports has been commendable and certainly far more so than the out-and-out parastatals such as Transnet and South African Airways (SAA). Yet it remains a monopoly without a benchmark so as to ensure that the community is getting full value for an important national resource. This is borne out in an article by Bruce

Whitfield in *Finweek*[10] in which it is stated that ACSA has over-capitalised on its R10bn projects in recent years, including 'going over budget on the much-criticised development of King Shaka airport at La Mercy, north of Durban.' This led to extraordinary demands; for example, it requested 133% increase in airport taxes from the regulator but was 'only' granted 59.9% over 2010/2011, 25% in 2011/2012, 3.7% in 2012/2013, 5.5% in 2013/2014 and 5.6% in 2014/2015.

## Sea ports

There is no such complexity with South Africa's eight commercial seaports: Richards Bay, Durban, East London, Nqura, Port Elizabeth, Mossel Bay, Cape Town and Saldanha. As mentioned above, the land and infrastructure are owned by the National Ports Authority, which also operates these harbours. In other words, the harbours are under full government control.

In an extensive feature article in the *Financial Mail*[11] it was reported that research by the Automotive Industry Development Centre found SA's ports amongst the world's most expensive to use. Amounts collected by port authorities per vessel call for Durban and Cape Town were $488,000 and R484,000 respectively, as against, say Antwerp at $182,000 and Buenos Aires at $57,000. Efficiency is also a problem, with the OECD noting that SA ports' efficiency levels for container and higher-value cargo are 50%-60% of similar ports elsewhere.

These ports meet the needs of the hinterlands they serve and there are no alternatives for South African importers and exporters – at least not in South Africa. But Maputo harbour, long moribund after departure of the Portuguese and the ensuing civil war, has been revitalised, and is starting to be a significant competitor to the eastern seaboard harbours of South Africa. The Government of Mozambique has retained ownership of the land and infrastructure, but has handed operations of the port to a consortium of local and foreign companies, led by a South African logistics company. In a radio interview in August 2010 the CEO spoke enthusiastically of expanding coal handling facilities, initially to 3 million tons per annum, and then to 25 million tons within 2 or 3 years.[12]

The main objective of these facilities is to ensure the optimally efficient throughput of goods and passengers. Users must feel that the

---

10 *Finweek*, 8 April 2010, p.20.
11 *Financial Mail*, 20 August 2010, pp.44-45.
12 Moneyweb, 16 August 2010.

services rendered represent value for money. This is especially so for air traffic to and from South Africa, as it is a destination or a starting point, not an interconnecting 'hub' like Heathrow or Singapore. People come to South Africa because they need to or want to, either on business or pleasure. South Africans flying overseas have no choice, but in both cases users must not feel deterred from using the service again. In the same vein, importers and exporters must get value in the services they are paying for. A seriously inefficient service not only increases costs, but can impede trade.

This is why competition for the operation of sea- and airports is vital to ensure efficiency, especially where port owners have the power in terms of concessions granted, to remove operators for noncompliance with the terms of the concession. Even if the main proposals of this chapter (the replacement of taxes by a system of rentals for the resources that belong to the people of South Africa) are not fully accepted, it still makes sense for sea and air port facilities to be operated by specialised private companies.

## Proposals for seaports

Limited-time concessions for harbours could be put out to tender with specific conditions such as black economic empowerment credentials, history of ability to operate such facilities, and so on. Bidders would be required to tender a price for the concession, or an annual rental, depending on the terms of the concession. Our preference would be for an initial payment plus an annual rental with escalation clauses.

## Landing slots

Related to airports is the question of landing slots that are allocated to airlines. We believe, however, that those airports that actually allocate specific landing slots to airlines are in the minority. Moreover, when they do, they seem to be given to airlines at no cost, even though slots at busy airports can be extremely valuable.[13] No South African airports seem to allocate landing slots.

Like land, landing slots are a national resource that attracts a value where demand outstrips supply and in our view should be subject to a resource rental where there is competition for specific time slots. This possibly does not yet apply to any South African airport, but could well do in future.

13 *The Economist* (March 29, 2008) reported that the American airline, Continental, 'has just paid over £100m for four slots'. These were presumably bought from another airline.

*The Economist*, in the report cited, deals with the problems at Heathrow airport in London (over-crowding, shabby facilities, an unacceptable amount of lost luggage and a large percentage of delayed and cancelled take-offs). The report considers the debates around proposals to extend the airport (advocated by British Airports Authority (BAA), the airport operator, and the airlines) against environmental issues relating to noise and air pollution and the need to expropriate a large number of surrounding houses. *The Economist* however, is of the opinion that one of the main reasons for Heathrow's problems is that it is far too cheap. It advocates breaking up BAA's monopoly, awarding some of the other London airports to other operators who could attract the less-profitable leisure and transit passengers, leaving the more expensive Heathrow mainly to business travellers.

However, *The Economist* does not say how Heathrow could become more expensive (other than by simply increasing charges) and it also notes that if its suggestions were adopted, landing slots at Heathrow might lose their value, presumably because passenger traffic through the airport could be reduced by as much as 60%, making slots more readily available.

## Proposals for airports and landing slots

While we agree with most of the suggestions in *The Economist*, our main proposal regarding the right to operate the nine airports now run by ACSA is that each one should, as a national resource, be awarded to an operator after a bidding process, for a limited time span (say up to 25 years) and on payment of upfront and annual licence fees. The same should apply to landing slots where demand is greater than supply, although the time span could be much shorter, say two or three years. The operator would manage the allocation/auction process for a commission, the amount of which would be part of its overall tender package. The licence fees (for the airport and the landing slots) alone would ensure that airports are correctly priced for the type of passenger the airport and the airlines wish to attract. Having more than one operator, instead of one for nine airports, with the resulting competition should facilitate greater efficiencies and this should be made a requirement of the process.

## Road networks

As mentioned above, a number of private companies have been granted concessions to operate tolls on portions of major routes. The conditions under which these concessions were granted are not known, but from the website of one concessionaire (Trans Africa Concessions (Pty) Ltd, or Trac4, which operates the N4 between Witbank and Maputo) it appears that there are no upfront or annual licence fees, and the only payments to government are company and other taxes such as VAT. This presumably applies to all concessionaires.

Toll fees are a controversial subject, especially in South Africa where the government also collects a 'road levy' included in the petrol price. Toll fees are supposed to be a payment for services rendered in the form of better-maintained and safer roads. In some cases the concessionaire is also required to build a new portion of the road, generally a dual-carriage highway that often shortens the route and the travel time for motorists. Nevertheless, the toll fee includes a profit for the concessionaire, and the perception among South African motorists is that the petrol levy is not used exclusively for the building and maintenance of the non-tolled routes, i.e. it is simply another tax. Initially, all toll routes were required to be adjacent to non-tolled 'alternative' routes, giving motorists a choice. However, many of these alternative routes were not properly maintained and became somewhat undesirable alternatives. For newer toll routes, there are often no alternative routes.

## Proposals for toll roads

Our proposal, therefore, is that toll route concessions should be auctioned and awarded to the highest bidder (who also fulfils all the other requirements). The concession, licence fee, or 'resource rental' should be paid on an annual basis and escalate over the period of the concession. We envisage that bidders would tender an upfront 'earnest fee' as well as the annual licence fee/resource rental they were prepared to pay. At the end of the concession, a new concession could be awarded to the existing operator or to a new bidder. In the case of a new bidder being successful, it would be required to purchase the infrastructure built and owned by the existing operator. This, in turn, implies that the valuations of the infrastructure are independently established prior to the bidding process. Alternatively, the existing operator could maintain ownership and lease this infrastructure to the new operator. The annual licence fee/resource rental would be in lieu of company taxation, as well as, in terms of our other proposals, taxes such as PAYE, VAT, and so on. In all of this we need to remember that good infrastructure, especially roads, raises land values all the way along. Our proposals will therefore automatically ensure that in any case, the community benefits from its own good work. Seen in this light, tolls can be viewed as user charges that not only ensure users value the resource used, but, in a sense, enable the community to get its money back twice!

## Other roads

Tolls, however, relate only to a small fraction of the country's roads and, in this regard, the Minister of Transport, Sibusiso Ndebele, stated in May 2010[14] that 'the total paved and gravel network at provincial level is 184,816 km. At least 40% of this network has reached crisis point when it comes to maintenance. The total paved and gravel network at municipal level is easily 9,849 km. We are developing mechanisms to quantify the backlog at municipal level in order to have accurate localised numbers. What we know is that our country needs R75bn over the next five years to address this decline in road infrastructure and this has been continuously emphasised since 1994.' The Minister's statement begs the question why on earth the inordinate delay, to which we would reply that had the government been aware of the revenue raising potential from rising land rentals along improved roads, the necessary spending would not only have been a no-brainer, but would have facilitated loan applications to the World Bank and other fundraising exercises.

## Proposal for other roads

Measure the increased land rentals likely from the roads and use these to facilitate the necessary fundraising. Then build them hell for leather, Mr Minister! That said, this need not preclude private-public partnerships in certain areas, rural or suburban, where the landowners themselves are willing to fund roads; for example, by way of levies (which would serve in lieu of increased land rental).

## Proposals for rail networks

Portions of the rail network could be treated on a similar basis, i.e. the concessionaire could either operate the line itself (as could have been the case with Sheltam Rail, which in early 2008 was rumoured to be about to operate the East London/Bloemfontein line), or it could allow other rolling stock operators to use the line for a fee. The concessionaire would be liable for maintaining the line over the period of the concession. As proposed for toll routes, the concession would be

14 Department of Transport: Special Edition 'SA On the Move' (featuring the King Shaka and OR Tambo airports), p.9.

awarded to the highest bidder for an annual (escalating) licence fee/resource rental. No taxes would be payable by the concessionaire.

## Status quo on rail

Transnet, the wholly government-owned freight operator 'wants to close or concession about a third of the national rail network', mostly branch lines now viewed as redundant. 'The remaining 12,000km will make up a high-performance corridor backbone that will ease congestion and provide capacity.'[15] Although Transnet denies responsibility, coal exporters claim that the country has missed out on untold billions of the export revenue due to its failure to match the capacity of the Richards Bay Coal Terminal of around 91 million tonnes per annum (mtpa). Meanwhile, in a commendably innovative R123bn contract, the state passenger rail agency, PRASA, plans to acquire 7,224 coaches over 20 years to replace its antiquated rolling stock. Even though this bodes well for improved services, PRASA still doesn't have to be the provider. Given the enormous demands for infrastructure spending on roads and energy, to mention but a few, it seems that there is no way the government can cope without leasing some or all of these rail assets to private operators.

Road and rail networks compete for freight traffic, the total demand for which is expected by Transnet to double within 20 years. Although most players are agreed it would be helpful if more road freight could be diverted on to the rail network, it is doubtful whether Transnet, on its recent showing, will be able to maintain its share let alone regain it. If it could, it would save considerable maintenance on the roads and make them safer for private motorists, taxis and buses. This, however, will only happen if the rail networks are more efficient than at present, and this in turn is more likely to happen under private operators working under the constraints of licence conditions, an annual licence fee/resource rental, competition and the need to operate profitably.

# Conclusion

In conclusion we should note that, to a large extent, well-planned and operated air and sea ports, together with efficient rail and road networks, would repay the Treasury many times over through the resulting increases in land values. So our advice for government: act the landlord; don't bother with running them, just rent them out!

15 *Financial Mail*, 23 April 2010.

CHAPTER 8

# RENTAL COLLECTION: MINERAL RESOURCES

*'The Ministers would also seek to ensure that ... the rents
arising from South Africa's mineral resources are used to
develop the economy.'*
Ministers Davies, Shabangu and Patel,[1] July 2010

## Mines

THE RENTAL COLLECTION on mineral resources and mines
forms an important potential source of state income and is
dealt with in Chapters 8 and 9.

Surface rights or ordinary land holdings often have a variety of
uses to which they can be put and, in any event, most have readily
determinable market values. This does not, however, apply so readily
to mining rights. Although developed and undeveloped mining
properties do of course change hands, which would facilitate the establishment of some kind of a database, the frequency of transactions is
much lower than in the case of ordinary properties. Moreover, it would
be much more difficult to distinguish between the current value of

---

1 Ministers Rob Davies (Trade and Industry),Susan Shabangu (Mineral Resources) and
Ebrahim Patel (Economic Development) commenting, according to a report in Creamer
Media's *Mining Weekly* of 22 July 2010, on the interim settlement they facilitated between
ArcelorMittal and Kumba Iron Ore regarding the contested cost plus 3% iron supply agreement between the two companies. Soon afterwards, however, ArcelorMittal agreed to pay
R800m to the little known but politically well-connected Imperial Crown Trading (ICT) for
prospecting rights it unexpectedly acquired in preference to Kumba Iron Ore which had been
mining the deposit for decades. ICT's success in 'flipping' the rights after a matter of months
laid bare the absence of any means of preventing this kind of rent-seeking behaviour (for
example, by the Treasury collecting the rental itself). See also Chapter 9.

'improvements' and unimproved site value. Therefore, in the case of land on which there are registered mineral rights and land on which there are established mining operations, the collection of land rentals as described in Chapter 6, would not be appropriate. Mining takes place where payable grades of ore exist, and this can occur on any land regardless of its potential commercial, residential or agricultural value.

For the collection of resource rentals in respect of established mining operations there is at hand a well established alternative, possibly unique to South Africa, and that is the gold mining profit to revenue ratio tax formula (GMF), the case for which we set out in a presentation to the DME (28 April 2006). Accordingly, we propose that this formula be rolled out to the rest of the mining industry. In contrast to the collection of other resource rentals (especially those on ordinary surface land), it could probably be achieved much more quickly. Confirmation of the value of this approach is the adoption of the EBIT[2]/revenue ratio formula basis for determining royalties in the Mining Royalties Bill.

In essence, the approach is to exempt marginal mines from tax, charge near marginal mines at a much lower rate and richer mines at a higher rate. The 2007 South African gold mining formula (GMF) tax was $Y = 45 - 225/X$ where Y is the percentage tax payable and X is the ratio of mining profit, after the deduction of all mining capital expenditure, to revenue from mining operations (depreciation is ignored for this purpose). The formula, in effect, defines marginal mines as those having a mining profit to mining revenue of less than 5%. As can be seen from Table 8.1 the rate of tax rises steeply initially, thus surpassing the company tax rate at a post-mining capex EBIT: revenue rate of 15% before levelling off markedly over 25%. Bear in mind, however, that capex is fully recoverable before any tax is payable. Thus, in June 2007 Gold Fields, for example, had R9.1bn in unredeemed capex as well as R4.9bn in tax losses available for offset against actual tax payable.

The merit of this system is that it provides enormous flexibility for the industry as well as the ability to cope with the endless volatility inherent in commodity prices. Moreover, the system we envisage would make this formula even more effective as it would also free the mining

2 Earnings before interest and taxation. After initially opting for EBITDA, the Treasury changed (correctly in our view) to EBIT, which takes into account the capital intensity of each operation.

industry from the enormous burden of indirect taxes it bears, not to mention PAYE. This would be of further assistance in enabling marginal mines, which are often large operations, to survive and hence be of great benefit to the economy and local community. Although there is some room for debate as to the structure of the formula, e.g. as to whether the slope should be as steep as it is, and so on, the underlying principle upon which South African gold mining taxation is based is, pardon the pun, rock solid.

### Table 8.1: Gold mining tax (2007) formula rates

| Post-Mining Capex EBIT: Revenue Ratio (%) | Mining Tax Rate (%) |
| --- | --- |
| 5.0 | 0 |
| 6.0 | 7.5 |
| 7.5 | 15.0 |
| 10.0 | 22.5 |
| 15.0 | 30.0 |
| 20.0 | 33.8 |
| 25.0 | 36.0 |
| 30.0 | 37.5 |
| 40.0 | 39.4 |
| 50.0 | 40.5 |

## Exploration rights

In the case of much sought-after rights (such as coal, at the time of writing), we propose that they be auctioned to the highest bidder. This would eliminate the current practice whereby licences are awarded to persons or entities incapable themselves either of exploring or developing the properties and who simply sell a slice of the action to those who can, i.e. another case of '*hic transit rentum populi* ... here goes the people's rent' again, into the pockets of the well connected! Since the existing 'use it or lose it' regime already stipulates active exploration and the Mineral and Petroleum Resources Development Act (MPRDA) provides for minimum BEE participation, there would be no need for further measures.

In the absence of other bidders we propose that the rights be granted as at present with no further rental, royalty or tax charges until sale or production commences and capex is recouped. Since sale of the property by the explorer (once it has moved the property up the value curve through successful discoveries) is more the rule than the exception, we propose that a once-off rental recoupment be achieved by applying the latest relevant industry sector average EBITDA/revenue formula rental percentage to the capital gain made by the explorer.

## Liquid fuels industry – crude oil refineries, synthetic fuels

We believe that the cumbersome and complex regulations governing the entire liquid fuels industry including retail distribution are an out-dated and unnecessary relic of the apartheid era that have resulted in many unintended consequences. These include ruinously high fuel prices, shortages of refinery capacity and misplaced retail outlets.

It follows, therefore, that the only question is how to collect resource rentals in this industry (which we regard as akin to the activities of smelting and refining of precious and base metal ores) that are often, but not always, conducted at the point of extraction. Since the profits and margins of these businesses fluctuate in line with the relevant com-modity prices, exactly the same basis of resource rental collection can be applied to crude oil refining with one difference: refineries, unlike mines, often take up valuable surface rights i.e. urban land, and we propose that they be assessed for these rentals in the normal manner. The same applies to the liquid fuels industry except to note, in the case of Sasol, that its coal mining activities are in any case to be treated as any other mines.

In rejecting a windfall tax on the liquid fuels industry, the report of the departmental task team acknowledged the phenomenon of eco-nomic rent and the merits of a progressive tax rate which it came close to recommending. It did, in fact, suggest on an *obiter dictum* basis – which was then hastily withdrawn after the ensuing hullabaloo in the press – that the gold mining tax formula be rolled out to the rest of the mining industry! In our response to the report, which included a response to the task team's discussion on rent,[3] we opposed the intro-duction of a windfall tax for various reasons. One of them was simply that, on its own, it would be out of context and would be perceived as an *ad hoc* opportunistic revenue-grabbing stunt by the Treasury. Clearly this objection now falls away. It is nevertheless useful to con-sider some of the issues raised by the task team

---

3 Meintjes, S.W.P. and Jacques, J.G.M., submission to the Treasury 'Response to the discus-sion document dated 14 July 2006, prepared by the task team appointed by the Minister of Finance to consider possible reforms to the fiscal regime applicable to windfall profits in South Africa's liquid fuel sector', 20 May 2007.

## The role and importance of the liquid fuel industry

The discussion document (DD) pointed out (section 6) the vast importance of a liquid fuels industry in a non-oil producing country like South Africa, and how the synthetic fuel industry had played a major role in reducing the country's dependence on crude oil imports. This importance is underlined by the government's reluctance to deregulate the oil and liquid fuel industry. This has resulted in a pump price of petrol and diesel that probably bears little resemblance to the actual cost of producing these fuels in South Africa, especially given the presence of the synthetic fuels industry.

South Africa is in a unique situation in that Sasol produces about 23% of the country's liquid fuel requirements.[4] This means that a large portion of the inland northern provinces' fuel requirements are met by Sasol. Yet inland consumers are burdened with an 'imaginary' cost of shipping fuel 'produced' at overseas refineries from the coast to inland sites. But with a fungible commodity like oil, chaos would probably ensue if refineries were allowed to sell refined product based on the actual cost plus shipping to the point of sale. It is unclear from the DD what a barrel of refined product costs Sasol (we believe it is currently around $75 per barrel), but with a breakeven at between $23 and $28 for a barrel of crude, their costs must be considerably less than those of the crude oil refineries.

## Taxes levied on liquid fuels

Another matter underlining the importance of the liquid fuel industry is the comparative ease with which the state is able to collect tax revenues on the sale of liquid fuels. In the year to 30 June 2012, Sasol alone paid R10.3bn in direct taxes and a net R17.7bn in indirect taxes, mainly customs, excise and fuel duty to government.

It is unclear whether VAT is levied before or after the imposition of the above levies, or what the VAT take is on liquid fuels in a fiscal period. Agriculture and mining enjoy rebates on (presumably) the general fuel levy, and this will affect the VAT if it is applied after the general fuel and other levies.

The DD (page 65) stated that the tax content of the fuel price in South Africa was about 40% and that this was relatively low compared with many other countries. However, it should be pointed out that the first ten countries (Turkey to Lithuania) with high fuel prices and tax takes are mainly small, developed countries with a variety of

---

4 Discussion Document, page 68.

transport systems. Australia (next after Lithuania) also has a high fuel price and a tax take, but in spite of being a very large country, the developed part of the country is probably less than 5% of the land mass. Most of the remaining countries are large, and with the exception of the USA and Canada, are developing countries with much lower tax takes. This is significant because for many of these countries, private motor vehicles comprise the most important (if not the only) means of transport. In South Africa, with a so-called 'low' tax take on fuel, this tax still has an enormous effect on the living standards of the rural poor. Studies by the writers show that the prices of basic necessities in rural shops can be between 30% and 40% higher than in urban supermarkets. In addition, most rural people have to take taxis to the nearest town or village to purchase food and clothing, and fares include a large portion for fuel and vehicle taxes. The same studies have shown that the poorest of the rural poor subsisting on either social grants or piece-work wages, spend at least 10% of their incomes on VAT (some of their purchases are on non-VAT food and school fees).

Thus, these indirect taxes compound upon each other, gathering more taxes until they reach their maximum effect on the lowest levels of society. It is little wonder that those who are able to do so soon make their way to the metropolitan areas in search of riches and a better life, leaving only the elderly and very young in the remote rural areas. These are the real unintended consequences of fuel and other indirect taxes.

## Sasol: potential for application of progressive tax formula (GMF)

Sasol is the only oil company whose financial statements are available to the writers, and we are using its income and value added statements for the three years to 30 June 2012 in order to illustrate a progressive formula tax that could be applied to Sasol and possibly to other oil companies.

Table 8.2 shows combined value added/income statements for the above three years. The format is one that the writers are working on in an attempt to incorporate value added information into an income statement that conforms to international financial reporting standards. All the numbers are taken from the Sasol financial statements and the only number that has had to be surmised is the amount for impairment of non-current assets.

## Table 8.2: Sasol value added/income statements

| Rm | Note | 2010 | Years Ended 30 June 2011 | 2012 |
|---|---|---|---|---|
| Turnover | | 122 256 | 142 436 | 169 446 |
| Purchased materials and services | 1 | 74 061 | 86 330 | 103 116 |
| Value added | | 48 195 | 56 106 | 66 330 |
| Employees | | −17 546 | −18 756 | −19 921 |
| EBITDA | | 30 649 | 37 350 | 46 409 |
| Providers of capital | | −7 605 | −8 432 | −11 839 |
|   Dividends | | −5 806 | −7 040 | −10 274 |
|   Interest | | −1 799 | −1 392 | −1 565 |
| Taxation | 2 | −6 985 | −9 196 | −11 746 |
| Depreciation | | −6 509 | −7 165 | −9 422 |
| Impairment* | | 4 757 | 4 505 | −1 314 |
| Retained profit | | 14 307 | 17 062 | 12 088 |
| Add back dividends | | 5 806 | 7 040 | 10 274 |
| Headline earnings | | 20 113 | 24 102 | 22 362 |
| Non-operating gains losses | 3 | 1 071 | 1 380 | 1 895 |
| Profit | | 21 184 | 25 482 | 24 257 |
| Attributable to minorities | | −446 | −426 | −674 |
| Attributable to shareholders | | 20 738 | 25 056 | 23 583 |

### Notes

**1 Purchased materials and services**

| | | | | |
|---|---|---|---|---|
|   Cost of sales | | 79 183 | 90 467 | 111 042 |
|   Marketing & distribution | | 854 | 1 088 | 6 701 |
|   Administration | | 9 451 | 9 887 | 11 672 |
|   Other operating exp. | | 4 043 | 6 424 | 4 689 |
|   Less salaries & wages | | −17 546 | −18 756 | −19 921 |
|   Depreciation | | −6 509 | −7 165 | −9 422 |
|   Write down of inventories to net real/val. | | −172 | −120 | −331 |
|   Impairment* | | 4 757 | 4 505 | −1 314 |
| | | 74 061 | 86 330 | 103 116 |

**2 Taxation**
Only company tax and STC

**3 Non-operating gains and losses**

| | | | | |
|---|---|---|---|---|
| 1  nvestment income | | 217 | 292 | 479 |
|   Non-trading income | | 854 | 1 088 | 1 416 |
| | | 1 071 | 1 380 | 1 895 |

*Balancing figure
**Source:** Sasol 2012 Annual Report, pp.48, 110, 187.

In Table 8.3 we show how the gold mining formula would work in Sasol's case, using the EBITDA (earnings before interest, taxation, depreciation and amortisation) to revenue ratios. Some may complain that the EBITDA formula does not allow interest, depreciation or amortisation as a 'tax deduction', but the point is that this is a formula for calculating a resource rental, not an income tax. In fact, the formula may be wholly inappropriate; more study is probably needed to arrive at a proper basis for the calculation of a resource rental in this instance. It appears that on this basis, Sasol would, because of its high margins, pay more resource rental (R16.6bn) than it does in all the taxes it pays at present, including PAYE (R13.5bn – see Table 8.4).

### Table 8.3: Progressive tax formula

|  |  |  | Years Ended 30 June | |
| Rm | Note | 2010 | 2011 | 2012 |
| --- | --- | --- | --- | --- |
| Y = 45 – 255/x EBITDA |  | 10 675 | 13 175 | 16 563 |

Source: *Ibid*, authors' calculation.

## Total taxes paid/collected by Sasol

Table 8.4 lists the total taxes paid by Sasol to the South African taxing authorities (taken from the statement of monetary exchanges with governments in the Sasol 2012 Annual Report p.49).

### Table 8.4: Total SA and foreign taxes paid by Sasol

|  |  |  | Years Ended 30 June | |
| Rm | Note | 2010 | 2011 | 2012 |
| --- | --- | --- | --- | --- |
| SA normal tax |  | 4 270 | 5 235 | 7 358 |
| Foreign tax |  | 726 | 1 192 | 1 861 |
| Dividend Withholding Tax |  |  |  | 16 |
| STC |  | 606 | 771 | 1 032 |
| Employees' tax |  | 3 028 | 3 571 | 3 921 |
| Property tax |  | 86 | 96 | 98 |
| Other levies |  | 4 | 8 | 46 |
| Net VAT received |  | –1 615 | –1 714 | –2 161 |
| Other |  | 928 | 1 036 | 1 353 |
| **Total SA taxes paid** |  | **8 033** | **10 195** | **13 524** |
| **Customs & excise duty (collected for government)** |  | 16 889 | 18 200 | 18 396 |

Source: *Ibid*, p.49.

Some of these numbers may be considered to be controversial: for example, employees' tax (PAYE) is generally considered to be paid by the employee as a separate taxable entity. However, the Sasol Value added statement shows that this tax comes out of the value added created by the business. In Table 8.5 we have merely subtracted the employees tax from employees share of value added and added it to the government share. This raises the government share of value added in 2012 from 15.2% to 21% and reveals that the employees share in reality was only 23.7% in 2012 and not the 29.5% as shown (albeit correctly so in accounting terms) in Sasol's value added statement.

The important fact is that Sasol (and most other companies) are paying considerably more tax than that shown in the income statement.

### Table 8.5: Value added statement

| Factor Share Adjusted for PAYE | 2010 | | 2011 | | Years Ended 30 June 2012 | |
|---|---|---|---|---|---|---|
| | Rm | % | Rm | % | Rm | % |
| Government | 8 630 | 17.3 | 10 769 | 18.8 | 14 188 | 21.0 |
| Government: direct taxes, STC | 5 602 | 11.3 | 7 198 | 12.5 | 10 267 | 15.2 |
| Government: PAYE | 3 028 | 6.1 | 3 571 | 6.2 | 3 921 | 5.8 |
| Employees: pay, net of tax deducted | 14 518 | 29.2 | 15 185 | 26.5 | 16 000 | 23.7 |
| Capital | 26 596 | 53.5 | 31 435 | 54.8 | 37 417 | 55.3 |
| Dividends | 5 806 | 11.7 | 7 040 | 12.3 | 10 274 | 15.2 |
| Interest | 1 799 | 3.6 | 1 392 | 2.4 | 1 565 | 2.3 |
| Reinvested in the group | 18 991 | 38.2 | 23 003 | 40.1 | 25 578 | 37.8 |
| **Wealth created** | **49 744** | **100.0** | **57 389** | **100.0** | **67 605** | **100.0** |

**Source:** *Ibid.*

## Treasury moots 'resource rental tax'

The discussion document refers to a 'resource rental tax' in section 3.3.1 (page 15) as follows:

> Direct tax (profit taxes)
> Resource rent tax – related to the economic rent generated by the difference between the market price and the cost of extraction (including an acceptable return on investment).

'Economic rent' is discussed in section 4.1 of the discussion document. The *Pocket Economist* (2000), however, describes it as 'the difference between what a factor of production is paid and how much it would need to be paid to remain in its current use.'

In Sasol's case we understand this as follows: if Sasol can mine coal and turn it into a form of crude oil for a cost of, say, $20 a barrel, when other refineries have to pay $70, then Sasol's economic rent is $50, given that the cost of converting crude into a petroleum product is similar for all refineries. This, as the *Pocket Economist* says, 'is a measure of market power'. In other words, Sasol, by virtue of its ownership of its technology, can bar all would-be competitors from entering its field.

Our view of a resource rental however, is that it should be charged on the use of all natural resources. Because there are two distinct stages of production, Sasol makes an interesting case study. In the first instance it is mining coal. Here the Mineral Royalty Bill specifically recognises South Africa's 'ownership' of its mineral resource patrimony and looks for additional payment for this in the form of a revenue-based royalty from anyone who wishes to extract, process and sell such minerals. Since our proposals are based on the same principle, but take it much further, the royalty would be redundant, and should be abolished. Sasol's coal mining operation would therefore pay the resource rental and the downstream operations either the same or whatever variant thereof is ultimately settled upon.

## CHAPTER 9

# MINING

> *'The return for capital from the poorest mine paying*
> *no rent would regulate the rent of all the other*
> *more productive mines.'*
> David Ricardo[1]

## Mining is different!

THE BUSINESS OF wresting minerals from the earth differs from all others in that it always means digging a hole, making a mess and then cleaning up. This applies whether it is a 2-million ounce gold open pit resource scooped out over a few years or a mighty multi-decade operation digging for 40 million ounces 4km underground.

In the past, alas, mines did not always have to clean up but they do now, and provision for rehabilitation is closely watched by the regulators. Manufacturing, on the other hand, may be liable for pollution but does not have to re-establish the landscape. Moreover, both the operational as well as product price risks are often much less than in the case of mining. Consequently, many a mining start-up has been aborted before it saw the light of day.

These risks, which include the long lead times involved, mean that security of tenure and clarity as regards the fiscal goalposts are particularly important in order to woo investors. In their absence, fabulous mineral potential in countries such as Angola and the Democratic Republic of the Congo went virtually untapped for decades.

---

1 Ricardo, D., *On the Principles of Political Economy and Taxation*, Dent, 1969, Ch.3, p.47.

## Exploration even more so!

The same applies to the more exciting and even riskier business of exploring for such deposits. Thus, while every diamond exploration company dreams of discovering another Venetia or Orapa, and while De Beers spends $90m a year on finding kimberlites (which it does every year), less than 1% are diamondiferous and less than 1% of those are viable. The long-established junior diamond mining company Transhex spent seven years looking for them in Angola without any luck. There are also hundreds of small operators digging all over the alluvial fields around the Orange River in South Africa, many of them second or third generation in the business. They are a special breed!

Then there are the dozens of exploration companies searching for gold, copper, cobalt and other minerals in many African locations in the hopes of another commodities boom. So, if commodity prices are right and the fiscal goalposts clear-cut, exploration companies will explore and mining companies will mine.

Because of these differences, however, it is not always possible simply to determine the unimproved site value with reference to neigh-bouring stands as is the case for agricultural, manufacturing, commercial, financial and residential land. Calculations of 'unimproved site value' in the mining context are usually only possible after exploration programmes beginning with desktop research and/or aerial surveys before moving on to expensive drilling programmes to delineate grade, depth and other characteristics of the ore body. In the early stages of exploration, a pre-feasibility report (costing say $20m for a small project) by in-house or consulting geologists would be used to generate risk capital for taking the project further via more exploration – perhaps including a pilot plant – to bankable feasibility stage. In South Africa, this would entail a Competent Person's Report, usually com-piled by external geologists. This would then be used by the miner's board and, if approved, used to raise debt and further equity capital.

The paradox here is, obviously, that although the valuable minerals might have been there all the time, much labour and capital has to be applied to prove their existence in a mineable state. This process of proving up the value, more commonly referred to by exploration companies as 'adding value' is typically depicted by them in the graphs that they show to investors or financiers.[2]

2 The whole exploration process is ably described by David J. Hall, a geologist who founded three exploration juniors after some 15 years experience in the field, in a presentation he gave in 2006 in Zurich entitled 'Grass-Roots Exploration to Production or from Rocks to Riches'.

# Cracking the exploration nod from the Department of Mineral Resources (DMR)[3]

It's very simple!

As we said earlier,[4] and in contrast to the current situation, we propose that where they are sought after, exploration rights should be auctioned to the highest of the bidders who meet the minimum criteria, including empowerment credentials, as regards capacity to do the job. In the absence of any contest, the exploration rights should be granted subject to the normal criteria. That way, resources are explored efficiently and timeously so as not to miss out on commodity booms. Needless to say, expiry dates must be realistic in relation to the work involved and retention throughout the period, subject to minimum progress achieved. This procedure would also curb the practice whereby successful applicants for exploration and mining rights simply hawk them, either wholly or partially, to *bona fide* exploration or mining companies thereby pocketing public rent themselves. In the likely event of an understandable reluctance to part with too much hard cash at this stage, the bids might well consist of a share of ultimate equity earnings if the exploration company went on to develop itself. Alternatively, as suggested earlier, if it sold out either wholly or partially at that stage, the proceeds of that sale (or more accurately, the value added being proceeds less exploration costs) would be subject to a once-off formula-based resource rental collection. We also believe in the Canadian system, whereby exploration companies benefit from a 'flow-through' allowance of exploration expenditure to shareholders of the exploration company concerned. In the event (as is possible under the natural resources rental system we are proposing) of the shareholders not being in a position to benefit from this, we see no reason why it should not be passed on to the ultimate miners of the property. There is, therefore, no need in our view for exploration costs on a particular property to be ring fenced; i.e. if unsuccessful, they can be offset against net proceeds of subsequent ventures.

3 After the appointment of President Jacob Zuma in 2009, the Department of Minerals and Energy (DME) was split into the Department of Mineral Resources and the Department of Energy.
4 See Chapter 8.

## Use it or lose it

One of the most successful aspects of the many changes introduced in mining legislation and regulation since transition in South Africa is the system whereby mineral rights holders in effect use them or lose them. This contrasts starkly with the previous system whereby the handful of mining houses that dominated the South African mining scene applied, as a matter of routine, for the mineral rights to almost anything that didn't move. One of us began his career in a mining house where management trainees were expected to 'do time' in the mining titles department but one look at an entire floor of moles burrowing amongst paper piles was sufficient to concoct a successful avoidance strategy! It served to show, however, that the mining houses were quite capable of accumulating valuable rights either to deny them to competitors or, as also happened, getting them and then forgetting them as they lay gathering dust in a bottom drawer. Soon after the 'use it or lose it' legislation, some enterprising entrepreneurs went to the mining houses and struck deals with them on those mineral rights that they weren't going to be able to use. They then listed on the stock exchange to raise capital in order to explore them properly – which is exactly what the legislator intended. It also explains why, at the time of transition the predecessor of Anglo-American Platinum, for example, had an overwhelming preponderance of rights to the world's greatest ever platinum group metals resource. Its competitor Impala Platinum, by contrast, had to content itself with a more limited extent of less attractive ground, whereas the great and technically highly competent gold miner, the then Gold Fields of South Africa, battled for years to keep going at Northam which was, and is, the quintessentially marginal platinum operation. It is ironic that the latter-day Northam Platinum Mines is at last, under the new mineral rights regime, getting some juicy scraps (Booysendal) from the still-sumptuous table of Anglo-American Platinum. The latter still had by far the greatest entitlement but has been forced, both by the mineral rights regime as well as black empowerment measures, to go into partnership with others in many parts of its vast holdings. Certainly the Bushveld Igneous Complex, which has been a hive of exploration activity by many foreign and local companies in recent years, is a far cry from what it used to be when Rustenburg Platinum, the predecessor of Angloplats, so to say, had it all!

## The great mining rights mix-up of 2010

Sadly, much of this progress in our mineral rights regime was marred by some spectacularly controversial decisions by the DMR, which came to a head in 2010. One of them concerned the separate award of associated minerals prospecting rights to a little-known company in respect of an area in which the London and JSE listed Lonmin Plc had the rights to mine platinum group metals. Although the source of the error lay in the mining rights regime not explicitly recognising that separability of these minerals was not economically and technically feasible, there were also other aspects of the award that raised concern. The other case arose from ArcelorMittal S.A. not applying timeously to have its share of the mining rights of Sishen Iron Ore converted from 'old order' to 'new order' rights. Despite the owner of the other share, Kumba Iron Ore, applying as soon as possible thereafter for these rights, prospecting rights in respect thereof were awarded to another little-known but politically well-connected entity that soon afterwards agreed to sell these rights to ArcelorMittal for R800m. The ensuing furore notwithstanding, the case was a useful illustration both of rental value as well as how our proposal (i.e. to auction sought-after prospecting rights) would eliminate this type of rent seeking. The same applies in the Lonmin case inasmuch as, assuming there were valuable rights (say, contiguous to its property) that had legitimately become available, it would at least have had the opportunity to bid for them instead of suddenly having them whisked away from it.

## Taking it from where we are now

In South Africa, of course, we are not only endeavouring to apply these principles to a well-established mining industry but one that is also grappling with the black empowerment requirements of the Mineral and Petroleum Resources Development Act, as well as the Mining Royalty Bill. Our proposals will therefore have to be tailored to phase in with the situation.

## Starting with the Rand, 'The Ridge of the White Waters'

Despite momentous changes and more than a century-and-a-quarter of mining, the Witwatersrand gold basin, albeit very deep down, is still the world's largest gold resource by far. It is therefore vital that we do not let taxation stand in the way of its exploitation and, although as we shall see, there are some harmful aspects of our current tax regime, we have embedded in the gold mines tax formula, the seeds of the answer to the question, 'How best to collect natural resource rentals from mining operations?'

That is because, as we explained in Chapter 8, South Africa has (over more than a century) evolved a unique system of gold mining taxation whereby, in effect, the rate of tax for the richest mines (say, with a profit-to-revenue ratio of 60%) can be as high as 41.3% whereas that for marginal mines (with profit-to-revenue ratios of 5% or less) can be zero.

## Why the roll-out to the rest of the mob?

Since we believe that South Africa has, with its gold mines, stumbled on a highly beneficial means of collecting resource rentals from all mines it behoves us to take a closer look at the background.

The beauty of the system is that it has two great advantages for mining. First, it encourages miners to develop mediocre to marginal deposits, as well as prime areas. Secondly, it reduces the rate of tax when the price of the commodity (in this case gold) slumps and vice versa. The Treasury might, of course, not see it quite like this because the system would also increase the volatility of its income. Nevertheless, it has broad shoulders with which to plan accordingly and can console itself with the knowledge that the system will generate it more income overall, as it encourages more development.

The system is not without its detractors, including some from among the ranks of the Treasury who seem to regard it as an unwarranted perk and feel that gold mining should be taxed on a flat rate like other mines. The belief that the fiscal regime should be consistent across all industries is, of course, widely accepted, including by ourselves! It's just that we believe that consistency should move the other way – that is, in the direction of following the lead of the gold mining industry which, in a rough and ready way, already has a kind of natural resources rental setup.

Needless to say, the reason for special treatment for the gold industry has been queried before, not least by some of the gold miners themselves. To appreciate this requires a little detour into the history of South African gold mining taxation, some of which is contained in the Marais Commission report.[5]

5 Report of the Technical Committee on Mining Taxation (Chairman: Dr G. Marais.) December 1988.

# Arguments for and against the gold mining formula (GMF)

Although the Margo Tax Commission (1986) questioned the gold mining formula (GMF) tax it recommended further investigation, as a result of which, the Marais Commission was appointed and it reported in 1988. Having duly considered a wide range of arguments against the GMF, not least from interests with high-grade mines, it firmly recommended retention, albeit with a lower tax tunnel, as well as other reforms. The gist of the arguments, and refutations by the commission, follows.

### Reduced efficiency
The Commission strongly refuted the assertion that the GMF system leads to reduced efficiency *per se* (supposedly due to complacency owing to reduced risk of failure).

### Encouragement of mining marginal ore is inefficient
The Commission found that the undue encouragement given at the time to mining marginal ore occurred because of the (then current) formulae coupled with the surcharge and lease formulae, which led to overall rates around 80% for some other richer mines. (We think at that stage, the apartheid government had given up on fresh investment and was content to squeeze the existing mines for all it could.)

### The GMF system leads to overproduction, thus thus depressing the price of gold
The Commission found that the formula led to increased gold production in the long term but reduced it in the short term by encouraging a lowering of the average grade of ore milled. Hence, the effect would have been the opposite of that alleged; that is, if anything, it would have tended to increase the price in the short term.

### GMF did not lead to a reduction of pay limit
The Commission found that this totally contradicted other criticisms. It agreed with the Holloway (1947) and Corbett (1936) Commissions that, although in certain circumstances the formula had little effect on the decision to mine marginal ore, in many cases it did.

## Reduction of risk in new, stand-alone, ventures

The Commission found the GMF reduced such risks because of its progressive nature and the 'insulation' it provided if part of a new venture failed while another part succeeded. Although this risk reduction effect could be limited, owing to substantial lead times, a flat rate system provided for no risk reduction at all.

## The lack of attraction to foreign investors

The Commission found that the possible lack of attraction due to reduced responsiveness of after-tax profits to changes in the gold price was largely due to the extreme characteristics of the then formula with its very high marginal tax rate (the probable reasons for which are explained above).

## Difficulty of administration

The tax officials concerned said the extra time and effort in calculating tax payable under the formula was immaterial.

## More volatile tax collections

The Commission pointed out that this was a statement of fact, not a criticism, and if anything illustrated the advantage of a formula system as it provided support to the gold mines when times were difficult and extracted a higher level of tax when things went well. In what might have been a dig at the increasingly feeble arguments of the critics (including high-grade mine owners) it said 'to state that this is a disadvantage is misleading.'

## Conclusion

Therefore, despite considerable opposition, the Marais Commission upheld a long tradition of encouraging the rational use of the nation's gold patrimony by ensuring that the exploitation of marginal ore was undertaken when economically feasible, i.e. even during times of lower prices, rather than being left unmined (possibly forever) by an insensitive tax policy.

The question of rolling out the GMF to the rest of the mining industry does not seem to have been debated recently. Since that might change because of our proposals, it is interesting to note the arguments used in earlier debates on the topic.

# Arguments for and against extending the GMF to other mines

## Arguments against

Both the Margo and Marais Commissions and others correctly point to the *difference between gold and other mines*. For example, although mining by its nature is a very risky operation, coal mining, with its thicker seams and shallower mining depths (as well as opencast operations in some cases) is less risky than most South African gold mines. Moreover, until recently, whereas most precious and base metals and minerals were sold into the export market which is extremely volatile, coal producers had been shielded to some extent from volatile world markets by the extensive share of production taken by local consumers. It was also said that, given the abundance of the platinum resource and South Africa's dominant position globally, there was no need to 'subsidise' foreign consumers. In addition, it was argued that on the grounds of simplicity there should not be more than one tax formula and that tax should be neutral between one industry and another, so one industry did not subsidise another; that is, that *ability to pay should specifically be excluded* as a criterion in company tax unlike personal tax.

## Arguments in favour

It is, however, 25 long years since the Marais Commission reported, and in that time the global appetite for resources has grown so voraciously that fears of exhaustion of the oil resource are growing, albeit tempered in 2014 by shale oil fracking. South African coal is therefore also being exported on an increasingly grand scale. Even as regards platinum, although the resource remains wonderfully abundant, times have changed together with the pickup in pace of global demand growth. Thus, increased depths with concomitant difficulty and danger have led to tougher regulations and legislation, in particular the 'use it or lose it' regime. This has had the commendable aim of opening up the industry to many more players as well as allowing a much wider range of grades to be exploited. Although some of the exploration companies currently enthusiastically promoting the prospects of their mineral rights may never get as far as mining, a relatively large number will. Inevitably, this will include more players on more marginal deposits. It will, therefore, readily be seen that the considerations that led to the application of the GMF to gold mining are now applicable to all mines.

The argument on utility and simplicity can therefore be turned on its head; i.e. one can argue that all mining should be on the same (GMF) formula base. We suspect that much of the aversion in the past by other mining sectors to the formula was based on a fear that, because of (in some cases) higher profitability, they might end up paying higher tax than at present. Needless to say, however, if the desire of the Treasury was to encourage more mining than merely to squeeze current operators harder, the average effective tax rate could be maintained, if necessary, by adjusting the formula downwards as has indeed happened in recent years. The same applies to ensuring that South Africa, in the event of adopting our proposals, does not price itself out of the global mining jurisdictions market by allowing the formula to have too high a result for the richer mines.

Another possible objection would be that miners would no longer get quite the same benefits of boom-time spikes in commodity prices. Well, apart from the likelihood that this would spark renewed demands for windfall taxes, the flipside for the miners is that when the booms eventually subside, as the miners know full well will happen, they will be taxed at lower rates. So to sum up, in the earlier stages, miners will benefit from reduced risk of failing to achieve the targeted rates of return, and in the later stages, from reduced volatility of income.

## Royalties

Even before the Mineral and Petroleum Resources Development Act[6] established state ownership of minerals in South Africa there was implicit recognition of this position in the gold mining lease payments, which included considerations of grade and depth, and were first imposed in the Transvaal after the Anglo-Boer War. Later on they were also imposed in the Union of South Africa, in addition to the GMF tax introduced in 1936.

In terms of the MPRDA, the government was obliged to impose a royalty over and above the mining taxation and, in 2006, it published its proposals in the draft mineral and petroleum resources royalty bill the preamble to which states, *inter alia*, 'South Africa's mineral resources are non-renewable and are part of the common patrimony of all South Africans, thereby entitling the nation to consideration for the value of those resources extracted and transferred ...' and 'South

6 Act no. 2 of 2002.

Africa's mineral resources belong to the nation and … the state is the custodian thereof.'

In doing so, it could have been argued that the proposed royalty was, in essence, a resource rental that needed to be paid over and above company tax for the use of a wasting part of the national patrimony. Indeed, in the government's press statement on the mineral royalty bill on 23rd of March 2003 it stated that, 'it is important to note that most non-marginal mines generate on extraction so-called resource rents, which are a function of the scarcity value of the minerals. These rents can be taxed/shared among the government and the operators without impacting negatively on the viability of the project.' We agree, except that resource rents are by no means only a function of the scarcity value of the minerals. It is of the utmost importance to note that they are also related to the specific quality of each deposit/site – that is, grade, depth, location (proximity of infrastructure, labour), security and governance and so on – in other words, site value.

The government's press statement continued, 'Resource rent refers to the surplus return over and above the input costs, including capital, labour and materials. Differently put, resource rents are excess profits over the minimum rate of return which is required to justify investment into a mining venture.' This is a most important statement with which we fully concur. And it is precisely because marginal sites yield only the minimum rate of return that there is no rent to be shared with the government. Any attempt to collect rent where there is none either renders the site non-viable or renders useless a greater or lesser part of its ore.

So rentals have, of course, to be related to the value of the assets leased. And the corollary of the definition of rent used by the government is that where there is no rent, i.e. the resources are marginal, there should therefore be no royalty or resource rental.

As the GMF formula is widely accepted as a proxy for rating a mine according to grade and depth etc., it ensures, with the minimum of fuss, that marginal operations are indeed exempt.

## Royalties crossed the Rubicon?
Given that the early drafts of the Royalty Bill recognised the need for some relief for marginal mines, the government proved amenable to reason in the debates that ensued (in which we participated) and replaced initial cumbersome attempts with, in effect, a version of the GMF insofar as the royalty rate varies according to the profitability of the mine. It retains, however, a fundamental defect as it is based on

revenue with a minimum of half a percent payable. It therefore impacts marginal mines in conflict with the principle that the Treasury has no business gathering revenue where there is no rent.

This partial recognition of the merits and nature of resource rentals in the Royalty Bill may nevertheless be seen to have been a crossing of the Rubicon from the wilderness of Eurocentric and Anglo-Saxon systems of taxation towards the beginnings of a world-leading fully fledged system of resource rentals collection. We, at any rate, will do our utmost to see that it was not just a fleeting and forgotten lucid interval.

The upshot of all this, of course, is that the principle now adopted in the Royalty Bill, instead of being an afterthought add-on, needs to become the basis of all mining taxation. In this event, the mineral royalty (with its defects) would in any event become superfluous because much fuller recognition of the principle of resource rental collection can be achieved by the GMF. We should note that the GMF defers tax until full recovery of capex by the gold mine whereas the royalty is EBIT-based (i.e. it is levied on earnings before interest and tax but after depreciation). The GMF would be more favourable to the mines from a cash-flow point of view but an EBIT-based resource rental system would in principle achieve the same goal. For the sake of simplicity, however, we have generally referred to the GMF.

## GMF benefits for rich mines too!

We have made so much of the vital importance of the formula-based tax for marginal mines that it might come as a surprise that richer mines can benefit too: after all, don't they stand in line to pay possibly more than under the current tax regime?

This line of thinking, however, merely serves to show how cleverly disguised the impact of indirect taxes on the value added of the enterprise has been. According to Harmony's 2012 annual report, employee salaries and wages were R5,763m and PAYE R949m. In addition, labour contracts cost a further R693m and, together with our estimated PAYE paid by the contractors of R104m, this amounted to R1,053m. This was 10.1% of production costs of R9.9bn or 8.7% of total costs of R12.1bn. Removing layers of costs such as these would have a significant effect on reducing pay limits and thereby freeing up more ore for exploitation for rich and poor mines alike. VAT is not payable by gold mines, but for other mines, net VAT payable can be a significant factor.

## Indirect taxes critical for marginal mines

Marginal mines would not only benefit from the GMF but, even more so, from the absence of indirect taxes.

## Super cat among Oz mining pigeons!

In May 2010 the Australian Government announced far-reaching changes to mining tax based on the report of a commission, widely known as the Henry Tax Review. The proposed Resources Super Profits Tax (RSPT)[7] was fiercely contested by the mining industry, despite several positive features from a miner's point of view. BHP Billiton claimed it would increase its effective tax rate on Australian operations from 43% to 57% and it (together with other large players) threatened to put on hold or cancel major projects, proclaiming loudly that Australia's status as a world-class mining jurisdiction and investment destination would be severely damaged.

There is no doubt in our view that a change of this magnitude should have been discussed and negotiated in depth with the industry prior to publication, instead of providing for extensive consultation after presenting the industry with what was essentially a *fait accompli*. In essence, the RSPT would have taken 40% of profits after operating costs and depreciation (EBIT), and allowing for a tax-free return on capital based on the long-term government bond rate (then 5.5%). These would have compounded from start of project to commencement of operations, and only then, as we understood it, would RSPT be levied, thus constituting a tax-free tunnel. The government justified this seemingly 'non-super' return of 5.5% on the basis that not only was all project and exploration expenditure of the company to have been transferable to its other projects, but also part refundable, in the event of project failure. The government therefore 'guaranteed' 40% of capex against loss and claimed it was a 'partner' to that extent. The industry remained unimpressed, pointing out that the government did not supply that share of the capital. Other features included the replacement (in effect) of the royalties payable in the various states (the Australian Government would pay existing royalties) and the tax deductibility of the RSPT. Yes, the miners would still have been liable for normal company income tax, which was to be reduced from 30% to 28%!

7 Australia's Future Tax System, Report to the Treasurer, December 2009 (www.taxreview. treasury.gov.au).

## Oz Government justification

The Australian Government pointed out, quite rightly, that it was an improvement on revenue or production-based royalties which, as we have pointed out earlier, tax a mine before it makes a profit and regardless as to whether the deposit is marginal or prime. It also stated:

> Mining inherently involves the extraction of community owned non-renewable resources, so it is appropriate that the community receives an additional return from mining above those taxes that generally apply to businesses, such as company tax ... Governments should not give away publicly owned resources for free – for example land – simply because a company pays company tax.[8]

Moreover, in Table 9.1, the government showed that the effective all-in tax rate under RSPT (right-hand column) would have been much lower (i.e. 28%) for marginal projects with operating profit margins of 6% than the present royalties and company tax system (i.e. 45.4%). For the more profitable mines with 50% margins on the other hand, the present tax regime would drop to 35.5% whereas under RSPT and company tax it would have risen to 53.3%. This would, of course, have made it somewhat easier for marginal mines to survive.

**Table 9.1: Effective tax rates on a hypothetical resource project**

| Rates of Return | Effective Tax Rate under Royalties Plus 30% Company Tax | Effective Tax Rate under RSPT Plus 28% Company Tax |
|---|---|---|
| 6% | 45.4% | 28.0% |
| 10% | 40.9% | 39.5% |
| 15% | 38.7% | 45.3% |
| 20% | 37.6% | 48.2% |
| 25% | 36.9% | 49.9% |
| 50% | 35.5% | 53.3% |

**Note:** Effective tax rates are for a hypothetical project that has average operating costs based on ABS data. This assumes a risk-free rate of 6% and royalty rate of 6%. These estimates ignore the risk-sharing aspect of the RSPT. Therefore, these estimates should be taken as an estimate of the tax rate applying to a project that generates, say, a 25% return with no risk. Effective tax rates under the RSPT are lower if the project involves risk, because the risk is shared with government under the RSPT.

**Source:** www.futuretax.gov.au as at 15 June 2010

8 FAQ on www.futuretax.gov.au as at 15 June 2010.

# The Petroleum Resources Rent Tax (PRRT)

The Australian PRRT was introduced in 1987 on petroleum projects at a rate of 40% on upgrading profits in excess of an 'uplift rate' generally based on the 10-year government bond rate plus a premium of either 5% (for project expenditure) or 15% (for exploration expenditure). This provided a proxy for the projects' required rate of return – a risk-free rate plus a premium to compensate for project risk. In this way, the PRRT regime ensures that the tax is levied only on a project's profits above normal returns (i.e. 'super' profits). The Henry Tax Review, however, had the following to say about it: 'The resource rent tax should not provide concessions to encourage exploration or production activity at a faster rate than the commercial rate or in particular geographical areas, and should not allow deductions above acquisition costs to stimulate investment.'[9] It seemed that the Australian government believed that some operators were making too much money on their projects and, therefore, that future petroleum and offshore projects should be governed by RSPT while existing PRRT taxpayers were 'invited' to move to the RSPT regime. Needless to say, the PRRT has its critics who claim that it delayed by many years the opening of Australian projects as more lightly taxed deposits were opened elsewhere.

# Did the Aussies nearly get it right?

The mismanagement of the introduction of RSPT led, by mid-2010, to the Labour Party unceremoniously replacing Prime Minister Kevin Rudd with Ms Julia Gillard, who in turn replaced the proposed RSPT with a watered-down version styled Mineral Resources Rent Tax (MRRT) – whose fate, incidentally, remained equally uncertain amid less than expected revenue yields and enduring controversy in early 2013. The Australian Government had, however, introduced the concept of resource rentals into the global mining tax lexicon. Was it, therefore, talking our language and had it nearly got it right?

No! The root problem for the Australian Government was its limited understanding of what constitutes 'resources'. For in truth, resources comprise (as we have said) *all* land, mining, agricultural and

---

9 Australia's Future Tax System: Final Report > Part 1: Overview > Chapter 12: List of recommendations (#46) http://taxreview.treasury.gov.au/content/finalreport.aspx?doc= html/publications/papers/final_report_part_1/chapter_12.htm.Accessed 30 May 2014.

urban resources, and much else besides. They comprise both 'non-renewable'[10] and ongoing. So it is not only on mines where the resource rents need to be collected, but on all land. There is no need for the confusion about this that led to the South African Government almost simultaneously introducing a 'land tax' (so called, despite being on agricultural land only) at the same time as abolishing site value (i.e. land only) rating in urban areas.

Moreover, it is not necessary for the government to determine the appropriate risk-adjusted hurdle rate of return. This will already have been taken into account by the land or resource rentals that users are prepared to pay. To discover this may, of course, be a challenge, and for this reason we have suggested auction mechanisms where appropriate and, in the case of mining, adaptations of the relatively simple South African GMF as a proxy for rent collection.

Ignoring this leads inevitably to the kind of complexity involved in the RSPT, MRRT and PRRT including the cardinal sin of double taxation! Remember, it is a fundamental principle of collecting natural rent to recognise the fact that there is no rent at the margin. In mining the margin is primarily a function of grade, depth as well as local infrastructure and good governance. Commodity price fluctuations, however, will also render median deposits marginal at times. Therefore marginal operations (e.g. 6% in Table 9.1) should not be taxed at all, let alone at 28%.

So we repeat: all land, all resources need to be subject to resource rental collection!

---

10 Rehabilitation techniques in the coalfields of Mpumalanga are such that some land is being restored not only for grazing, but maize farming as well. The Treasury would therefore be able to collect normal land rentals again.

## CHAPTER 10

# LEGACY RENTIERS, LUXURIES AND POLLUTERS

*'Taxes upon luxuries have no tendency to raise
the price of any other commodities.'*
Adam Smith[1]

I N SOUTH AFRICA, as in many other countries, the non-collection of rent over many decades has led to the establishment of powerful entities that have benefited thereby. For want of a better term, we refer to them as the 'legacy rentiers'. Some of them we have already dealt with, e.g. the liquid fuels industry, telecoms, mining and the transport network.

## Barriers to entry

Many businesses and professions in South Africa are subject to barriers to entry: doctors, pharmacists, lawyers and auditors (among many others) have to pass stringent exams and registration processes before they are allowed to practise in the public domain. Restaurants and food shops have to meet health requirements before they are issued with a licence to open shop, and professional drivers must have the correct driving licences and specific training. All of the regulations that govern these, and other similar businesses, are in the interests of protecting the public. In other cases, the sheer amount of capital required (for example in mining or telecommunications) is, in itself, a huge barrier to entry to just anyone who thinks such businesses would be 'nice to be in'.

---

1 Smith, A., *An Inquiry into the Nature and Causes of the Wealth of Nations,* The Modern Library, New York, 1994,, Book V, Ch.11, Part 2, p.940.

For other businesses in the manufacturing, distribution, wholesale and retail industries there are few specific barriers to entry other than ability, capital and the will to succeed. However, once they are established, there are often attempts to restrict new entrants through collusion and dodgy business practices. Even Adam Smith observed this over 200 years ago: 'People of the same trade seldom meet together, even for merriment and diversion, but the conversation ends in a conspiracy against the public, or in some contrivance to raise prices.' While Smith did not agree with such practices, he considered any law to prevent such collusion to be inconsistent 'with liberty and justice'?[2] He said that 'the real and effectual discipline which is exercised over a workman (businessman) is not that of his corporation (trade association), but that of his customers'.[3]

While many such professions and businesses could be considered to be legacy entities, they are not rentiers in the same way as the businesses mentioned above, and they would be treated in the same way as any other owner or occupier of land.

## Proposals in the case of ongoing barriers to entry

Barriers to entry have certainly applied in regard to parastatals such as Transnet, SAA and the Post Office and, to the extent that these continue, they should certainly remain subject to company tax in addition to land rentals.

### Banks

In banking, however, there are old legacies that maintain the existing players in their dominant position and deter new entrants. As late as the 1970s, South African banks openly operated a cartel-type agreement (Rocco) on their fees charged and it is possible that collusion may have extended beyond that. In 2008 the competition authorities publicly scrutinised bank charges for signs of collusion, but one gets the sense that the banks do indeed compete with one another; the cosiness consists rather in the *de facto* barriers to entry created largely by their heavily entrenched positions. These are, in turn, a function of historical factors including levels of regulation and the isolation of the apartheid years. In the early years of this century, however, it could be argued that the disappearance of one of the larger banks (BOE) and

2 *Ibid.*, Book 1, Ch. 10, Part I, p.148.
3 *Ibid.*, p.149.

the demise of a smaller one (Saambou) was due to the way in which their problems were dealt with at the time by the authorities. Instead of allowing the field to expand so as to create more competition, the opposite occurred. Consequently, we feel that the banks are able to earn higher than average returns on capital and hence should continue paying tax until a much better populated and more competitive landscape is evident. Until then, we also propose that newer entrants below a certain threshold pay resources rental only.

Historically, banks came about when goldsmiths, as men of 'fortune, probity and prudence',[4] took in for safe-keeping the gold and silver coins of other wealthy people. The receipts they issued for such deposits could then be used to purchase goods and services as a proxy for the gold held by the goldsmith. As these receipts were seldom redeemed, the goldsmith could issue further receipts (or promissory notes) up to ten times the value of the gold and silver held by him plus his own capital. These promissory notes could then be lent to business people at a certain rate of interest. Theoretically, such loans would be on the basis of a sound business plan and the business person's ability and integrity.

However, following the non-collection of rent arising in the wake of the agricultural and industrial revolutions, it became far less onerous for banks (as the goldsmiths had become) to lend on the basis of the security of the borrower's property. This would include improvements, but for the most part the collateral would comprise land value, or, as we could now say, the capitalised value of the uncollected rent. While initially the banker may have taken into account the integrity of the borrower and his ability to service the loan and repay it in time, relying mainly on land-value collateral led to an easy and somnolent banking practice. As land values grew in real terms over long periods at the same time as the economy it eventually led to the fiction, subscribed to by Greenspan and Bernanke, that 'house prices never decline'. Needless to say, the present value of uncollected rent, like anything else, can become the subject of a buying mania and price bubble. The downward spiral to the sub-prime crisis, where loans were made to people without integrity or ability to service the loans, became almost inevitable.

Be all that as it may, banks globally (as evidenced by the sub-prime crisis) remain very much involved in lending, with property as collateral. Home loans and commercial mortgages typically comprise

---

4 *Ibid.*, Book 2, Ch. 2, p.318.

nearly half the lending of the Big Four[5] South African banks, for example.

Absent the ability to lend on this basis, and home lending reverts to what it should have been in the first place: a sober calculation of the ability of the borrower to repay the costs of the bricks and mortar. It is indeed sobering to reflect on the extent to which the current global financial calamity could have been thereby avoided. American banks, in effect pushing land values to unsustainable heights so that Americans could borrow even more in order to import vast quantities of consumer goods (thereby pushing their trade deficit to unsustainable levels), were hardly conducive to a healthy balance in the global economy. Perhaps one could even speculate that, were both the US and Chinese Governments to have collected rent over the past decade, the US Government would have had the wherewithal for (and hence paid more attention to) its ageing infrastructure. The Chinese, on the other hand, would have been able to afford a social welfare net so as to encourage more consumption and a less paranoid rate of saving.

## Proposal for banks

Our proposal for revenue collection from banks would therefore be that they be subject to site value resource rentals in the same way as all other land owners. In addition to this, they should be liable for normal company taxation on non-core banking activities without any deduction for site value rentals. However, assuming that, say, half the collateral for mortgage lending comprised land values and the rest bricks and mortar, the evaporation over a short period of time of about a quarter of all its collateral could, of course, have repercussions as regards capital adequacy, since the favoured 50% risk weighting for mortgage loans might well be reviewed. In this event, banks would have to be given some leeway and a phase-in period of 5 to 10 years may be necessary. Finally, quite apart from the legacy aspect of our banks, we take a fresh look later on (Chapter 16) at the sector in the light of the global move to re-regulate it following the universal opprobrium heaped on it for its role in the crisis that began in 2007. There, we also distinguish between core and non-core activities.

## Steel manufacturers

ArcelorMittal South Africa (formerly the state-owned Iscor and now part of Lakshmi Mittal's global empire) has been the subject of many

5 Standard Bank, Absa, Firstrand and Nedbank.

enquiries and complaints on competition issues, not to mention some major differences of opinion with SARS on tax deductibility of special business improvement payments to its controlling shareholder, ArcelorMittal plc. Long before it was privatised and listed in the late 1990s it was overtly monopolistic and, in the 1960s, Anglo American had to undergo a long process of negotiation with the government before its Highveld Steel (now Evraz Highveld Steel) was allowed to enter the field. We suspect the latter succeeded only because of the limited market share for which it aimed as well as the special features of its process which incorporated the production of vanadium pentoxide and ferrovanadium using raw material from its Mapochs Mine some 70km from Witbank. Although we do not recall any allegations of collusion with Iscor, neither was it exactly renowned for furious competition with the latter for market share. It may, therefore, also be said to have benefited from a *de facto* barrier to entry situation. Not only was Iscor protected from internal competition, but it was also notorious for its strong arm tactics in discouraging its customers from resorting to imports. As a favoured state-owned entity, it also owned its own iron ore deposits at Thabazimbi in the Limpopo province and Sishen in the Northern Cape. When the latter were split off into a separate company, Kumba Iron Ore, at the time of listing on the JSE, it was stipulated that Kumba would continue to provide Iscor with most (6.25 mtpa) of its ore requirements at cost plus 3%. This non-arm's length transaction (which Kumba disputed in 2010) constituted another barrier to entry measure but was replaced by a more arms length transaction in November 2013.

### Proposal for steel manufacturers

Suffice it to say that the existing steel manufacturers fall foursquare into the category of legacy rentiers and should continue to pay company tax, albeit perhaps at reduced rates, in addition to resource rentals as determined elsewhere in our proposals.

## Proposals for liquid fuels, natural gas and selected telecoms

### Proposal for liquid fuels

That Sasol was incubated over decades by the apartheid state for strategic reasons is not open to dispute. Its synthetic fuel (synfuel) and gas-to-liquid technologies are a direct result, and together with its leading position in the South African market, constitute a major barrier to entry to any would-be synfuels producer on the Highveld. In addition, it is also arguable that the complex web of regulations governing the liquid fuels industry is at least partially skewed in its favour. Pending the deregulation that we propose, it should continue to be subject to (a lower rate of) company tax in addition to the resource rentals proposed.

## Proposal for natural gas

In our view, similar considerations apply to the state-owned PetroSA, which is derived from the former Mossgas (exploiting offshore gas near Mossel Bay) and the state oil exploration entity, Soekor, and is planning a new oil refinery at Coega. In early 2013 South Africa was still mulling over the basis on which its world-class resources of shale rock would be exploited. We trust that the principles propounded here will be heeded, and that where appropriate, auction mechanisms will be used for allocation of exploration and/ or exploitation rights. In passing, it is interesting to note that in 2010 Shell paid prices of around $4,500/acre for so-called tight gas acreage in the Marcellus Shale area around the Appalachian Mountains in the North-eastern United States.[6]

## Proposal for selected telecoms

As noted in Chapter 7, the incumbent landline operator, Telkom, together with the cell phone players, Vodacom and MTN, have bene-fited from restricted competition, to say the least, which constitutes a legacy rentier situation for these entities. In the case of Telkom this has been to the serious detriment of business as well as individuals, especially in the last decade. The fact that competition is at last looming cannot make up for the lost years. As regards the cell phone opera-tors, they benefited from the delays in introducing a third player and, as we have discussed, have been paying company tax instead of resource rental. However, should our proposals be adopted, any tax still payable would be priced into the licence auction bids. And yes, we propose that these three players continue to pay corporate tax, albeit at a lower rate, for a limited period up to, say, 10 years or at least until the expiry of their current licences. Finally, despite our comments about the lack of competition in the past, regulators should take care not to let the sector become overtraded otherwise they won't be getting decent bids at their auctions!

6 *Financial Times*, 29 May 2010.

# VAT on high-value luxury items: alcohol and tobacco products

Adam Smith was not keen on consumption taxes: 'The state', he wrote, 'not knowing how to tax, directly and proportionably, the revenue of its subjects, endeavours to tax it indirectly by taxing their expense, which, it is supposed, will in most cases be nearly in proportion to their revenue.'[7] However, he got caught up in a web of complications attempting to distinguish between what he called 'necessaries and luxuries'. Although he spent many pages describing what he considered to be the difference between necessities and luxuries, in essence he said that necessities should not be taxed, but luxuries should be.

'A tax upon the necessaries of life operates exactly in the same manner as a direct tax upon the wages of labour. The labourer, though he may pay it out of his hand, cannot, for any considerable time, be properly said even to advance it. It must always, in the long run, be advanced to him by his employer. His employer will charge upon the price of his goods this rise of wages, together with a profit; so that the final payment of the tax, together with this overcharge, will fall upon the consumer.'[8] And, we might add some 230 years later, this manifests in a downward spiral that adds considerably to the price of necessities borne by those who can least afford them: the rural poor.

But a tax on luxuries, argued Smith, will not increase wages. Nevertheless, he gets into a long and convoluted argument as to what consumables are, which are necessities, and which are luxuries. For example, Adam Smith, who (as previously noted) was a vegetarian, argues that 'butcher's meat' is a luxury, because he has shown personally that anyone can live quite adequately without it. This is not an argument that would go down too well now.

## Proposal for luxuries

Our proposal is that whole classes of consumables are classified as either necessities or luxuries and are taxed accordingly. So if tobacco and alcohol products are classified as luxuries, all products within this definition would be taxed, not exempting some because of their low alcohol or low tar content. The present regime of exempting some items within a single classification, for example, brown bread (exempt),

---

7 Smith, A., *An Inquiry into the Nature and Causes of the Wealth of Nations*, The Modern Library, New York, 1994, Book V, Ch. 2, Part II, Article IV.
8 *Ibid.*

versus all other types of bread (not exempt), makes no sense. The differential between the price of a brown loaf of bread and the price of a white loaf of equal weight and size reflects, in all probability, merely the cost differential between the two products. Arguments as to what is a luxury or a necessity will go on forever; simplicity, in our view, is always best.

## Carbon emissions

Carbon emissions by industries such as coal-fired power stations, metal, and oil refineries, are considered to be a major source of green-house gases, and therefore of climate change. The Kyoto Protocol is a global attempt by the United Nations to get all countries to agree to reduce carbon emissions. The protocol was agreed on 11 December 1997, entered into force in 2005 and ran from 2008 to 2012 when a number of Annex 1 countries agreed to further reductions in green-house gas emissions by the end of 2020. Only 'Annexure 1' countries (mainly developed countries) are required to cap emissions by their industries. Other countries (including South Africa) are required only to monitor and report on carbon emission levels in their territory.

Annex 1 countries that are required to reduce their emission levels in accordance with the Kyoto Protocol used a carbon credit trading system (known as cap-and-trade) as an incentive for specific industries and companies to reduce their carbon emissions levels. Companies received one carbon credit for each ton of emission permitted up to their cap. If their emissions are above this cap they may either install equipment that will reduce emissions to or below the cap, or they may buy 'carbon credits' from companies that are below their own cap. Carbon credits are traded on financial markets and their price, like any other financial instrument, depends on supply and demand.[9]

Given that the voluntary emission targets set out by President Zuma at the time of the Copenhagen conference in December 2009 were subject to certain conditions which were not fulfilled, South Africa remains exempted from having specific emission cap levels (and thus the emissions trading scheme), but it is required in terms of the protocol to monitor and report on emission levels. Nevertheless the question remains, should South Africa take more active steps to reduce carbon emissions? This is especially important as South Africa is in the process of planning new coal-fired power stations and Sasol is

9 Information: https://unfccc.int.kyoto_protocol/items/2830.php

considering a new coal-to-oil plant. South Africa has abundant supplies of coal and it makes sense to use this relatively cheap source of
fuel. However, there should also be incentives to make new coal-fired
plants as efficient as possible. While large public companies such as
Sasol and PPC take their responsibilities in this respect very seriously,
government policy at this stage seems to be based on the Air Quality
Act of 2005. This provides for licensing of facilities (both public
and private) that produce carbon emissions and for penalties for not
conforming to the licensing requirements. It is not clear to us how
successful this policy has been.

In the February 2013 budget, the Minister of Finance stated that
'Government proposes to price carbon by way of a carbon tax at the
rate of R120 per ton of $CO_2$ equivalent, effective from 1 January 2015.
To soften the impact, a tax-free exemption threshold of 60% will be
set, with additional allowances for emissions-intensive and trade-
exposed industries.' In the 2014 Budget further phase in and carbon
offset measures were announced and the imposition of the tax post-
poned until 2016 to allow further consultation and preparation. If
South Africa is to provide more incentives for the mitigation of emissions, beyond the 'licence-and-punish' regime of the Air Quality Act,
the closest to collection of resource rentals is, in our opinion, the
Emissions Trading Scheme (ETS) as used in the European Union and
other developed countries. An ETS provides an incentive for companies to reduce their carbon emissions, but at the same time also
provides a choice to either install mitigation technology or purchase
carbon credits on the ETS open market. In addition, there are social
and environmental pressures on companies to reduce their carbon
emissions.

As mentioned above, many large companies in South Africa already
take these responsibilities seriously. In its 2013 annual report PPC
states that it 'achieved a 16% reduction per unit of cement produced
from 1990 to 2010. PPC's plans include targets for further improving
electrical efficiency by 10% and thermal efficiency by 5%, resulting in
a further 5% reduction of our carbon footprint by 2017.' According
to the company it has invested considerable time, effort and money in
reducing its carbon footprint.

## Proposal for emission trading schemes
While this is laudable, we believe that South Africa should be preparing
now for the creation of a local ETS. While such liabilities for polluters
are not based on liability for natural resource rentals, they are based

on the related obligation to keep the resources used in good condition. We also note that, based on the principle that the only real justification for tax is to discourage behaviour where necessary, some form of carbon tax may well be justified. Nevertheless, as asserted vehemently by many of those likely to be affected, it does need to be realistic in terms of its potentially negative effect on the economy.

## Tax on high-income individuals

Here we again follow the Adam Smith philosophy, this time on the taxation of wages. 'In all cases a direct tax upon the wages of labour must, in the long run, occasion both a greater reduction in the rent of land, and a greater rise in the price of manufactured goods, than would have followed from the proper assessment of a sum equal to the produce of the tax partly upon the rent of land, and partly upon consumable commodities.'[10]

In this short paragraph Adam Smith sums up what we are proposing in this book: the revenue of the nation should be confined to collecting the resource rents and by taxing luxury goods. Although Adam Smith says simply '[a tax partly] upon consumable commodities', he means, as we show above, only on luxuries.

So Adam Smith is saying that taxes on wages and consumable goods (and services) are destructive and inflationary, and this is a position with which we concur. This problem is amply demonstrated in South Africa with its high levels of unemployment and endemic poverty. And it is those who are unemployed and living in poverty who suffer the worst effects of destructive and inflationary taxation policies.

In South Africa at present, the historical and legacy discrepancies in education and business opportunities may justify a tax on incomes at a high threshold (say, R2 million per year). While this may indeed include some highly-paid government officials, it is mainly aimed at all who have benefited from superior education and better business opportunities, both in the old and new South Africa. It is important to note, however, that this is a legacy situation; the need for which should be eliminated after a decade or so during which resource rental collection should have levelled the playing field.

10 Smith, A., *An Inquiry into the Nature and Causes of the Wealth of Nations*, The Modern Library, New York, 1994, Book V, Ch. 2, Part II, Article III.

## New-look SARS

The South African Revenue Service has established a formidable reputation garnering revenue for the Treasury. In doing so, the learning curve has been steep. Quite apart from the likelihood that the legacy taxes proposed in this chapter will still have to be gathered, we feel the Department should be capable of continuing its learning curve into the new realm of rental collection indicated in this book.

## CHAPTER 11

# COMMERCIAL AGRICULTURE

*'As soon as the land of any country has all become private property,
the landlords, like all other men, love to reap where they never
sowed, and demand a rent even for its natural produce.'*
Adam Smith[1]

## What the land can carry

To townsfolk travelling through the Karoo after good rains, the land
may appear deceptively underutilised, with boundless views of lush
grazing interrupted only by the occasional farmstead or glimpse of
sheep and cattle. Yet every district has its own well-researched carrying capacity, to exceed which would contravene the flip-side of the 'pay
the full rent' principle, that is, to 'keep the land in good condition'.
Thus in the Venterstad area it would be 13 ha/LSU (13 hectares
required to support 1 large stock unit). One large stock unit (such as
a mature cow or horse) is the equivalent of seven small stock units
(such as sheep or goats). In the Barkly East area the carrying capacity
is better, requiring only 10 ha/LSU, and in the grazing lands of the
Free State, it improves further to 8 ha/LSU. In parts of KwaZulu-
Natal (KZN) the carrying capacity of the veld approaches 1 ha/LSU.
Whereas the latter probably represents the higher end of the range,
Pofadder in the Northern Cape (at 15 ha/LSU) and Beaufort West in
the Great Karoo (at around 20 ha/LSU) represent the lowest.

Farm prices vary accordingly, with current levels estimated at around
R2,500/ha around Venterstad and R4,000/ha in the southern Free
State. In the Kuruman district, north of Beaufort West, the land price
may be as low as R500/ha.

1 *Ibid.*, p.56.

# Crop farming

Moving up the range to the more valuable and scarce arable land results in farm values of around R3,500/ha in the more marginal maize-growing area of Theunissen to around R4,000-R8,000/ha in a prime area such as Delmas. Bear in mind here that these prices include the farmstead, barns, other outbuildings and dams as well as fencing, all of which constitute vital improvements. Under our proposals, these improvements would be subtracted from the farm value for the purposes of calculating the unimproved land, natural resource or site value rental.

# Horticulture, forestry

Dryland cane farming land in the Dalton area of KZN could typically sell for around R30,000-R35,000/ha while the rich alluvial land with irrigation rights on the Umfolozi Flats (where no fertiliser is needed) would go for around R90,000/ha. Forestry land, with its long-term nature and more specialised economics, probably sells at around R10,000-R15,000/ha in KZN.

# Capital intensity

With arability, of course, comes a massive increase in capital intensity with, for example, the very expensive cultivating and harvesting equipment needed for maize farming, not to mention R7,000/ha input costs, as well as the major expenditure of establishing orchards in the case of horticulture e.g. R300,000/ha for grapes.[2] Since we do not propose that capital expenditure be deductible from the resource rental, the market would adjust land values accordingly. This would not only counter complaints at the loss of a traditional means of minimising tax liabilities, but eliminate the over spending on the likes of dams, vehicles and equipment such as harvesters, which has sometimes featured in the past. Moreover, farmers contemplating major capital expenditure could do so secure in the knowledge that it would not raise unimproved land values and hence rentals.

2 Chris Stimie, Director, Rural Integrated Engineering.

# Land use

As shown in Table 11.1[3] a few stark factors dominate land in South Africa:

- Only 13.7% is arable;
- 70.5% of the total land area is comprised of 35,000 commercial (mainly white-owned) farms;[4]
- 11.8% is occupied by 1.3 million farmers in the former Homelands (typically 2ha/farmer); and
- 10.7% is used for nature conservation and forestry leaving only 6.9% for everything else!

So all other economic activity takes place on the remaining 6.9% of the land, i.e. it supports all mining, manufacture, commerce, finance and so on as well as residential and infrastructure.

### Table 11.1: Land utilisation in South Africa (1991)

|  | Commercial | | Former Homelands | | Total South Africa | |
|---|---|---|---|---|---|---|
|  | m.ha | % of total | m.ha | % of total | m.ha | % of total |
| Arable land | 14.2 | 13.5 | 2.5 | 14.6 | 16.7 | 13.7 |
| Grazing land | 72.0 | 68.4 | 11.9 | 69.6 | 84.0 | 68.7 |
| **Farm land** | **86.2** | **81.9** | **14.4** | **84.2** | **100.7** | **82.4** |
| Nature conservation | 11.0 | 10.5 | 0.8 | 4.7 | 11.8 | 9.6 |
| Forestry | 1.2 | 1.1 | 0.3 | 1.8 | 1.4 | 1.1 |
| Other | 6.8 | 6.5 | 1.6 | 9.4 | 8.4 | 6.9 |
| **Total** | **105.2** | **100** | **17.1** | **100** | **122.3** | **100** |

**Source:** Development Bank of South Africa.

Consequently, over two-thirds of the total area of South Africa is grazing land while nearly 10% is for nature conservation and only 1% for forestry. Despite taking up no less than 82.3% of the total area of South Africa, agriculture (according to Statistics South Africa) comprised a mere 2.6-3.5% of the total value added by the economy between 1995 and 2000. Note, however, that in 2000/2001, value added by agriculture comprised roughly one-third of total agricultural

---

3 Since transition in 1994, data, which would have been used for the former Homelands, is now gathered by the various Provinces and relevant government departments, so no updates are available.
4 This includes the vast dry area of the Northern Cape with 2km?/farmer required, which skews the picture.

revenue of R48bn. Its importance to the economy should not be underestimated, despite comprising only 2.3% of Gross Value Added in the third quarter of 2011.[5] Some experts claim that, taking into account backward and forward linkages, it accounts for up to 20% of GDP[6] Moreover, it currently contributes 8% of total exports. Even so, the contribution to GDP is far less than in many other African countries (such as Ghana at around 70%), which demonstrates both the relative productivity of its agricultural land as well as the advances of other industries in South Africa.

It follows from all of this that over 96% of total value added in South Africa was on less than 7% of the land. Now that's saying something about relative land values!

The apparently humble contribution of agriculture to the economy is (as is well known and we shall see later) in inverse portion to its political importance. If mishandled, it has a capacity, as we have seen elsewhere, to derail everything.

Whilst the disparity between value added per hectare on land used for agriculture and the rest of the economy is vast, Table 11.2 shows that between arable and animal production (grazing) it is also great.

### Table 11.2: Commercial agriculture: income per hectare across various categories

|  | Field Crops | Horti- culture | Forestry | Animal Production | Mixed Farming | Total Commercial Agriculture |
|---|---|---|---|---|---|---|
| Number of farming units | 11 992 | 8 039 | 796 | 31 442 | 5 711 | 57 980 |
| Hectares (m) | 9.53 | 3.9 | 1.56 | 63.38 | 4.39 | 82.76 |
| **Gross income (Rm)** | | | | | | |
| Year to March 2008 | 23 818 | 26 743 | | 51 314 | | |
| Year to March 2009 | 37 800 | 31 076 | | 58 727 | | |
| **Gross income (R per ha)** | | | | | | |
| Year to March 2008 | 2 499 | 6 857 | | 810 | | |
| Year to March 2009 | 3 966 | 7 968 | | 927 | | |

**Source:** Census of Agriculture, 1993: Agricultural survey 1996 and Statistics South Africa and Economic Overview: Department of Agriculture Annual Report 2008/9, p.6.

In the 2008/2009 year, for example, gross revenue per hectare on land used for field crops was more than four times that on land used

5 South African Reserve Bank Quarterly Bulletin: December 2010.
6 John Lishman, head of Nedbank's Agriculture Division, quoted in the *Financial Mail* of 7 May 2010.

for animal production. Whilst income on land used for horticulture was nearly nine times greater, it is likely that of the total of 1.35m ha under irrigation (in 1993), for field crops and horticulture, a higher proportion of the latter was under irrigation. Putting land under irrigation, of course, constitutes a marked improvement so a large proportion of the extra productivity is due to the capital expenditure involved. Nevertheless, not all land lends itself to irrigation, so to some extent the extra productivity is, indeed, due to the higher value of the underlying raw land. Moreover, there is not much scope for developing new land for irrigation as our water resources are already under stress.

## It's in the prices

As one would expect, these vast differences in productivity are factored into the prices paid for land. Unsurprisingly, the land value data (see Appendix) indicates that a 'land value map' of South Africa would correlate well with one of rainfall.

## Snookered by distance...

In addition to poor climate and soil conditions, many agricultural areas suffer from great distances from markets. Upington, capital of the Northern Cape, is 800km from Johannesburg and 900km from Cape

### Table 11.3: Gross agricultural income, inputs and value added in 2007

|  | Rbn |
|---|---|
| **Total income** | **79.5** |
| Feed | 9.8 |
| Fertilisers | 4.3 |
| Fuel | 4.2 |
| Repairs & maintenance | 3.2 |
| Packaging material | 2.6 |
| Seed, plants | 2.5 |
| Dips, spray, other | 2.4 |
| Buildings, dams, fencing | 1.6 |
| Transport | 1.6 |
| Electricity | 1.5 |
| Purchases of animals | 8.9 |
| Other expenses | 6.9 |
| **Inputs** | **49.5** |
| **Value added** | **30.0** |

**Source:** Preliminary agricultural census for 2007: Department of Statistics S.A.

Town. Louis Trichardt and Thohoyandou in Limpopo are 430km and 500km respectively from Johannesburg, while Mafikeng, capital of the North West Province, is nearly 300 km from Johannesburg and over 1,300km from Cape Town. Communal farming areas in the Eastern Cape might be close to East London but are far away from major markets in Gauteng. The same applies to large areas in north-eastern KwaZulu-Natal. As can be seen in Table 11.3, fuel is the fourth largest single farm input. (Note that field crops, horticulture and stock farming would each have their own unique distribution of input costs, so this table gives the combination of these sectors as an overall picture.)

## …and snookered by tax

To make matters worse, the disadvantages of distance are exacerbated by taxation. The fuel tax of 150c/l and customs and excise duty of 4c/l (or more if the Road Accident Fund and transport levies of 64c/l and 0.15c/l are taken into account) comprise 28.5% of the retail price of 765c/l.[7] We presume that the fuel costs data is net of the diesel rebate of 33.6c/l (46c/l[8] less a 20% margin to allow for incidental non-primary use) for use of diesel on the farm which would benefit mechanised operations in particular. As the census does not distinguish, we have assumed that for the industry as a whole, the incidence of fuel tax would have been reduced by up to 5%. Taxes on fuel, therefore, raise input costs by 2.5% on average, and certainly more for the marginal remote areas, which is precisely where it shouldn't. All the other inputs, of course, also include a hidden fuel tax component, which could easily be another 2.5%, although we cannot estimate it with any degree of accuracy. Consequently, it is interesting to note in Table 11.4 that, if our assumption of a 28% income tax rate is anywhere the mark, the government gets a healthy 18% of the value added by agriculture. This would be more for prime land and less for marginal sites.

While operations on good arable land might be able to handle this as a matter of course, many of the others (which could in any case easily have a much higher than average proportion of fuel input costs)

7 In February 2013 the fuel levy was 197.5c/l and the RAF 88c/l. The four items comprised 23.6% of the Gauteng 95 Unleaded Petrol price of 1 227c/l according to the AA website on 9 March 2013.
8 In April 2012 these amounts were 56c and 70c, respectively (KZN Agicultural Union website, accessed on 9 March 2013).

would find that an extra, say, 4-10%, could well make the difference between survival and demise. This is especially the case when bearing in mind that where the grant of security of tenure confers no special advantage there is no rent to collect, let alone any case for any tax whatsoever.

**Table 11.4: Distribution of value added by agriculture (2007)**

|  | Rbn | % |
|---|---|---|
| Value added per census data in Table 11.3 | 30.0 | |
| Add back estimated fuel tax | 1.2 | |
| Add output less input VAT (R4.4bn-R4.0bn) | 0.4 | |
| **Gross value added** | **31.6** | **100** |
| Distribution to: | | |
| **Labour (as per 2007 preliminary agricultural census)** | **8.6** | **27** |
| **Capital** | **17.3** | **55** |
| Owner's return before income tax | 13.5 | |
| Owner's income tax (say 28%) | −3.8 | |
| Interest | 2.8 | |
| Depreciation | 3.5 | |
| Rental, grazing rights | 1.3 | |
| **Government** | **5.7** | **18** |
| Taxes, rates, excise | 0.3 | |
| Fuel taxes | 1.2 | |
| Income tax (say 28%) | 3.8 | |
| Output less input VAT | 0.4 | |

**Source:** Authors' estimates based on Table 11.3 and preliminary agricultural census 2007.

## Gross value added

To the extent that input VAT is recoverable, it does not appear in company accounts, and we have assumed that this also applies to the 2007 census figures. But with a very substantial R4bn paid by the farmers on non-fuel inputs (and hopefully, recovered) and R4.4bn paid by their customers in respect of their own value added, it is very much the unseen elephant in the agricultural room. We have therefore added it on to the value added as per the census data because, since the customers paid the gross amount (i.e. R35.6bn), it must have constituted at least that amount of value for them. Commercial farmers can, of course, claim back their input VAT against output VAT paid but we suspect that unclaimed VAT constitutes a significant cost burden on smaller farmers.

## Rental and grazing rights? Tell us more!

One of the most intriguing and potentially useful bits of information in the 2007 agricultural census is the R1.3bn shown for rental and grazing rights, which we have included in returns on capital. If this were to be broken down to a per hectare basis for different categories (i.e. grazing, crops and horticultural), it would go a long way towards establishing a national agricultural resource rental matrix.

## Owners' salaries change the distribution picture

The owners' return after tax of some R9.7bn or 27% of gross value added may well have been inflated by the inclusion of a 'salary' element, which has not been shown separately. An average salary for example of, say, R15,000 per month on each of the 40,000 units included in the 2007 agricultural census would amount to R7.2bn. Since this would make an enormous difference, we have shown it in Table 11.5 below.

### Table 11.5: Distribution of value added, including salaries

|  | Rbn | % |
|---|---|---|
| **Gross value added** | **31.6** | **100** |
| Distribution of value added: |  |  |
| **Labour** | **13.8** | **44** |
| Per 2007 preliminary agricultural census | 8.6 |  |
| Add authors' salaries estimate | 5.2 |  |
| **Capital** | **12.1** | **38** |
| As per Table 11.4 | 17.3 |  |
| Less estimated salaries after tax (72% of R7.2bn) | 5.2 |  |
| **Government** (as per Table 11.4) | **5.7** | **18** |

Source: Authors' estimate based on preliminary agricultural census 2007.

This reduces the share of capital from 55% to 38% and boosts the share of Labour from 27% to 44%.

## Higher returns are needed to lure investment

The apparent returns on assets, deduced from the census data in Table 11.6, are way below what is required to maintain – let alone expand – South Africa's agricultural production so as to restore food sufficiency and boost exports. The returns (which are before tax and have not even had the salaries deducted as in the value added study) range from –0.6 in 1993 to a still abysmal 9.4% in 2007.

### Table 11.6: Apparent returns on assets

| Rbn | 2007 | 2002 | 1993 |
|---|---|---|---|
| Gross farming income | 79.5 | 53.3 | 19.6 |
| Current expenditure | 54.1 | 45.0 | 16.4 |
| Salaries, wages | 8.6 | 6.2 | 3.6 |
| Apparent net income | 16.8 | 2.1 | –0.4 |
| Market value of assets | 178.6 | 98.4 | 66.9 |
| **% Return on assets** | **9.4** | **2.1** | **–0.6** |

**Source:** Authors' estimate based on preliminary agricultural census 2007.

## Low wages

The *per capita* wages in Table 11.7 that we have deduced from the 2007 census data vary enormously from region to region, and although this could be due to the nature of work involved (with more skills being involved in capital-intensive operations), the broad trend is unmistakable. The lowest wages occur in the more remote and arid provinces such as the North West and the highest in the higher-rainfall areas such as Gauteng. The Free State is, however, a puzzling exception, possibly due to the preponderance in the Province of low capital-intensive grazing lands as opposed to field crops. In general, however, even the

### Table 11.7: *Per capita* wages (2007)

| | Full-time | Casual and Seasonal | Full-time | Casual and Seasonal | Full-time | Casual and Seasonal |
|---|---|---|---|---|---|---|
| | Remuneration | | Remuneration | | Remuneration per capita | |
| Province | Number of employees | | R'000 | | Rand | |
| Eastern Cape | 34 253 | 30 565 | 510 404 | 106 497 | 14 784 | 3 484 |
| Free State | 53 944 | 45 150 | 737 796 | 98 996 | 9 901 | 2 193 |
| Gauteng | 22 979 | 11 957 | 534 083 | 93 461 | 23 242 | 7 816 |
| KwaZulu-Natal | 66 685 | 34 383 | 968 455 | 154 286 | 14 523 | 4 487 |
| Limpopo | 35 728 | 31 833 | 625 436 | 124 159 | 17 505 | 3 900 |
| Mpumalanga | 46 520 | 32 826 | 853 396 | 176 363 | 18 345 | 5 373 |
| North West | 53 741 | 32 008 | 574 596 | 75 250 | 10 692 | 2 351 |
| Northern Cape | 26 871 | 47 874 | 339 948 | 123 723 | 12 651 | 2 584 |
| Western Cape | 90 943 | 98 546 | 2 029 275 | 485 108 | 22 314 | 4 923 |
| South Africa | 431 664 | 365 142 | 7 173 389 | 1 437 843 | 14 909 | 3 938 |

**Source:** Authors' estimates based on preliminary agricultural census 2007 data.

higher income levels fall below the income tax threshold; although, as we have noted elsewhere, VAT can easily take up to 10% of the income of the poorest.

In late 2012 the issue of low agricultural wages burst onto the scene at De Doorns and elsewhere with a vengeance, and while it was common cause that the previous minimum was too low, it was also noted that the farmers' capacity to pay more varied enormously – which is what we have been talking about all along! One of the authorities' responses was to encourage farmers to apply for exemption from the new minimum of R105 per day. To the extent that marginal farmers are exempted, it will be recognition of this fact. What needs much more attention, however, is that this is pointing to the lack of taxable capacity of marginal sites!

## Inadequate data

For the reader who is by now wondering why this examination of data keeps taxiing around the runway without ever taking off, the answer is that although they are a whole lot better than nothing, the per hectare data (which are indispensable for determining the relative value of land in southern Africa) are not supplied. The good news is, of course, that it should be readily forthcoming if the need for it were to be appreciated.

## No burp taxes needed in the Karoo!

To illustrate the sort of analysis required, in Table 11.8 we have attempted a 'bottom up' approach, showing data from a typical Karoo sheep farm of around 9,450 ha.

The bottom line is that even for 1 dry hectare in the Karoo battling to create wealth of even R50 per annum, the government still takes R10 (or 20%). In truth, as we have explained in the case of marginal land, it has no business taking even one cent. We have no doubt that, since this particular farm may or may not be average for the Karoo, there are many farms there and elsewhere in the country where the government takes an even higher proportion of value added. So, if it is bad for Karoo farmers, imagine how much worse it is for farmers, commercial and emerging, in other, drier, areas. While governments in high-rainfall areas such as New Zealand with much higher value added per hectare can enjoy the luxury of conjuring up 'burp taxes' to protect the environment, the South African Government finds that VAT, fuel taxes etc. do even better.

## Table 11.8: Per hectare analysis for typical Karoo sheep farm

|  | Land value | R1 250/ha |
|---|---|---|
| Estimated value of plants, equipment & vehicles | | R1 025 000 |
| Infrastructure | | R250 000 |

|  | R/ha |
|---|---|
| **Revenue** | **74.67** |
| **Input costs** | **−33.69** |
| Fuel (less diesel rebate as explained above) | 4.6 |
| Stock feed | 0.88 |
| Stock dips & sprays | 0.52 |
| Fertiliser & seed | 0.02 |
| Rations & clothing | 3.44 |
| Woolpacks & shearing | 2.25 |
| Repairs & maintenance | 6.19 |
| Farm services | 3.46 |
| Transport | 0.48 |
| Rent | 4.23 |
| Electricity & water | 2.23 |
| Administration | 5.39 |
| **Revenue less input costs** | **40.98** |
| Output VAT (10.45) less input VAT (4.71) | 5.74 |
| **FULL VALUE ADDED (i.e. incl. net VAT)** | **46.72** |

**TYPICAL SHEEP FARM (ignoring salary)**

| Distribution of value added to: | (R/ha) | % of total |
|---|---|---|
| **LABOUR: wages & Workmen's Compensation Assistance** | **7.55** | **16.2** |
| Farming profit before tax, interest & depreciation | 33.43 | |
| Providers of capital: | 9.09 | |
| Interest paid on loans | 0.02 | |
| Depreciation | 9.07 | |
| Farming profit before tax | 24.34 | |
| **TAXATION** | **9.40** | **20.1** |
| VAT on input costs | 5.74 | |
| Income tax on farming profits | 3.66 | |
| Farming profit less income tax and VAT | 20.68 | |
| **CAPITAL (20.68 plus interest and depreciation)** | **29.77** | **63.7** |
| **FULL VALUE ADDED (i.e. incl. net VAT)** | **46.72** | **100.0** |

**TYPICAL SHEEP FARM (including salary of R15,000pm)**

| Distribution of value added to: | (R/ha) | % of total |
|---|---|---|
| **LABOUR (incl. salary)** | **26.59** | **56.9** |
| Farming profit before tax, interest & depreciation | 14.39 | |
| Providers of capital: | 9.09 | |
| Interest paid on loans | 0.02 | |
| Depreciation | 9.07 | |
| Profit before tax | 5.30 | |
| **TAXATION** | **9.40** | **20.1** |
| VAT on input costs | 5.74 | |
| Income tax on farming profits and salary | 3.66 | |
| Farming profit after tax | 1.64 | |
| **CAPITAL** | **10.73** | **23.0** |
| **FULL VALUE ADDED (i.e. incl. net VAT)** | **46.72** | **100.0** |

**Source:** Data from farm in the Graaff Reinet district.

# We've come a long way from sheep farming

Agriculture has come a long way since the days when sheep and cattle farming were mainly what it was all about in South Africa, so value added analyses for maize, cane and fruit farms would look very different and, if we had the data, would provide very many chapters of interesting reading – for the industry if not the reader of this book! In the meantime, just to illustrate a totally different land use in the industry, the figures in Table 11.9 for a full-feed dairy operation in the Southern Cape yield a gross profit per hectare nearly 100 times higher than the revenue/ha for the sheep farm. While value added per hectare on a free-range dairy farm would be much lower – and some might carp that a feedlot is more akin to a manufacturing operation – those are different issues. The bottom line is that the numbers are still valid examples of different yields for different uses for different land.

### Table 11.9: Full-feed dairy operation

**500 head of cattle on 223 ha at Rolhoek near Witsand, Southern Cape, dryland grain farming area**

| Cost per day of feed per cow (R) | R | R/ha |
|---|---|---|
| 17 kg @ R1.15 | 19.55 | |
| Feed pills; 5kg @ R1.44 | 7.20 | |
| | 26.75 | |
| Income per cow | | |
| 23L @ R1.98 | 45.54 | |
| Gross margin % | 70 | |
| Average days lactation | 208 | |
| Cows milked in Jan '06 | 234 | |
| **Total GP from cows** | **1 582 870** | **7 098** |

Source: *Landbou Weekblad*, 5 January 2007.

# Value added per hectare data is required nationwide

Assuming for a moment that value added of R47/ha is indeed the average per annum for South African grazing lands, it follows that there must be many thousands of farms adding much less value/hectare. Equally, of course, there will be others producing much more, even before we move on to arable and horticultural land, where the value added/hectare is likely (as we have seen) to be many multiples of this figure.

What we can readily see from this study, however, is that for the majority of farming areas taxation is a major challenge and, in many cases, would make agriculture unviable.

## Industry idiosyncrasies

The 80:20 principle is alive and well in agriculture inasmuch as (with regard to the 59,000 commercial farmers in 1993), well over 80% of production came from much less than 20% (i.e. less than 12,000 of the total number of farmers). Another quirk is that land prices in some areas – such as viticulture, for instance – seem to be of 'Clifton Beach' proportions, making it highly unlikely that they could yield anything like a commercially reasonable return on capital. When first we began to investigate this anomaly, industry comment was 'they get it back when they sell.' The fact that this occurred in the face of a global red wine lake raises suspicions of some bubble process which will, in any event, end in tears at some stage. Game farm prices, albeit not as stratospheric, appear to be another category where considerations of (for example) lifestyle, leisure and prestige could be playing a major role. If this is indeed so and proves to be sustainable, then of course we cannot complain on behalf of the people, because this will enhance the rent they receive! 'If it ain't broke don't fix it!' We strongly suspect, however, that while some wealthy land-owners (such as successful, retired, multi-millionaire businessmen) might be happy to pay 'non-economic' rentals (that is, including lifestyle and prestige values), the majority would come down to earth resulting in more realistic rentals as well as more economically rational decisions regarding usage. Thus arable land converted to, say, game farming to reduce risking more capital and avoiding labour hassles would probably be cultivated again.

## Land restitution and land reform

Not much of this pussyfooting approach is, however, to be observed in regard to some of the utterances over the years from government and the DLA (Department of Land Affairs) in response to various factors such as impatience on the part of potential beneficiaries at the slow pace of land restitution and land reform as well as the generally more politically charged atmosphere following the Zimbabwean land grabs. Organised agriculture has even had cause to complain that some ministerial statements are contributing to the serious and steadily increasing number of farm murders. To outsiders such as ourselves, it seems clear that there is, for example, an urgent need for the DLA to stop using organised agriculture as a scapegoat and to address its manifest lack of capacity to implement all the transactions involved, let alone ensure that beneficiaries are properly equipped for the task. Farmers, on the other hand, need (with equal urgency) to be more proactive in areas such as mentoring emerging farmers and publicising their successes and/or problems in this regard. Simply pointing to government ineptitude is very far from a winning strategy.

There have, however, from time to time been signs of such a proactive approach as illustrated by the Renosterrivier Project, a comprehensive set of proposals by a group of prominent farmers in regard to cattle farming presented in person to President Mbeki in 2007. In June 2010 a promising initiative, The Standard Bank Centre for Agri-Business Leadership and Mentorship Development, was launched by the bank in partnership with Stellenbosch University. The bank also established a R500m black economic empowerment (BEE) fund that offers to assist black farmers with a track record of at least three years and the aspiration to farm on a sustainable commercial scale. The Dean of AgriSciences at Stellenbosch University, Mohammad Karaan, said the centre will engage with agri-businesses to develop leaders and systems necessary for 'competitive, equitable and environmentally sustainable agricultural production.'[9]

The many reasons for the failure to achieve the target of transferring 30% of white-owned agricultural land to blacks by 2014 have been well documented; but, at the outset, it is now clear that the task of developing capacity on the part of the new owners to continue operating efficiently was not merely underestimated, it was completely overlooked. In a report prepared for the Queenstown District Land Reform Office of the Department of Land Affairs (DLA) the writers state:

> Other than the slow pace of LR (land reform), the major concern is the lack of post-settlement support that is largely responsible for the failure of many LR projects. DLA, for too long, saw LR as transfer of land to beneficiaries as job done. While this was to some extent acceptable in a focus on provision of land rights to HDI (historically disadvantaged individuals) cases, it was disastrous in an economic context for establishing black commercial farmers. Grants to cover part of the purchase price of a farm are only the beginning of the support required.

9 *Financial Mail*, 11 June 2010, p. 30.

An empty farm without basic implements and equipment, without short-term finance for operations, without transport, without extension and expertise, without market information, without the local farmers association, without legal and administrative support, is not likely to succeed. The current effort by the Minister of Land Affairs requesting national parliament to approve the funding of equipment and operations during the purchase of farms is certainly the way to go.[10]

The Cabinet's recent estimates are that up to 90% of the 5.9 million hectares of commercial agricultural land, including some highly successful export-orientated operations, is not being farmed productively.[11]

The DLA has accordingly devised comprehensive strategies, not only in an attempt to speed up the process, but to increase capacity. For example, in the 2008/2009 budget allocation, R500m was allocated for the next MTEF (medium-term expenditure forecast) period to train 5,000 agricultural extension officers. The DLA has also estimated the cost of transferring the remaining 25.5% of land at R60bn. Had our resource rental collection proposals been in place all along, however, the cost would have been only half this amount, on the assumption that about half the values concerned was for improvements. The aim of redistributing 30% of all white-owned agricultural land into black hands by 2014 has also been extended by 25 years.

Recalcitrant farmers, and the willing buyer/willing seller principle are but a few of the many challenges facing the DLA, which include inadequate coordination between Central, Provincial and Local Governments, especially as regards planning, lack of capacity in the latter, and the DLA. Moreover, its responsibilities extend beyond land reform, restitution and redistribution, but also relate to land-use regulations.

All these issues have, however, been well documented elsewhere, and suffice it to say that while we support the restitution and reform objectives, we believe that the fundamental and overriding principles that we are highlighting will not only boost agriculture generally, but will facilitate both land restitution and reform as well. Certainly they point to the responsibility of all involved to ensure not only optimal rent for the 'People's Land', but to make sure that it is kept in the best possible condition as well.

All of this may seem perfectly obvious, but the constitutional approach of the government is under threat from the intensity of

10 Area Based Plan, Sectional Analysis Report prepared by Kula Development Facilitators, June 2008.
11 *Finweek*, 1 April 2010, p.19.

feeling amongst, not only rural, but also urban blacks because of an underlying resentment at real and perceived historically unjust dispossession. Deep-seated cultural ties to land persist in the minds of what is nowadays the urban majority, a fair proportion of whom still maintain links with their rural origins.

We have commented on the benefits to land reform and redistribution from our proposals but it is worth noting, in addition, that they would eliminate many of the complexities and red tape facing new entrants to the industry. Not the least of these would be the recently introduced land tax imposed on farmers by local authorities who could instead charge directly for any services rendered.

Moreover, insofar as collecting the rent on our land goes to the very heart of grudges, grievances and anger on this issue, it is not unreasonable to expect that it will militate against farm murders. We also believe, therefore, that it would vastly improve relations between the DLA and organised agriculture and encourage the promising trend for mentorship by established farmers of their new neighbours. Certainly, the rising levels of prosperity we envision for the rural areas generally would strongly reduce the motivation for stock theft.

## Collecting the rent: modus operandi

As a point of departure, we believe the standard model of annual site value rates should apply. Initially, these would be based on relative land values prior to the introduction of the proposed changes. As noted elsewhere, should the proposed reforms indeed succeed in capturing the full rent, capital values of unimproved land would tend towards zero, with farms effectively changing hands at improvement value. The latter would, in time, provide a useful gauge as to the extent to which farm prices included payment for uncollected rent (i.e. current rates paid undervaluing land). Alternatively, where the prices were patently less than the value of improvements, they would indicate that rates were too high. All of this data would be captured so as to provide for regular 'marking to market' of the rates collected by the state. Given the volatility of many agricultural product prices, these reviews would probably have to be fairly frequent, and would possibly include moving average mechanisms to cater for fluctuations. The process would also have to include opportunities for hearings of objections, with provision for independent arbitration or legal appeals.

A possible alternative approach would be to allow large or mainly export-orientated farming units to apply to have their site value rentals replaced by a progressive formula tax based on either EBIT or value added, kicking in at above the agreed cost of/return on capital. This would be on the basis that farms, like mines, are also primary industries, the net returns on which can be hugely influenced by extraneous factors such as commodity price and currency volatility.

We have a difficulty in that this analogy breaks down in some fundamental respects:

- While it is relatively easy to establish the unimproved land value of a farm, 'unimproved site value of a developed mine' is a contradiction in terms;
- Unlike crop farming, which can often be switched among a wide variety of crops, mines are generally restricted to one particular metal or mineral with by-products; and
- Mines are wasting assets.

We conclude, therefore, with a preference for a rating based on unimproved land value including appropriate mechanisms for rapid marking to market to cater for currency and commodity volatility.

## Data wish list

It is beyond the scope of our resources to produce the data in Table 11.10, but between government and industry it should be possible to begin data gathering along such lines – certainly as far as the current tax regime is concerned.

### Table 11.10: Authors' data wish list

| Farming Activity | | Current Tax Regime | | | |
|---|---|---|---|---|---|
| R/ha | Land Value | Wealth Created | Labour | Tax | Farm Return |
| Extensive | ? | ? | ? | ? | ? |
| Intensive/crop | ? | ? | ? | ? | ? |
| Horticulture/viticulture | ? | ? | ? | ? | ? |
| Game | ? | ? | ? | ? | ? |
| Other | ? | ? | ? | ? | ? |

**Source:** Authors.

Pending general availability of such data, a good start was made in a *Finweek* cover story[12] which tackled ministerial rumblings about agri-

12 *Finweek*, 'Sticking Our Necks out for Game Farms', 1 April 2010,p.14

cultural land being switched to game farms by pointing to research[13] that indicates that the economic value of indigenous species is higher than that of exotic species in regions with less than 700 mm of rainfall per year. South Africa's average annual rainfall is 464 mm (against a world average of 860 mm) with very few regions regularly getting more than 700 mm. The Namibia Nature Foundation conducted a comparative study on the income per hectare for different uses that showed that the financial gross return from tourism was R165/ha whereas that from communal livestock farming (probably a few goats and a couple of cattle) was only R4.71/ha, and the return from commercial farming was R15/ha. Dr Chris Brown, Executive Director of the Namibia Nature Foundation said 'the wildlife of no other continent even closely approaches the actual and potential value of that of southern Africa. The beauty of the situation is that wildlife, if carefully managed, will always be Africa's comparative advantage.' In South Africa, the Kruger National Park covers around 2,000,000 ha and the SA National Parks report indicates gross income of around R500m or about R250/ha – which is much more than achieved by neighbouring cattle farmers. The article also gives another perspective on land use, shown in Table 11.11 (attributed to the Council for Scientific and Industrial Research and Agricultural Research Council: National Land Cover 2000).

### Table 11.11: SA land use perspective

| Category | m/ha | % |
|---|---|---|
| Bare and degraded areas | 5.45 | 4.5 |
| Cultivated areas | 12.76 | 10.5 |
| Grasslands | 24.30 | 19.9 |
| Indigenous forests | 0.52 | 0.4 |
| Mines | 0.20 | 0.2 |
| Forest plantations | 1.72 | 1.4 |
| Shrub lands and herb lands | 42.27 | 34.7 |
| Urban areas | 1.85 | 1.5 |
| Water bodies | 0.68 | 0.6 |
| Wetlands | 0.87 | 0.7 |
| Woodlands and bush lands | 31.34 | 25.7 |
| Total | 121.96 | 100.0 |

**Source:** Finweek, 'Sticking Our Necks Out for Game Farms', 1 April 2010.

13 Namibia Nature Foundation: *Namibia's Conservation Paradigm* by Chris Brown, 2010.

## Conclusion

The upshot of all this is that in some cases tax is clearly not an issue, whereas in others it renders otherwise viable operations intensely marginal and elsewhere simply pushes them off the playing field. We offer no prizes for guessing which is which, and note that locational advantage is reflected in current unimproved land values which, of course, can be used for replacing the current onerous system of taxation with land value rates.

As to the overall effect on the economy, we believe the following factors would come into play:

- A host of underutilised marginal sites would increase (or return to) production;
- Underutilised prime sites would be incentivised to optimise operations;
- Land with a lifestyle and prestige bias in its pricing might in certain areas retain this premium, while in other cases there is likely to be a steady reversion to purely economic criteria, but in any event, the incentive to optimise operations will take effect;
- Increased levels of employment on farms;
- Increased viability of farmers would contribute to the revival of currently depressed small towns in the rural areas;
- Small towns themselves would be the major beneficiaries of the reforms proposed here, which would in turn benefit farmers;
- To the extent that the new approach led to the de-politicisation of land holding and greater security of tenure, this would lead to increased investment and productivity; and
- Inefficient or idle owners would tend to be weeded out, thus making farmland more freely available.

## CHAPTER 12

# RURAL AREAS

*'... for a long distance beyond the city, land bears a speculative value, based upon the belief that it will be required in the future for urban purposes ...'*
Henry George[1]

## Forestry

THIS SECTOR of primary industry (i.e. excluding indigenous forests of 0.5 million ha), occupies some 1.7 million ha or 1.4% of the surface area of South Africa. It is unique in that its harvest time of up to 30 years requires special attention. It is also a valuable national resource in regard to which the consensus is that not enough land has been made available to meet the growing requirements of mass housing and industry. One of the problems in some traditional areas of the Eastern Cape, which are otherwise well suited, has to do with complex land tenure issues. Considerations of national interests are also cited by Safcol as a *raison d'être* for itself as a state-owned entity. According to its (March 2008) Annual Report, its wholly owned subsidiary, Komatipoort Forests owns 190,000 ha including at least 141,000 ha of plantations (excluding 17,000 ha in Mozambique) and is considering an additional project of 50,000 ha. Pulp and paper producers Sappi and Mondi also own large plantations for their own needs, with the former owning 550,000 ha (of which only 66% is for timber production with the rest managed as conservation areas), while Mondi has 327,000 ha. Together, therefore, these three entities own some 45% of South African forestry land. Safcol states, however, that considerations of competition in forestry and processing have been

1 George, H., *Progress and Poverty*, Robert Schalkenbach Foundation, New York, 1992, p.257.

identified by the state as key principles in the privatisation process. Interestingly enough, Safcol increased its plantations valuation by over R500m to R2.46bn thanks (according to its private sector critics) to its ability to set prices almost at will. The land on which this valuable timber stood was valued at a risible R4m! Of course, if we resist the temptation to conflate the worth of this long-term harvest and the land on which it stands, there will have to be some serious rethinking if the basic principles of resource rental collection are to be applied. Once these are understood, however, we believe industry experts will not take long to come up with solutions. If the government were to privatise Komatipoort, this would be an ideal opportunity to split it into several entities using rental auctions as a basis for allocation.

After establishing the amounts to be paid for the standing timber via independent valuations of its net present value, the bids could comprise:

- A combination of upfront payments for land; and
- An EBIT/revenue-based rental.

Although the interests of traditional communities in the relevant parts of the Eastern Cape need to be respected, it may well be necessary to allow some major commercial players to participate in the process to achieve market-related rentals and get the process going at last.

As far as the ongoing collection of land rentals from the sector is concerned, we believe that a site value rental method would be by far the best, although no-one is pretending that there are no complexities involved. Useful discussions of the technicalities are to be found on the website of Professor Mason Gaffney[2] including the following comments: 'The urgency to minimise the downtime of land between crops of trees is a function of its value: no value, no hurry. A tax that lowers site rent and value therefore delays restocking.'[3] Owners incentivised via tax systems (e.g. taxing eventual harvest yield) to leave restocking to nature could delay the turnaround by anything between 10 and 20 years, during which time a valuable natural resource is left lying idle.

Moreover, yield or harvest taxation 'affords a 100% loophole for owners who never cut their stands, but use them for amenities, recreation, or nothing at all' and 'the income tax rate required to raise the same revenue as a yield tax must be at a substantially higher figure,

2 www.masongaffney.org, along with many other aspects of land taxation and resource rental collection in general (accessed January 2011).
3 http://www.masongaffney.org/publications/O11aTaxes on Yield Property Income_and_Site.CV.pdf. (accessed January 2011).

at least, where rotations are medium or short. This high rate leads to strenuous contortions motivated by tax avoidance. The deductibility feature leads easily to padding expenses and gold-plating of capital equipment.'[4]

## Traditional agriculture

We desperately need to move beyond subsistence agriculture and the outmoded practices, which, together with taxation, have created sink-holes of poverty in the former Homelands.

Together with the improved rural infrastructure that we envision, security of tenure (as we have commented elsewhere) needs to be finally and firmly established. In this regard, traditional leaders need to take a firm lead. There is absolutely no need for the backwardness of these areas. South Africa can no longer afford it.

In this regard, the Community Land Rights Act of 2004, which allows local communities to choose between communal and individual tenure, has not had the desired effect, owing, apparently, to cumbersome and costly procedures including: surveyors having to document the land, town planners having to draft a development plan and conveyancers having to make the legal transfer followed by the opening of a deeds register.[5] While it is certainly not for us to prescribe a detailed solution to the problem, it is worth noting that not only was the original system of tribal land tenure thoroughly distorted by more than a century of colonial, republican and apartheid administration, but as a result, many misconceptions as to its nature have arisen. According to Essy Letsoalo[6] the potential for patronage and misallocation of land that arose under the latter situation did not prevail previously. 'By implication, allocated land was the tribesman's – he owned it. The chief was *mongmabu,* but the man given the land owned it, because the link between the land and individual tribesman was stronger than the link between the land and the chief.' Tribal ownership, of course, was subject to use and membership of the tribe; land could not be bought or sold although it could be passed on to descendants. In principle, however, had the land not been interfered with, there would have been nothing to prevent the tribesman developing

---

4 http://www.masongaffney.org/publications/A3-AlternativeWaysofTaxingForests.CV.pdf. (Accessed January 2011.)
5 Grube, L., *Communal Land Rights Act Needs to be Revised*, Free Market Foundation website, accessed March 2010.
6 Letsoalo, E.M., *Land Reform in South Africa*, Skotaville Publishers, Johannesburg, 1987, p.21.

his land without fear of 're-allocation' by a corrupt state agent (as, in the end, some of the so-called chiefs became). The need and opportunity for the State or community to collect some rent should also act as a spur to speedy resolution of the stalemate.

Given basic support and proper incentives – including minimal rentals for marginal land instead of taxation – there is little doubt in our minds that rural people will seize the opportunity with both hands. This includes the menfolk for whom, for more than a century, migration to the cities appeared to be the only solution. The possibility that our proposals would rejuvenate the towns in these areas would also be a boon to the surrounding communities.

In this regard the decade-long controversy surrounding the proposed Wild Coast Highway illustrates both a unique challenge and opportunity. The former is to preserve the magnificent and relatively unspoilt natural beauty and the latter is, in doing so, to develop its undoubted potential for tourism as well as general economic development. Given the validity of environmentalists' concern, it is clear the project should be approached on an integrated basis; i.e. construction and conservation going hand-in-hand and designated tourism and other sites being made available at market based land rentals.

## Country towns

To city travellers, whether passing through commercial or traditional areas, two features of the towns stand out: first, rows and rows of RDP houses, many of which stand empty with no doors or windows, and, secondly, the absence of any industry or other sources of employment. In addition, these towns very often reek of 'marginality' as we define it.

We have a very different vision.

First and foremost, the many taxes borne by these marginal areas will either be eliminated or reduced, thus encouraging entrepreneurs to settle and take advantage of the tax haven status. With this in mind, we expect the local authorities to steadily refurbish the often decaying infrastructure including, in many cases, neglected schools. If so, they will be rewarded in due course, because rising prosperity leads to rising rentals, even if they remain way below those in metropolitan areas.

Take, for example, the decision by First National Bank to close 31 of its branches in towns in the Free State and Northern Cape.[7]

7 As reported in the *Beeld*'s Sake24 on 21 April 2010.

Undoubtedly, one of the factors in its cost reckoning would have been the PAYE element of their salaries bill (see calculations in the next paragraph) which would be absent under our proposals. In addition, one way or another, VAT bedevils the situation – either by non-recoverability or by inflating bank charges. The same applies to all businesses employing those salaried people who are indispensable to the core infrastructure of small towns.

## Manufacturing

The accelerated decline in the global economy in the fourth quarter of 2008 wrought havoc with the South African manufacturing sector, which declined 22% despite a sharply weaker Rand (which often helps this sector). To make matters worse, the Rand – possibly bolstered by the South African Reserve Bank's conservative stance on interest rates – began to strengthen in the second quarter of 2009. One of the casualties was the once mighty Frame Group, which in its heyday in the 'old' South Africa employed 65,000 textile workers. In announcing further major closures with the loss of 1,400 jobs in April 2009, Johnny Copelyn (the Chairman of the parent company Seardel) expressed great disappointment at the government's decision not to help the company which, as he pointed out, was paying hundreds of millions of Rand in VAT and PAYE. Most of the operations are located near the major metropoles of Durban and the Western Cape.

It is possible, therefore, that the scenario that we envisage (i.e. free from VAT, PAYE, company and petrol tax and subject instead only to a modest site value related rental) would probably apply mainly to a small part of its operations, e.g. in Newcastle, and to a lesser extent elsewhere.

Of course, the business model of Mr. Philip Frame was controversial from the 1960s onwards, and no doubt part of his success was due to extensive tariff protection, which (understandably if somewhat precipitously) was dismantled in 1994 by the incoming minister of Trade and Industry, Trevor Manuel. To make matters even less politically correct, several of his operations were located in the so-called 'border areas' such as Qwa Qwa near Harrismith and in the Transkei. Nevertheless, it is our contention that to some extent, the reprobate apartheid government was actually doing some of the right things, albeit for a very wrong reason (apartheid). Thus the tax breaks and subsidies were tantamount to a handing back to those operations some of the much lower levels of indirect taxation applicable at the time.

The Ciskei Government added to these attractions with particularly low levels of direct tax. In effect, therefore, it was a recognition (albeit by a political fluke) of the principle that governments should not try to extort tax from otherwise viable operations in marginal locations (i.e. areas with little locational advantage).

Frame was, of course, not the only manufacturer to avail itself of border area concessions that resulted in the creation of thousands of jobs. In the little town of Butterworth in the Transkei, for example, there were about 43,000 people employed in industry (albeit derided as sweatshops) in the early 1990s, compared to some 4,000 now. 'Tax harmonisation' of the former Homelands with the rest of South Africa following transition in 1994 saw the imposition of the full South African tax regime with no recognition for lack of locational advantage. Many thousands of jobs were lost, leading to a flood of rural migrants into informal settlements around South African cities. This whole episode could, we believe, do with a lot more research. Yes, urbanisation is a global phenomenon, with taxation playing its part everywhere as well. It's just that in South Africa, it would appear to have been given a sudden (and probably unintended) impetus in the mid-1990s.

Getting back to Frame's woes, they elicited scant sympathy from Nick Steen, chairman of the SA Household Textile Manufacturers Association, who said South Africa did not have enough cotton to compete with the huge economies of scale that China and Pakistan have with their massive textile mills. He said that the vested interests of the unions controlling Seardel blinded them to this reality, and that their doomed effort to prevent the removal of the 22% duty on imported fabrics not only failed to save the 1,400 jobs but 'put the jobs of many more thousands on the line.' This was to the severe detriment of the textile industry as a whole where 'the bulk of jobs are on the make-up side, namely the sewing and cutting. The potential for creating jobs here is enormous because the necessary skills levels are not very high, and this is one part of the industry that can be competitive and profitable.'[8]

So how can we realise the enormous job-creation potential Steen was talking about?

Well, ironically enough, although Seardel's operations (which include the parent company's clothing operations as well as Frame's textiles) are for the most part not in marginal locations, its Annual Report for

8 *Sunday Times*, 26 April 2009.

the year to June 2008 is, nevertheless, of great interest and not just for the usual array of fetching models either![9] It includes, on a cash basis as shown in Table 12.1, one of the more meaningful value added statements to be found in the published accounts of JSE-listed companies.

### Table 12.1: Seardel cash value added statement

| Year Ended June 2008 | Rm |
|---|---|
| Cash derived from revenue | 3 848 |
| Paid to suppliers for materials and services | 2 393 |
| Cash value added | 1 455 |
| Interest received | 31 |
| **Total wealth created** | **1 486** |
| **Distributed as follows:** | |
| **Employees** | **1 037** |
| Administration | 280 |
| Production | 639 |
| Sales | 118 |
| **Providers of capital** | **124** |
| Interest paid on borrowings | 113 |
| Dividend to shareholders | 11 |
| **Monetary exchanges with government** | **319** |
| Taxation (including customs and excise duty) | 101 |
| PAYE | 119 |
| VAT | 114 |
| RSC levies | 0 |
| Incentives | −15 |
| Used in operations/retained to develop growth | 6 |
| **Total wealth distributed** | **1486** |

**Source:** Seardel Annual Report 2008.

Seardel made a loss in 2008, so 'taxation' in that year did not include the usual company tax at 28%, but was comprised solely of customs and excise duty (although we doubt if it included taxes on fuel purchased). RSC levies had been phased out by 2008 but were substantial a few years earlier. However, what is indeed striking is the amount of tax borne by the enterprise despite its marginality.

This analysis also puts paid to the myth that individual employees of enterprises pay tax out of their own pockets. Both the PAYE and the VAT have to be paid for by the wealth created by the businesses, otherwise they fold!

9 Discontinued by the new management, no doubt in deference to more doleful circumstances!

Although Seardel's marginality was probably as much due to industry structural issues as location, its value added statement is a very important pointer to the potential Nick Steen is talking about.

Both revenue and value added (wealth created) were static in nominal terms at around R3.8bn and R1.5bn per annum between 2004 and 2008.

**Table 12.2: Percentage distribution of Seardel's wealth created**

|                  | 2008 | 2007  | 2006 | 2005 | 2004 |
|------------------|------|-------|------|------|------|
| Employees        | 69.8 | 77.9  | 65.6 | 67.3 | 63.4 |
| Government        | 21.5 | 26.5  | 21   | 17.9 | 13.2 |
| Retained/utilised | 0.4  | −12.3 | 8.5  | 8.9  | 15.7 |
| Lenders          | 7.6  | 6.0   | 4.1  | 4.7  | 6.5  |
| Shareholders     | 0.7  | 1.9   | 0.8  | 1.2  | 1.2  |
|                  | 100  | 100   | 100  | 100  | 100  |

**Source:** Seardel Annual Report 2008.

As Table 12.2 clearly shows, from the start of this period shareholders received a measly 1.2% of value added and this diminished to 0.7% in 2008! Employees' share rose from 63.4% to 69.8% but guess what – government share increased from 13.2% to 21.5%! How is it possible that a professed jobs-for-the-people government could grind such a large employer into the ground?

Here's how this could be avoided.

Just imagine some of Steen's cutting and sewing operations setting up in rural locations (think Uniondale, Winberg, Warden, Cradock, Venterstad, Makhado, Butterworth and dozens like them), all of which have much lower land values or locational advantages than the metropolitan areas. With low (or minimal) resource rentals to pay and no PAYE, VAT, company tax, fuel tax and excise duties, it is not hard to imagine that many would flourish.

To assist the imagination, we have gone back to the Seardel accounts and assumed them to be for a marginally located operation (the fictitious Uniondale Clothing), which is 1/10 of the size. In Table 12.3 we have located it in Uniondale, but you could imagine it in any other marginal rural town.

So at the operating level, Uniondale Clothing made a loss in 2008 of R1m (2007: profit R12m) and, after impairments, restructuring and retrenchment costs, finance expenses and taxation, a loss of R18m (2007: profit R5m). Needless to say, in a recessionary environment it becomes a prime candidate for closure adding to unemployment.

## Table 12.3: Uniondale Clothing Manufacturing Co. saved by moving from taxation to resource rentals

| Year ended June (Rm) | 2008 | 2007 |
|---|---|---|
| **Sunk by taxation!** | | |
| **Revenue** | **387** | **379** |
| Costs of revenue | 315 | 300 |
| **Gross Profit** | **72** | **79** |
| Other income | 9 | 13 |
| Distribution costs | –34 | –35 |
| Admin and other expenses | –48 | –45 |
| **Operating loss/profit before impairments, restructuring and retrenchment costs** | **–1** | **12** |
| Impairment of assets | –11 | –1 |
| Restructuring and retrenchment costs | –4 | 0 |
| **Operating loss/profit before finance costs** | **–16** | **11** |
| Finance income | 3 | 2 |
| Finance expenses | –12 | –8 |
| **Loss/profit before taxation** | **–25** | **5** |
| Taxation | 7 | 0 |
| **Loss/profit for the year** | **–18** | **5** |
| **Saved by resource rentals!** | | |
| **Add back monetary exchanges with government** | **32** | **35** |
| Taxation (including customs and excise duty) | 10 | 11 |
| PAYE | 12 | 13 |
| VAT | 11 | 13 |
| RSC levies | 0 | 0 |
| Incentives | –1 | –2 |
| **Profit before resource rental charges** | **14** | **40** |
| Resource rentals (say 2ha @ R0.31m$^2$) | 0 | 0 |
| **PROFIT AFTER RESOURCE RENTALS** | **14** | **40** |

In a resource rentals environment, however, there is a sharp turn-around from a loss of R14m to profit of R28m.

This comes about by adding back the indirect and other taxes of R32m, as well as the impairments and restructuring (and so on) of R15m, which in all likelihood would not have been necessary under this scenario. One could also argue the same in respect of finance charges, but we have left them in place on the basis that a healthy operation would require some working capital.

We have assumed that Uniondale Clothing would use 20 ha, which we have charged at one-third of the manufacturing average resource rental assumed in national budget (Chapter 14).

The upshot of this is that we think that not only would Uniondale Clothing be an attractive proposition, but that the same would apply to many other light industries.

Is it too far-fetched to see here the renaissance of normal economic activity and job creation in our far-flung rural areas? In our view, clearly it is not. Would it take long? Well, in some ways it would amount to a reversal of the impetus that accelerated the rural exodus in the 1990s, and so, one could argue, could be quite quick to occur. As against that, there have been a plethora of regulations governing business in general, so it might require (in the absence of a general simplifying of regulation) the designation of past and present rural nodes with potential as having some kind of regulatory free IDZ[10] status. Ideally, however, one would try not to have to do this, as our approach has been as far as possible to avoid exceptions, such as in the case of legacy rentiers. In other words, we are proposing the general application of the principle so as not to have distortions caused by selective implementation. One major difference from the apartheid-era rural Homeland tax breaks (which attracted numerous enterprises despite the political opprobrium and controversy surrounding these areas) would be that if anything, the new dispensation could be seen as part of the re-building of the New South Africa.

So, thanks are owed to Seardel's finance team for an enlightening value added statement, and let's hope all JSE companies follow suit soon.

---

10 Industrial Development Zone.

## CHAPTER 13

# URBAN AREAS

*'Fancy comparing these healthy processes [i.e. of production] with
the enrichment which comes to the landlord who happens to own
a plot of land on the outskirts of a great city, who watches
the busy population around him making the city larger,
richer, more convenient, more famous every day, and
all the while sits still and does nothing.'*
Winston Churchill[1]

URBAN AREAS cover less than 2% of the surface area of the country but support over half the population and generate the bulk of wealth created. Here too, we have the highest natural rent, with land prices indicating the huge productive potential of land ranging from that in the heart of the Central Business Districts (CBDs) of Sandton and Cape Town through suburban shopping centres and industrial areas (often less than 15km away) as well as a wide range of residential land values. Estimated values of prime land in the Sandton CBD of around R18,000/m$^2$ are indeed priced at 400,000 times more per square metre than the bottom-of-the-range sheep farms near Pofadder of around R450/ha. Moreover, whereas the latter will pay little or no rental, Sandton landowners will pay accordingly for the most productive land South Africa can provide. The Gautrain that connects it with the Johannesburg *or* Tambo International Airport, the nation's capital at Pretoria and the old Johannesburg CBD gives it yet another major boost. Thus, only the very best and most productive commercial, financial and other tertiary businesses will be able to afford locating there.

1 Speech to the House of Commons on Land Monopoly on 9 May 1910. Winston Churchill, *The People's Rights*, reprinted by Jonathan Cape, London, 1970, p.118.

Elsewhere in Greater Johannesburg, office sites come down to more mundane levels such as in Witkoppen, Sandton (R2,133/m²), or Northgate, Randburg (R1,308/m²).

## Manufacturing[2]

The Wynberg industrial area is a mere 4km away from Sandton City, while within a range of 15-35km, there are serviced industrial stands to be found at Olifantsfontein for R650/m²; Devland, south of Johannesburg for R300/m²; Lanseria (next to a regional airport) also for R650/m². Not very much further afield there are industrial stands aplenty in the East Rand towns of Germiston (e.g. Raceway Park at R400-600/m²), and Brakpan (R125/m² for land with 'industrial zoning soon').

Moeletsi Mbeki[3] points to the de-industrialisation of South Africa, citing various factors – all of which are valid. He also points, in contrast, to the relatively favourable position of the mining and energy complex during the global commodities boom, as opposed to the manufacturing sector that declined in the face of rising competition from the East (and is largely responsible for South Africa's very high unemployment levels). Since we agree that this is a problem area of the economy, readers may well ask why we have not dedicated a separate chapter to it, when we have done so for mining and agriculture. The reason is that we believe manufacturing can be resuscitated not only in our metropolitan areas but in the rural areas as well. In the foregoing paragraphs we have just pointed to the enormous difference in land values (and hence, likely rentals payable) as between metropolitan, commercial, financial and other business areas on the one hand and industrial areas on the other. In the taxation versus natural resources rental study for Uniondale Clothing in Chapter 12, we showed how immensely positive the absence of PAYE, VAT and other indirect taxes will be for manufacturing generally.

In our Resource Rentals Budget in Chapter 14, we suggest that the average industrial rental could be R3.10/m². With a range of, say, a hundred-fold, one could envisage a rental in a currently rundown rural area for as little as around 31c/m² up to, say, R31/m² in City Deep, Johannesburg. So a 1,000m² stand in the former would cost R310 per annum, whereas the same sized stand in the latter would cost R31,000.

2 Data from www.saland.co.za website, accessed on 18 April 2010.
3 Mbeki, M., *Architects of Poverty*, Picador Africa, Johannesburg, 2009, Ch.3.

Even a heavy industrial enterprise on 10 ha paying R3.1m or more could well be getting off lightly. So, yes, resource rentals collection is likely to give the manufacturing industry the boost it sorely needs. Notwithstanding all the other problems faced by manufacturers (including Asian competition, lack of skills, regulatory rigidity and so on), we feel that this relatively tax-free regime would go a long way towards revitalising industry nationwide.

In return for the massive benefit of paying land rental instead of tax, manufacturers would have less temptation to gear excessively (no tax from which to deduct interest!). Our proposals would, however, increase incentives for lending to manufacturers by commercial banks as well as the provision of equity capital (including by venture capital and private equity entities).[4]

## Informal settlements

With most urban dwellers running hard to make money or just survive, they probably haven't really sat down to consider why our cities continue to attract the best brains and skills, as well as (a few kilometres away) millions of economic refugees from our rural areas and other African countries, who huddle together in makeshift shacks. There are many reasons for this, but one of the most important is that the full natural rent has yet to be collected in urban areas, whereas in rural areas, our taxation system attempts in effect to collect rental where it does not exist – and in the process merely grinds all attempts at economic activity into the ground. We referred briefly in the preceding chapter to the role played by taxation in all this, but it warrants further comment. Prior to the transition to democratic government in 1994 and the introduction of value-added tax in the early 1990s, South Africa had a General Sales Tax (GST) of 4%. GST could relatively easily be evaded, and hence often was. The former Homelands also had tax incentives for industry and generally lower levels of personal and company tax, while petrol taxes were also less onerous. So by a kind of political fluke, the erstwhile apartheid government of the day was at least not busy exterminating economic activity in these areas as, ironically enough (and albeit out of a misguided intent to abide by the best of the West's fiscal proprieties), is the 'government of liberation.' Then, of course, with impeccable timing, the gods suddenly visited upon South Africa a transition from a relatively benign situation for

4 See 'Our Credit' Chapter 16.

these areas to one where VAT was introduced and all the tax breaks eliminated in terms of 'harmonisation' of the former Homelands' systems with the South African tax regime. It did not help the industries there that tariff protection was also eliminated and that there was increasingly no chance of escape from the growing efficiencies of SARS. The only hope – albeit desperate – for the people from the resulting factory closures and unemployment was the cities. The data on this phenomenon could easily be collected and would be a fruitful area of research for Economics students. It does not require rocket science to understand this, however; and most South Africans above the age of 20 would have observed with their own eyes the huge influx into the cities, if not the simultaneous rural exodus.

While many of the rural and other immigrants compete legally and illegally for jobs or contribute to the informal economy, many remain without work and resort to begging or worse. In any event, the need to provide housing and other facilities has provided an enormous challenge to metropolitan and other municipalities with which they are patently not coping. In a rental collection system, many of those with jobs and feet on at least the lower rungs of the ladder of economic prosperity would be contributing to the city and national coffers. If nothing else, it would be easier to collect rentals from landlords than fly-by-night tenants.

## Backyard landlords

Where the Treasury does not collect the natural rent, someone else will! Hence the phenomenon of 'shoebox' houses in the townships with tenants, legal or illegal, in backyard shacks paying the owners. The same applies to the flat lands of Hillbrow and the Johannesburg CBD, where tales abound of overcrowding to the benefit of landlords including (in some cases) those who have hijacked empty buildings for this purpose.[5]

If nothing else, exploitation by slum and other landlords is yet further testimony to the fact that natural rent is not fully collected in

---

5 Nobukhosi, (not her real name), a Zimbabwean mother who peddles maize and makes table-cloths to pay for her daughter's schooling, pays R115 per week to stay in a 4-bedroomed flat in the Noord and Wanderers Street area of the CBD. Tenants (who fluctuate between 20 and 50) sleep on the floor and queue throughout the night to use the kitchen and bathroom. We doubt whether SARS gets much of the indicated mean monthly rental of nearly R15,000 per month, let alone peak rental of nearly R25,000 per month from this and the 30 other flats in the 8-storey building. But then it would be much easier just to collect one cheque from the landowner/body corporate!

urban areas. Were it to be so, and the rural areas freed from intolerable taxation, economic activity would be less unevenly distributed.

## Gladiators and the rest

The best professional skills, brains and businesses already occupying the best sites in the country might have to pay higher rentals *in lieu* of taxation but would continue to reap the benefits of those locations. Others might prefer to relocate to less challenging rentals, either in the metropolitan areas or to renascent country towns. Homeowners wanting their own gardens for children or pleasure would pay according to the size and value, while those choosing the security and convenience of lock-up-and-go townhouses and flats would pay lesser land rentals via their landlords or body corporates. Retailers, freed from income tax and the chore of collecting VAT, will face higher rentals, as their landlords recoup the land rentals payable to the Treasury. They will need to see, in their lease negotiations, that their landlords do not penalise them for their own success through unduly onerous turnover clauses. Heavy road transporters will no doubt take big stands in industrial areas near motorways. These may not cost them much, but they are already, in effect, also paying user charges via toll roads.

## No more leapfrogging holdouts[6]

We refrain from inserting the word 'greedy' in front of holdouts because they are, after all, merely playing according to the rules of the game. People buying large stands for their homes, with a view to later subdividing and selling off, are a normal phenomenon in the Western world. This does, however, impose huge costs in terms of forcing developers to open up new suburbs further afield, as well as unnecessarily extensive municipal infrastructure – not to mention the extra and unnecessary wear and tear on individuals and vehicles toiling to and from their work past these sites, often on inadequate roads. Similar pressures would be brought to bear on the notorious phenomenon of small stand owners in the CBD holding out for extortionate prices and thus obstructing more rational land use. Owners of ramshackle buildings on valuable sites would be encouraged to sell or redevelop.

---

6 See also Prof Mason Gaffney: *After the Crash – Designing a Depression-Free Economy*, Wiley-Blackwell, Oxford, 2009, Ch.1.

## The property industry

This industry would, in effect, take over from many of its tenants the chore of collecting revenues for government, making the lives both of the latter as well as retailers and countless other VAT-registered businesses a lot easier! The opportunities would, however, be immense. The return, if you like, of site value rating with a vengeance to the Gauteng and other cities (which until recently enjoyed it) would stimulate the need for more rational land use, and hence redevelopment. There would be much more work, which would probably be reflected in more JSE listings. In the event of bidding mechanisms being required to establish market-related land rentals or prime sites, there would be no shortage of the necessary expertise and competition. Since we envisage that public sector entities would most certainly have to pay full land rentals, a useful by-product would be a much more powerful incentive for them to use their land much more efficiently. Yes, in our demolition job on some of the insanities of taxation (Chapter 5), we referred to the strange phenomenon of government taxing itself; but in this case, the land rentals would be a real measure of the nation's natural resources taken up by the parastatal or bureaucracy concerned. Nor should it be beyond the wit of the Treasury to devise incentives for government departments to eliminate unnecessary costs in this respect. The Public Works Department, in particular, would have to be fully commercially orientated, and, like every other land owner, fully transparent in all its transactions.

## Infrastructure payback

Finally, instead of big city developments like the Gautrain and improved motorways being regarded purely as a taxpayer-funded expenditure, the budgeting process would reasonably have an eye to the natural land value increases that attend every appropriate infrastructural outlay. Indeed, if they did not appear likely to pay for themselves over an appropriate time period, the projects should be canned. Viewed in this light, the tunnel between England and France under the English Channel, which has battled to recover its costs via fees alone, would have been a much happier prospect. In one of the most public-spirited acts ever by a land owner, Don Riley, a New Zealander who owned land in Southwark in the path of the new Jubilee Line Extension of the London Underground went so far as to write a book[7] 'complaining' about being enriched through no effort on his part! In a study he conducted in the area, he concluded that the £3.5bn spent on the extension had enriched property owners like him by about £13.5bn (although he didn't allow for inflation which probably reduced the gain to around £7bn in real terms).

## Urban planning

Like the property industry, this discipline will assume additional importance as one of those responsible for fine-tuning the ability of the resource comprising 2% of South Africa's surface area to deliver top productivity, and hence top rentals. Planning regulations are one of the more obvious ways in which the community can add value to land, or sometimes even subtract from it! For example, property developers in the CBD typically think in terms of (and so buy or sell) 'bulk square metres' rather than so many square metres of land. Thus, a prime site of, say, 1 ha, where planning regulations permit 90% coverage, and a floor area ratio of 80% and 16 stories, would provide 115,200 bulk m². At the (not uncommon) bulk rate of R4,000/m², this would be worth R461m or over R46,000/m². Just as the various South African governments, since transition, have had the foresight to ensure that the tax-gathering authority (SARS) had the necessary capacity to rake in ever-increasing revenues from both willing and unwilling taxpayers, so will the metropolitan and other urban authorities need to ensure that their planning departments have the capacity to enhance the value of their territory by both sensible and sensitive regulations attuned to the varied and complex requirements of modern cities.

## Vision

Given the masses of informal settlements around our cities, it could take time, maybe a decade or so, before our vision of a balanced spread of economic activity in the country materialised. Moreover, while we do not envisage a reverse flow of population from the metropolitan areas, the recent flood of rural immigrants (both local and foreign) would abate to a manageable flow. In addition, as soon as the metropolitan authorities upgrade the infrastructure of informal settlements and ensure that normal land ownership is facilitated, market forces would immediately ensure a flow-back on land rental income.

7 Riley, D., *Taken for a Ride*, Centre for Land Policy Studies, London, 2001.

Although we cannot claim to have done the study ourselves, the sums paid to backyard landlords would provide a good pointer. The latter can easily be observed by anyone driving from the N2 through Alexandra to Sandton. The people are indeed paying rent both for their makeshift dwellings as well as the land they occupy; it is just that the land rental component goes to the landlord instead of the community. So, instead of being dead weight, these areas would soon swell the coffers of the local authorities as their inhabitants increasingly contributed to the metropolitan economies, not least of all by taking up the jobs on offer from the recovery in manufacturing industry, which we believe our proposals will bring about.

## CHAPTER 14

# RESOURCE RENTALS BUDGET FOR SOUTH AFRICA

*'Year after year they voted cent per cent,*
*Blood, sweat, and tear-wrung millions – why? For rent!*
*They roar'd, they dined, they drank, they swore they meant*
*To die for England – why then live? – for rent!*
*The peace has made one general malcontent*
*Of these high market patriots; war was rent!*
*Their love of country, millions all mis-spent,*
*How reconcile? By reconciling rent!*
*And will they not repay the treasures lent?*
*No: down with every thing, and up with rent!*
*Their good, ill, health, wealth, joy or discontent,*
*Being, end, aim, religion – rent, rent, rent!'*

Lord Byron[1]

## Tips for Nhlanhla!

DEAR NHLANHLA,

Having endured scepticism for decades when talking about replacing taxation with collection of economic rent, it is with great pleasure that we finally present you with some suggestions

---

1 Lord Byron belonged to the second generation of Romantic poets born around the onset of the French Revolution. Although not directly affected by its commotion, 'the revolutionary ideas … could not possibly have left them untouched.' Byron's 'aristocratic individualism' enhanced the 'free and rebellious element to be found in Byron's unmoral cynicism.' (Legouis, E. and Cazamian, L., *A History of English Literature*, Dent, London, 1926, p.1042). Being one of them, he knew full well the aristocrats were fighting to preserve their enjoyment of unearned land rentals as much as anything else. We have little doubt that he would have approved of our proposals here to collect them in South Africa!

as to how it could be done. Needless to say, once these concepts have been publicly floated and interested parties given the opportunity to respond, we are sure that with the proven expertise at your command, you will be able greatly to refine and improve upon them.

Yours sincerely,

Michael Jacques and Stephen Meintjes

South Africa's long-serving and celebrated Minister of Finance, Trevor Manuel, famously invited the public to make suggestions every year ahead of budget time. Since we felt we had a lot of explaining to do, we did not take him up on it. However, here goes, as his successor, Pravin Gordhan, has continued with this commendable practice! We hope Nhlanhla Nene will too!

Table 14.1 shows how the revenue budget for the fiscal year 2012/2013 could have been replaced by a combination of resource rentals (RR) plus some retained taxes in line with the proposals made earlier. Note, in particular, the sharp reduction in the destructive personal and company taxes and VAT, and also how this is made up by the recovery of resource rental revenues, which is strongly enabling to enterprise and employment.

The following notes explain how we arrived at the proposed numbers:

1　**Personal income taxes**

The proposal assumes that 15% of all personal income tax is paid by persons earning over the given threshold (say R2 million p.a.). This number could be refined with access to more detailed data on taxes paid by individuals. According to the estimates for 2013/14 in the 2013 Budget Review, 148,468 individual taxpayers (2.3% of the total), who earned over R1 million p.a., were expected to pay R95 million (or 30.9% of the personal income tax total).

2　**Companies**

The proposals assume that companies we have termed legacy rentiers and who pose a barrier to entry to new entrants, would, for a certain period, continue to pay company tax (in addition to any resource rentals). Examples would be the five major banks, ArcelorMittal SA, Evraz Highveld Steel and Vanadium and Sasol. The proposed number assumes that these companies will continue

## Table 14.1: South Africa's 2012/13 revenue budget converted to resource rentals

| | SA Budget (Rbn) | Note | Changed to Resource Rentals |
|---|---|---|---|
| **Taxes on income and profits** | **453.5** | | **48.3** |
| Persons | 274.0 | 1 | 41.1 |
| Companies | 156.4 | 2 | 14.1 |
| STC/dividend withholding tax | 21.0 | | 0 |
| Interest on overdue tax, small business amnesty levy | 2.2 | | 2.7 |
| **Taxes on payroll and workforce** | **11.4** | | **0** |
| (Includes Skills Development Levy) | | 3 | |
| **Taxes on property** | **8.2** | **4** | **0.9** |
| (Donations tax, estate duty, MST, transfer duties) | | | |
| **Domestic taxes on goods & services** | **298.9** | | **76.0** |
| VAT | 217.0 | 5 | 46.7 |
| Excise duties (Includes alcohol, tobacco, petrol) | 28.4 | 6,7 | 28.4 |
| *Ad valorem* excise duties | 2.2 | 7 | 0 |
| Fuel levies | 40.5 | 7 | 0 |
| Other | 10.9 | | 0.9 |
| (Includes air departure tax, plastic bags, electricity levy, mining leases, Universal Service Fund, CO2 tax on vehicle emissions, incandescent light bulb levy) | | 8 & 9 | |
| **Taxes on international trade and transactions (mainly customs duties)** | **38.1** | **10** | **38.1** |
| **Total tax revenue** | **810.1** | | **163.3** |
| **Mineral royalties** | **5.0** | | **0** |
| **Other non-tax revenue** | **9.4** | | **9.4** |
| **Less Southern African Customs Union payments** | **−42.1** | | **−42.1** |
| **NATIONAL BUDGET REVENUE** | **782.4** | | **130.6** |
| Municipal rates | 24.6 | 11 | 0 |
| VAT & PAYE on government expenditure | −145.0 | 12 | 0 |
| **RESOURCE RENTAL REVENUES** | **0** | **13** | **531.4** |
| Land (excluding mining, ports, roads) | 0 | | 480.4 |
| Mining | 0 | | 25.0 |
| EMS | 0 | | 2.5 |
| Fishing | 0 | | 0.6 |
| Airports/seaports/toll roads | 0 | | 22.9 |
| **TOTAL TAXES & RESOURCE RENTALS** | **662.0** | | **662.0** |

to pay corporation tax at half the current rate (i.e. 14%) and the number used is our estimate of their tax for 2013 on this basis.

### 3  Skills Development Levy

This is a tax levied on employers and in our view should be abolished. At present, employers can recoup their actual expenditure on skills development from their tax liability. Although in terms of our proposals such taxes will no longer exist, deductibility against resource rentals remains an option.

### 4  Property taxes

In our view, all these taxes should be abolished – with the possible exception of Estate Duty at a higher threshold, on the basis that it addresses legacy issues. The Deeds Office should make a charge to cover its costs (as opposed to levying an extortionate tax!) in registering transfers of land and this should be its main source of income.

### 5  Value-added tax

In terms of our proposals this would be abolished for all goods and services on which VAT is currently charged, except for alcohol and tobacco products and some high-value luxury goods. We have estimated this at 12.5% of the present VAT collections, but no doubt SARS could establish a more refined number.

### 6  Excise duties on alcohol and tobacco products

These taxes should be consolidated with the VAT on these goods into a single tax.

### 7  Excise tax on petrol, ad valorem duties, and fuel levies

These should all be abolished. The Road Accident Fund should be returned to the private insurance industry, and all vehicles obliged to be insured in terms of the law. This includes foreign vehicles visiting South Africa and vehicles driven by visitors.

### 8  Air departure tax

The Treasury recovers resource rentals from ACSA and airlines in terms of our proposals but the security obligations of the state regarding air traffic are onerous so a user contribution is warranted. So it could be retained but restyled 'Air Departure Security Charge'.

### 9  Mining leases

These should be replaced by the resource rentals on mining companies.

## 10 Customs duties

Despite pious promises not to indulge in protectionism at the G20 and elsewhere, vigilance will still be required against unfair and predatory trade practices. Long-term planning should, however, assume the success (in due course) of efforts within the World Trade Organisation to eliminate them. For the time being, we have left the contribution unchanged.

## 11 Municipal property rates

This is the only other 'tax' not included in the central government budget proposals. The amount shown comprises the rates revenue of the seven largest metropoles (taken from their 2012/13 budgets). These amounts, together with rates income from small municipalities, would be included in the 'Land' resource rentals, and would be paid over to municipalities by central government.

## 12 VAT, PAYE (etc.) paid by government

As explained in Chapter 5, Treasury would have recovered an estimated R145bn on its expenditure of R971bn in 2012/13.

## 13 Land resource rentals

This is a balancing number for Table 14.1, but when reduced to an average amount per square metre for the area of the country that would be liable for such resource rentals, it can be shown that this amount is not unrealistic. Further details are given in Table 14.3, which gives a notional estimate of how the various categories of land use might contribute to a resource rental budget, as well as some indication of how they currently contribute to GDP. However, in order to make the latter comparison, we have first to re-group some of the economic activity categories used by the South African Reserve Bank under the broader, land-use categories used by Statistics South Africa. This is done in Table 14.2, where we have assumed that the land on which manufacturing, electricity and water provision, construction, transport, storage and communication activities take place (all of which are separately estimated for GDP purposes by the Reserve Bank) fall under the broad category 'Industrial', for statistical purposes. The same applies to wholesale, retail, catering, accommodation finance and insurance, real estate, as well as 'business and personal services' – all of which we have assumed to fall under 'Commerce and finance'.

175

## Table 14.2: Gross value added by economic activity
## (at basic prices in 2012)

|  | Rbn | % |
| --- | --- | --- |
| **Agriculture, forestry and fishing** | **72.7** | **2.6** |
| **Mining and quarrying** | **262.7** | **9.3** |
| | | |
| **Industrial** | **800.5** | **28.2** |
| Manufacturing | 351.1 | 12.4 |
| Electricity and water | 79.1 | 2.8 |
| Construction (contractors) | 112.6 | 4.0 |
| Transport, storage and communication | 257.7 | 9.1 |
| | | |
| **Commerce & finance** | **1 229.4** | **43.4** |
| Wholesale and retail trade, catering and accommodation | 452.7 | 16.0 |
| Finance and insurance, real estate and business services | 608.5 | 21.5 |
| Community, social & personal services | 168.1 | 5.9 |
| | | |
| **General government services** | **469.8** | **16.6** |
| | | |
| **Total value added at basic prices** | **2 835.1** | **100** |

**Sources:** SA Reserve Bank Quarterly Bulletin, March 2013, S-107; SA Reserve Bank: Economic and Financial Data for South Africa, www.reservebank.co.za, accessed 11 February 2010, data reformulated in Table 14.3.

Transferring the broad categories from Table 14.2 to Table 14.3 (p.178) gives us just three revenue-producing divisions for the 5.2% share of total South African land area taken up by the urban areas. In addition to Commerce and finance and Industrial, we have introduced 'Residential' with an initial 7.1% contribution to the resource rentals total, or R37.7bn for a relatively modest R5.39/m².

The resource rentals percentage share of Industrial at 33% is somewhat higher than the 28.2% share that it contributes to GDP. The 22.5% 'contribution' by government to GDP is therefore paid for by it together with the residential sector, as well as an increase of 7.5% in the resource rentals contribution of Commerce and finance, compared to its 37.4% contribution to GDP.

We have left agriculture at the same miniscule 2.6 percentage share of GDP (which it happened to have in the 2012 SARB data used in this table) as well as introducing an initial contribution from National and provincial game parks.

The 'Mines, ports, roads, EMS (etc.)' category is shown at 9.6% for contribution to GDP and 11.7% to resource rentals. This would not necessarily entail a higher contribution from mining to resource rentals, given that ports, roads, EMS and so on are not at present contributing anywhere near as much in taxation as we envisage they will in resource rentals.

Although this budget, on the face of it, represents a 'big bang', 'cold turkey' or 'switch at midnight at the end of the current financial year' approach to the changeover, it nevertheless has phase-in features such as what is envisaged as temporary retention of taxes on legacy businesses and wealthy individuals. For that matter, too, the exemption on informal settlements would no longer apply once they have been formalised with the implementation of marketable security of tenure. Elsewhere we have spoken of ways and means of phasing in the introduction of resource rentals.

We emphasise that these are illustrative estimates only, and that much work remains to be done before they can be implemented. We expect that all owners of natural resources – as well as government and the public at large – will have valuable inputs to make and we fully intend to conduct further research ourselves so as to participate in the debate. As we have said before, this debate around the value and uses of all our natural resources will inherently be more productive than the sterile discussions around tax avoidance and evasion of the past.

Finally, we believe strongly that although these numbers are merely illustrative, they nevertheless contain what will be a dramatic rewiring of the DNA of the South African economy, unleashing the talents and creative energy now bottled up and utterly frustrated by hugely debilitating taxes. Not only will holders of our land and other natural resources be incentivised to 'use it or lose it' in a big way, but land will become much more freely available for all forms of economic activity. This applies as much to land in our city centres as to that in far-flung rural areas and informal townships. Just think of the relief to small business that the abolition of VAT and PAYE will bring in terms of paper work alone! Think of it: PAYE is a payroll tax, a penalty for employing somebody! On the other hand, what do you think will be the effect on a business owner of a land rental? Will he pay one cent more tax if he hires another worker? So what do you think he will do? All things being equal, will he not take on some more workers? Now multiply that event a few million times and what do you think it will do to unemployment? Yes, we have other barriers to employment but this is the biggest. This rudimentary budget shows the way to remove it, once and for all!

## Table 14.3: Notional land resource rental contribution to SA (2012/13 budget).

| Land Category | Area | | GDP Share | Resource Rental Share | | Average |
|---|---|---|---|---|---|---|
| | Million ha | % | % | % | Rbn | R/m² |
| **Urban areas** | **6.4** | **5.2** | **88.1** | **85.0** | **451.7** | **7.06** |
| Commerce & finance | 0.7 | 0.6 | 37.4 | 44.9 | 238.6 | 34.09 |
| Industrial | 2.2 | 1.8 | 28.2 | 33.0 | 175.4 | 7.97 |
| Residential | 0.7 | 0.6 | | 7.1 | 37.7 | 5.39 |
| Informal settlements | 1.2 | 0.9 | | 0 | 0.0 | 0.00 |
| Government | 0.1 | 0.1 | 22.5 | 0 | 0.0 | 0.00 |
| Municipal | 0.4 | 0.4 | | 0 | 0.0 | 0.00 |
| Education & religion | 0.3 | 0.3 | | 0 | 0.0 | 0.00 |
| Open spaces | 0.8 | 0.6 | | 0 | 0.0 | 0.00 |
| **Arable land** | **16.7** | **13.7** | **2.6** | **2.6** | **13.8** | **0.08** |
| Commercial | 14.2 | 11.6 | | 2.4 | 12.8 | 0.09 |
| Developing | 2.5 | 2.0 | | 0.2 | 1.1 | 0.04 |
| **Grasslands** | **83.9** | **68.6** | incl. in arable | **0.5** | **2.7** | **0.00** |
| Commercial | 72 | 58.9 | | 0.45 | 2.4 | 0.00 |
| Developing | 11.9 | 9.7 | | 0.05 | 0.3 | 0.00 |
| **Forestry** | **1.5** | **1.2** | incl. in arable | **0.05** | **0.3** | **0.02** |
| **Nature conservation** | **11.8** | **9.6** | **0** | **0.15** | **0.8** | **0.01** |
| SA National Parks | 3.7 | 3.0 | | 0.08 | 0.4 | 0.01 |
| Private & provincial game reserves | 3.3 | 2.7 | | 0.01 | 0.1 | 0.00 |
| Other | 4.8 | 3.9 | | 0.01 | 0.1 | 0.0 |
| **Total (excl. mines etc.)** | **120.3** | **98.4** | **90.7** | **90.4** | **480.4** | **0.4** |
| **Mines, ports, roads, EMS (etc)** | **2.0** | **1.6** | **9.3** | **11.7** | **62.2** | **3.1** |
| **Total area of South Africa** | **122.3** | **100.0** | **100.0** | **100.0** | **531.4** | **0.4** |

**Sources:** http://soer.deat.gov.za/themes; *South Africa at a Glance – 2007/8*, Editors Inc., Johannesburg; Stats in Brief – 2004 Statistics South Africa, Pretoria, 2004.

CHAPTER 15

# WHAT ABOUT ME?

*'If one were to set out with a specific, stated objective of designing
a tax system which would penalise and deter thrift, energy and
success, it would be almost impossible to do better than
the one which we have in this country today.'*
Lord Soames[1]

NO PRIZES FOR guessing that one of the most frequently-asked
questions raised when we talk about collecting economic rent
is, 'How will it affect me?'

Another is, 'Who will the winners and losers be?' The answer is that
we will all be winners, except for the hard-core rentiers who cannot
(or will not) respond to the new incentives by using the natural
resources they own properly.

## Tax advisers and collectors

Yes, we can certainly envisage there will be grumpy tax advisers as well
as tax collectors, horrified at the thought that much of their hard-won
expertise will be useless. This category, of course, includes bankers,
lawyers, auditors and other financial advisors permanently employed
in dreaming up tax efficient schemes and structures, as well as the

---

1 Extract from a speech in the House of Lords on 3 July 1978. Obtained via Wikipedia
Hansard search 16 October 2010. Still holds true of most tax systems, despite best efforts of
Thatcher and others since then. Lord Soames was Governor of Rhodesia in the transitional
period between the guerilla war and independence in 1980 and, according to his obituary
by Steve Lohr in the *New York Times* of 17 September 1987, played a vital role in insuring
Britain's entry into the European Economic Community as Ambassador to France from 1968
to 1972.

SARS experts adjusting the tax net to catch them. However, provided that all these folk are prepared to redeploy their expertise into more productive services, or to be retrained, they should fare well since SARCS (South African Rental Collection Services!) will, as we have said before, have plenty of work. As for the tax avoidance experts, they can apply their minds to real wealth creation, i.e. finance for production. If this includes ways and means of minimising resource rentals so much the better, because this means that their clients will be using land more efficiently, leaving more available for other uses. In other words, this becomes an economically productive exercise – a win-win situation – which is a little different from their usual pastime of minimising what SARS could, should, or might have got from them otherwise!

## Rentiers and game farms

Rent seekers among the elite might be a little peeved to see rent going to the people instead of into their own pockets. Hard-core rentiers might well include some large land owners who underutilise their assets because they view their farms as their retirement or holiday homes. Alternatively, they might not need the money and have therefore given up on the hassles of labour-intensive arable farming in preference for the relative ease of stock or game farming. Many of these will, however, respond with alacrity to the new incentives to produce. Recent ministerial concerns about the proliferation of game farms would be laid to rest, since if game farming occurred on valuable agricultural land and didn't yield enough to pay the rental, the owners would no doubt switch to crops or sell to someone who would. In any event, as we have noted earlier[2] there may be sound reasons why land would have more economic value when used for game rather than cattle, in which case, the rentals paid would in any case be higher: end of argument. Moreover, we have no doubt that established game farmers would be happy to mentor Black farmers aspiring to join their ranks.

## Upmarket leisure and golf estates

While the mega-wealthy with properties in Clifton or Pezula near the Knysna Heads may take the big increase in site value rates in their

2 Chapter 11, in the penultimate paragraph 'Data wish list', p.150.

stride, the market will no doubt adjust in the direction of more intensive use of such land. While our present tax regime encourages foreigners to buy such properties (without encouraging them to do business here) the reverse would now apply. As regards the many wine farms where (as noted elsewhere) prices already make for uneconomic returns, some owners will be able to afford the 'lifestyle premiums', whereas others will sell, making way for new entrants. The same would apply to golf estates on valuable agricultural land. If they couldn't pay the rent, they would be ploughed under by farmers who could. And if they could, that would mean the people were better off because they were getting more rental for their land.

## Little old ladies

Special provision might be necessary for the elderly, whose pensions do not cover the site value rates for the family home, including allowing the rates to accumulate – ultimately as a claim against the deceased estate. Prior to the American Civil War these 'little old ladies' (whose wealth was tied up in the slave who looked after them) and other hardship cases were used as arguments against the abolition of slavery! In such instances, pragmatic arrangements will have to be made.

## The poor

The poor will be winners all the way – with no VAT on most of their purchases, cheaper petrol and better job prospects including in rural areas. They would undoubtedly benefit from the tendency of skilled people to escape the stress and higher rentals of urban life for the tranquillity and lower rentals in the countryside. In their wake would come the entrepreneurs to employ them, quite apart from the opportunities for the newly liberated locals to get off the ground themselves!

## Government is smarter than you think!

Most people are sceptical about government's service delivery but accept (if somewhat ruefully) that SARS is a remarkable exception! Few of them realise, however, that in this respect government is even smarter than they think as regards its ability to pluck 'the goose so as to obtain the most feathers for the least hissing.'[3] To illustrate this, we

3 Ascribed to Jean-Baptiste Colbert, treasurer to Louis XIV of France.

have compiled Tables 15.1 and 15.3 based on the tax rates in the 2013/14 Budget, showing all taxes paid by South Africans, from the very poor to wealthy. In estimating the category spending, we took note of the Statistics of South Africa Household Expenditure survey as well as a similar exercise in the UK.

### Table 15.1: Estimated percentage of individual incomes paid in all taxes

| Expenditure | The Poor | | Workers | | Black diamonds | | Middle Class | | Well-off | | Wealthy | |
|---|---|---|---|---|---|---|---|---|---|---|---|---|
| | % | Rpm | % | Rpm | % | Rpm | % | Rpm | % | Rpm | % | Rpm |
| Rent/mortgage payment | 16 | 160 | 18 | 900 | 19 | 2 079 | 19 | 6 823 | 17 | 8 160 | 17 | 17 000 |
| Light, water, rates | 5 | 50 | 5 | 250 | 6 | 611 | 6 | 2 100 | 7 | 3 360 | 7 | 7 000 |
| Food, beverages (incl. alcohol), tobacco | 6 | 60 | 14 | 700 | 19 | 2 079 | 12 | 4 200 | 9 | 4 320 | 6 | 6 000 |
| Food non-vatable | 22 | 220 | 8 | 420 | 1 | 122 | 0 | 0 | 0 | 0 | | 0 |
| Clothing & footwear | 8 | 80 | 7 | 350 | 7 | 734 | 5 | 1 750 | 4 | 1 920 | 3 | 3 000 |
| Household furnishings, equipment | 10 | 100 | 10 | 500 | 7 | 734 | 5 | 1 570 | 4 | 1 920 | 4 | 4 000 |
| Health | 0 | 0 | 1 | 50 | 2 | 245 | 3 | 1 050 | 3 | 1 440 | 4 | 4 000 |
| School fees, books | 6 | 60 | 4 | 180 | 3 | 367 | 5 | 1 750 | 4 | 1 920 | 4 | 4 000 |
| Transport | 16 | 160 | 18 | 900 | 16 | 1 712 | 16 | 5 600 | 15 | 7 200 | 13 | 13 000 |
| Communication | 5 | 50 | 5 | 250 | 4 | 489 | 2 | 700 | 2 | 960 | 2 | 2 000 |
| Recreation, culture, restaurants, hotels | 2 | 20 | 2 | 100 | 2 | 245 | 2 | 700 | 2 | 960 | 2 | 2 000 |
| Miscellaneous goods & services | 4 | 40 | 8 | 400 | 6 | 611 | 3 | 1 050 | 2 | 960 | 2 | 2 000 |
| Income tax | nil | nil | nil | nil | 8.8 | 973 | 22 | 7 707 | 31 | 12 445 | 36 | 33 140 |
| **TOTAL INCOME** | 100 | 1 000 | 100 | 5 000 | 100 | 11 000 | 100 | 35 000 | 100 | 48 000 | 100 | 100 000 |

**Tax estimates**

| | | | | | | | | | | | | |
|---|---|---|---|---|---|---|---|---|---|---|---|---|
| Non-vatable expenditure (%) | 48 | 480 | 38 | 1 900 | 29 | 3 179 | 8 | 2 800 | 6 | 2 880 | 6 | 6 000 |
| **VAT** | | 72.8 | | 431 | | 1 095 | | 4 508 | | 6 317 | | 13 160 |
| Fuel estimated at 28% of transport costs: additional tax component 28.5%–14% | 3.63 | 6 | 1 | 33 | 1 | 62 | 1 | 203 | 1 | 261 | 0 | 471 |
| **Income tax** | | | | | | 18 | | 973 | | 7 707 | | 12 445 | | 33 140 |
| **Transfer duty** | | | | | | 52 | | 333 | | 500 | | 833 |
| Other* | | | | 5 | | 30 | | 100 | | 250 | | 400 |
| **TOTAL EST. TAXES (%/Rpm)** | 7.9 | 79 | 9.4 | 469 | 20 | 2 212 | 37 | 12 851 | 41 | 19 773 | 48 | 48 005 |

\* 'Sin' taxes, customs duty on imported goods, etc.

Table 15.1 shows that even the Poor, with an income of, say, state grants of R1,000 per month, have to give the government back at least 7.9% (elsewhere we have estimated this at 10%), which is regressive to say the least. Moreover, this calculation assumes as much as 22% of their income going on non-vatable food and other items. To the extent that this is overstated, they will be paying more tax.

The next category is 'Workers' earning just below the income tax threshold for under-65-year-olds of R67,111 per annum or R5,000 monthly. We reckon that, even though they pay no income tax, they *pay at least 9.4% of their income* in other taxes.

Moving on to the lowest category of the 6.4 million income tax payers in South Africa (i.e. the 'Black Diamonds' and others) with incomes of R11,000 per month (R132,000 per annum), we find that *total tax paid currently jumps to 20%* of their relatively low incomes.

The percentage of tax for the next three categories – 'Middle Class', 'Well-off' and 'Wealthy' – ranges from 37% to 48%. But if we include the cost of private security owing to the inadequate provision of law and order (which is, of course, the primary function of government), then we could safely say *the wealthy, and probably the well-off, pay about half or more of their income in taxes.*

## The good news!

As we have said before this is an intolerable situation, so now for the good news!

**Table 15.2: Estimated savings for individuals: rentals vs. all taxes**

|  | % | Rpm |
| --- | --- | --- |
| The Poor | 100 | 79 |
| Workers | 100 | 469 |
| Black Diamonds | 60 | 1 362 |
| Middle Class | 68 | 8 251 |
| Well-off | 52 | 9 423 |
| Wealthy | 22 | 8 905 |

See Table 15.3

The savings from a switch to rental collection instead of taxation, both in percentage and Rand per month terms, are shown in Table 15.3 in detail.

Of course, we have had to make assumptions again in doing this, which explains why the Wealthy save less than the Well-off and Middle Class. That is because we have assumed a big jump in the average plot size to 4,000 m² (1 acre) for the Wealthy as opposed to only 1,500 m² and 1,000 m² for the Well-off and Middle Class respectively.

**Table 15.3: Estimated reduction in individuals' payments: rentals vs. all taxes**

| | The Poor | | Workers | | Black diamonds | | Middle Class | | Well-off | | Wealthy |
|---|---|---|---|---|---|---|---|---|---|---|---|
| | % of inc. | Rpm | % of inc. | Rpm | % of inc. | Rpm | % of inc. | Rpm | % of inc. | Rpm | % of inc. | Rpm |
| INCOME | | 1 000 | | 5 000 | | 11 000 | | 35 000 | | 48 000 | | 100 000 |
| Current tax | 7.9 | 79 | 9.4 | 469 | 20 | 2 212 | 37 | 12 851 | 41 | 19 773 | 48 | 48 005 |
| **Rental calculation** | | | | | | | | | | | | |
| Stand size m² | | 125 | | 250 | | 500 | | 1000 | | 1 500 | | 4 000 |
| Land value R/m² | | 100 | | 200 | | 350 | | 550 | | 750 | | 1 000 |
| Land value R | | 12 500 | | 50 000 | | 175 000 | | 550 0000 | | 1 125 000 | | 4 000 000 |
| Rental Rpm at 1% | | 125 | | 500 | | 1 750 | | 5 500 | | 11 250 | | 40 000 |
| Less rebate | | 900 | | 900 | | 900 | | 900 | | 900 | | 900 |
| **Rental payable** | 0 | 0 | 0 | 0 | 8 | 850 | 3.1 | 4 600 | 22 | 10 350 | 39 | 39 100 |
| **Reduction – %** | | >100% | | >100% | | 62 | | 64 | | 48 | | 19 |
| **Reduction – Rpm** | | 79 | | 469 | | 1 362 | | 8 251 | | 9 423 | | 8 905 |

For the Black Diamonds, we have assumed an average stand size of 500 m², which may be overstating the situation since many of them are living in apartments – which would mean that the land rentals they pay via their landlords would be less, owing to their participating in more intensive use of land. For Workers and Poor we have assumed stand sizes of 250 m² and 100 m² respectively.

As regards land values, we have assumed that the Middle Class live on stands valued at R550 m², which is close to what according to the *Financial Mail*[4] was 'FNB's[5] new vacant residential land price index' in the third quarter of 2009 of around R542/m². From there on out we have assumed that the Well-off and Wealthy live in plusher suburbs with land valued at R750/m² and R1,000/m² respectively. Conversely, the Black Diamonds, Workers and the Poor live on land valued at R250/m², R200/m² and R100/m², respectively.

The rental rebate of R900 per month – which roughly equates the 2013/14 income tax threshold of R67,111 per annum (R5,593 per month) – means that the Poor and the Workers pay no rent, while the Black Diamonds kick in at R850 per month.

---

4 *Financial Mail*, 5 November 2009.
5 First National Bank.

## So what's the catch?

Since thus far we have established that most individuals are the winners, presumably this means businesses are the 'losers' as, one way or the other, they will pay more. On the face of it this is so but bear in mind the following:

- When we handicap racehorses do we fill their nosebags with lead? Of course not! The weights are strapped around their girths, so at least they can still compete. In the same way, businesses will no longer have their input costs raised by tax or their sales reduced by VAT; instead they will be paying for valuable resources received from the community (e.g. land);
- Just as businesses get a whole lot more creative about fuel and energy efficiency when their prices soar, so will they if they suddenly find their natural resource rentals are high; instead of nagging management about 'lazy balance sheets', investment analysts will be asking about their lazy hectares;
- Although Mark Twain's quip 'Buy land son, they ain't making any more of it!' retains some validity, natural resource rentals will strongly boost the supply of land, making it much more readily available for economic activity;
- The relatively tax-free status of most rural areas, as well as all the other advantages mentioned here, will kick in to boost economic growth;
- Given that resource rentals are established by the market, all income in excess thereof is tax free. In other words, the marginal tax rate is zero. Given that resource rentals for commercial or industrial land would be based on what average returns are for efficient use, this would be a huge incentive to work smarter and harder, i.e. to apply above average labour and capital; and
- The same would apply to individuals who, after paying their rentals, would have no further claims on their earnings from the tax man.

## How about sectors?

As regards the outlook for various sectors, we have discussed Mining and Banking elsewhere. The former are likely to benefit from a transparent and clear-cut jurisdiction, with resource rentals geared in line with mine specific attributes as well as commodity price fluctuations benefiting marginal and richer mines alike. Banking will be incentivised towards more proactive financing of businesses and less towards playing with securities. That leaves Manufacturing, where, in Chapter 12, we described how clear winners would be those situated in rural areas, while in Chapter 13 we suggested that those in core metropolitan areas could also benefit. The incentive, of course, will be to use land much more efficiently. While we fully intend to look at this in more detail, it is beyond the scope of this work to do so here.

## How about companies?

In passing, a look at a few JSE-listed industrials might be instructive. To begin with we revert to Seardel, where, in Chapter 11, we showed how in its 2008 financial year government took R1,037m of its total cash value added of R1,486m, whereas only R124m went to providers of capital. Yes, it would be wonderful for shareholders if that R1bn went to them instead, but the catch is that we do not know how much land Seardel was using, nor what the rentals would be. However, judging from the valuation in 2008 of land and buildings at cost of R588m out of total assets of R2.6bn (including plant and machinery of R1.3bn) it is likely to be highly significant. The return on total net assets at the time was −13% for textiles and −90% for apparel and household textiles, which did not bode particularly well for its ability to pay market-related land rentals.

In the case of the smaller packaging manufacturer Bowler Metcalfe, however, the switch over looks more likely to be beneficial.

In Table 15.4 we have assumed that the company's 40,000 m² of factory space translates into 51,250 m² of land and that the average land value was R622/m². Taking, say, a 30-year purchase factor, this would translate into an annual rent of R20.75/m². This is much higher than the average of R7.13/m² suggested for industrial land in the notional resource rentals budget in Chapter 14, which is as one would expect, since Bowler Metcalf is situated on relatively prime land in metropolitan areas. Since current land prices are (in effect) the market's best estimate of the present value of uncollected land rental, we have to remember that where the full rental is being collected instead of taxation, land rental could be much higher than at present. Nevertheless, even if it were ten times higher, the land rental would still be much lower than tax paid in 2010. Once again, even if one allows for the possibility that Bowler Metcalfe was using its land more intensively, i.e. efficiently, than average, it points to the likelihood of industrial land rentals being lower than tax currently paid. Needless to say, however, more research is required here.

**Table 15.4: Comparison of tax paid/m² with notional land value rental/m² for Bowler Metcalf[6]**

| Company | y/e | PBT | Tax | PAT | Land | Tax | Land Value[3] | LV Rental |
|---------|-----|-----|-----|-----|------|-----|----------|--------|
| | | Rm | Rm | Rm | m² | R/m² | R/m² | R/m² |
| Bowler Metcalf | Jun-10 | 98.3 | 28.9 | 69.4 | 51250 | 564 | 622.5 | 20.75 |
| | Jun-09 | 100.2 | 27.7 | 72.5 | 51250 | 540 | 622.5 | 20.75 |

In addition, we note that Amalgamated Appliances (a Small Cap JSE-listed stock focused on the sales and marketing of branded household durables) also has a very instructive value added statement for both its 2009 and 2010 financial years, in which distribution to government, including company tax, PAYE, customs duty, excise duty, VAT and import surcharge as well as *ad valorem* charges, amounted to 43.6%. As against this, employees received 51.1% in 2010 while providers of capital received only 5.3%, including 4.7% reinvestment in the group (11.8% in 2009). Equally interesting is the fact that it has negligible land and buildings, implying that it is already paying land rental to some landlord. The chances are, therefore, that it is an efficient land user and would benefit from the switch over, despite the fact that we do propose the retention of some customs duties. Incidentally, because the company is a big importer, customs duties and so on comprise a big share of value added. This does inflate the government's share, but because we have proposed that the current customs system remain in place, it will stay that way for a while.

Just in case readers think all JSE-listed companies suffer from pathetically low shares of value added, consider Adcock Ingram in Table 15.5, which shows a healthy 47% in the 2010 financial year for providers of capital. This includes increasing both the total value added, as well as the government's share, by net VAT. Since its customers have paid for this, it is a more accurate measure of actual value added. In addition to thoughtfully providing the net VAT (which is not yet a JSE requirement) management has also shown the PAYE, which has enabled us to correct the accounting fiction whereby employees' share of value added is often inflated by including PAYE and government's share understated by excluding it.

6 Bowler Metcalfe 2010 Annual Report www.bowlermetcalf.co.za

Finally, as regards Adcock's positioning in the event of a switch over to resource rental collection, we note that land and buildings is a relatively modest R204m of total assets of R4.76bn, including plant and equipment of R576m. Although the company has probably held much of its property for many decades, and it is thereby undervalued, it nevertheless seems as though the company is also an efficient land user. This means that it may well pay a lot less land rental than the R740m government share of its current value added, in which case it is likely to be better off.

### Table 15.5: Adcock Ingram value added statement adjusted for PAYE and VAT

| Adcock Ingram | Rm | Rm |
|---|---|---|
| Year ended 30 September | 2010 | 2009 |
| Value added per accounts | 2 335 | 2 037 |
| Add net VAT paid | 266 | 206 |
| Economic value added | 2 601 | 2 243 |
| | | |
| **Distribution of value added:** | | |
| Providers of capital | 1 227 | 1 101 |
| Finance costs | 50 | 56 |
| Dividends | 280 | 215 |
| Reinvested | 967 | 967 |
| Percentage share | 47 | 49 |
| | | |
| Employees | 635 | 561 |
| Salaries (etc.) | 772 | 670 |
| Less employees' taxes | 137 | 109 |
| Percentage share | 24 | 25 |
| | | |
| Government | 740 | 580 |
| Taxation | 315 | 248 |
| Customs and excise | 3 | 3 |
| Rates (etc.) | 19 | 14 |
| Add net VAT | 266 | 206 |
| Add employees taxes | 137 | 109 |
| Percentage share | 28 | 26 |

**Source:** Adcock Ingram Annual Report for 2010.

We therefore have no doubt about it. We would all be winners. The apparent shift of the tax burden from individuals to businesses would almost immediately be made up for by the more efficient use of natural resources and the immensely incentivising effect of the new system, leading to faster, healthier economic growth.

## CHAPTER 16

# OUR CREDIT

*'... borrowing dulls the edge of husbandry.'*
William Shakespeare[1]

## Trust us to produce?

THE WHOLE REALM of money and banking has to do with the innate trust and belief in each other that naturally exists between fellow human beings under the thick veneer of this cynical and fraud-ridden age. At the same time, it covers the need for this to manifest in the credit (finance) needed for the endless realms of specialised production we want. In brief, the non-transactional part of banking is, or rather should be, more about providing credit for production and trade, rather than speculation or foisting credit for consumption on individuals.

Pillorying bankers has gone global in a big way without getting down to earth about where it went wrong in the first place, and we offer no prizes for your guessing it has to do with land. Whereas the English Agricultural Revolution spurred on the land enclosures – which, incidentally, created surplus labour for the Industrial Revolution – the whole thing need not have been so inhumane had the vastly increased land rents, both rural and urban, been collected by the government. This would have provided funds for urbanisation without slums.

## The somnolent model

The eighteenth century bankers, meanwhile, instead of having to provide credit for production based on their assessment of the viability of projects using the newfangled technology, were able to lend

---

1 Polonius' advice to Laertes, Hamlet, Act III, Scene III, line 75.

on the security of the land values arising from the uncollected rents. The latter also provided a source for the necessary risk capital, which was facilitated by the invention of the limited-liability company and secondary markets, which developed for its shares such as the London Stock Exchange. Thus commenced the somnolent model, which has prevailed to this day. Instead of having to do due diligence analysing new project business models, banks often found it far easier to use property as collateral, the bulk of which comprised land value. So a practice that arose out of an unnatural phenomenon (allowing a few to appropriate the rents created by everybody else) became an established system, the origins of which few bothered to consider. For much of the twentieth century, therefore, the safest banks were boring, i.e. they stuck to this model and maintained the quality of their lending books together with conservative gearing ratios.

## Masters of the Universe

Then along came the heyday of globalisation, and the Washington Consensus, after the fall of the Berlin Wall. This enabled giants such as Citibank, Deutsche Bank and Barclays, together with clever (erstwhile) investment banks such as Goldman Sachs, to leverage their leading positions in global finance in a lax, light-touch regulatory environment where they could deal in a multitude of new financial instruments and finance mega-corporate transactions including many instigated by hedge fund players. Not to be outdone, lesser players the world over also cottoned on to the game of securitising (mainly) mortgage bonds, so as to have repeated bites of the raising and on-selling commission cherries. So vast was the playing field, that when Bobby Godsell led a march of gold miners to the Union Buildings in a successful[2] protest against Goldman Sachs *et al.*'s game of borrowing gold from the central banks, dumping it on the market and buying it back lower down, they hardly blinked as they had a whole bagful of other new tricks to play.

## Back to boring banking?

So what are we saying? No more consumer loans or playing with mortgage-backed securities, LBO's, CDS's or other securities? Just back to

---

2 Following this and other protests from emerging country gold producers, the leading European central banks undertook in the Washington Agreement of 1999 not to sell more than 500 tons p.a., which enabled the bullion price to recover.

transactional banking and boring hold-to-redemption mortgage loans? Not at all. As a matter of fact, now that bankers have dropped the pretence that they have no appetite for risk, we'd like them to focus their undoubted ingenuity on innovative ways of providing credit for production – including the admittedly risky realm of start-ups and small, medium and micro-sized enterprises (SMME's). This is something that has recently been left to parastatal entities such as the Industrial Development Corporation (IDC), Development Bank of South Africa (DBSA) and Khula Enterprise Finance. Setting aside any assessment of results, the scale has in any case been inadequate. Banking is no more for bureaucrats than the somnolent! Moreover, in getting down to lending for production, bankers also have to face the fact that full collection of economic rent eliminates the land value element of their collateral! No doubt this will initially cause something akin to apoplexy amongst bankers, regulators, investors and homeowners alike until they appreciate that the benefits far outweigh the problems. In any case, economic rent, like human beings, is not a proper subject for private ownership. Obviously, however, timing is an issue and elsewhere (Chapter 10) we have pointed to the need to make allowances, albeit temporarily, for lower capital requirements while we all adjust to the new setup. To those who fear that comfortable homes will no longer be affordable, we respond that what we cannot afford, we cannot have. In the new setup, however, the stimuli to production and greater prosperity will be such that there could well be even more of them. For new buyers, of course, the big difference will be that the purchase price will be lower, because in principle, they only have to buy the bricks and mortar.

## Credit for production

Before we spell out how we envisage the world of finance in a world of economic rental collection, we need to step back up to the global level and look at the current state of the mess there as well as some of the proposals for getting out of it. So we also need to clarify some of the terms used, for example:

- Commercial banks – Traditional deposit takers from, and lenders to, individuals (retail banking), small- and medium-sized businesses (business banking) and large companies (corporate banking). More often than not, this would include trade finance (merchant banking) and, of course, they keep our money safe, give it back when we want it, and do our payments for us (transactional banking).

- Investment banks – As the name indicates, the bank would itself take positions in securities, currencies and derivatives (proprietary trading) as well as in unlisted companies (private equity). Typically it would also advise large companies as to how to raise finance for expansion (corporate finance) either organically via more money from shareholders (rights issues) or the capital market (via debentures and so on). Alternatively, and more controversially, since there is an inherent bias towards preening corporate egos because of the lucrative fees, they could advise on deals (mergers and acquisitions, or M&A).

- Hedge funds – Many moved far from the original concept of covering bets on securities movements one way with positions to benefit from movements the other way – to basically doing anything. Since they raised capital from wealthy investors, they would not have become controversial had they not borrowed aggressively from the banks for what (in many cases) were perceived as anti-social operations such as short selling or massive speculation in commodities.

- Private equity funds – Although often included in the activities of investment banks, they can just as easily operate on their own by raising their own capital from assorted types of investors, albeit generally not from members of the public (retail investors). Whereas hedge funds tend to be short-term and higher risk, private equity tends to be lower risk, longer-term and can sometimes be closer to the ideal of financing production.

- Venture capitalists – Prominent in the heyday of the Silicon Valley start-ups, they seem to have been overshadowed by the huge returns obtained by hedge funds prior to the global meltdown. They have always been popular, and are by all means to be encouraged.

- Moneylenders – When Muhammad Yunus saw the plight of the poor villager Sophia Begum, which led him to found the Grameen Bank, she was being exploited by one of those knee-cappers who operate amidst poverty all over the world at extortionately high rates of interest.

- Microfinance – Although famous now and emulated in many poor countries, Grameen Bank-type operations are still relatively unknown in the West.

## So what went wrong?

The above looks harmless enough so what, apart from the well-known sub-prime phenomenon, went wrong? Many errors as well as suggested remedies were summarised in a reprint of key articles in the *Financial Times.*[3]

There, Gillian Tett for example, describes the debilitating effect of the silo mentality in banks and financial institutions which 'will not be easy to beat. For one bizarre paradox of the modern age is that while technology is integrating the world in some senses (say, via the Internet), it is simultaneously creating fragmentation too (with people in one mental silo tending only to talk to each other, even on the Internet). And as innovation speeds up, this is creating a plethora of activities that are only understood by 'experts' in a silo – be that in finance or in numerous other fields.' She cites the example of the fixed-income department of Lehman Brothers, which was so alarmed by the American real-estate market, that it was hunting for ways to go short. Meanwhile, 'other departments, such as the mortgage securitisation team, were so aggressively bullish that they were increasing their exposure and the different departments were in such rivalry that they barely knew what the other was doing, with disastrous consequences.' This example is supportive of John Kay's view that 'the crisis was not caused by bad regulation, but by greedy and inept bank executives who failed to control activities that they did not understand.'

In George Soros's contribution,[4] he asserted that, far from the efficient-market hypothesis (whereby financial markets tend to equilibrium and accurately reflect all available information about the future), they always present a distorted picture of reality and have a tendency to develop bubbles. Amongst remedies, he suggests (unlike Greenspan) that central banks should accept responsibility for preventing bubbles and, for example, where they think a particular sector is overheated, they could instruct commercial banks to restrict lending to it or freeze new listings. In addition to control of money supply, they should also control credit via margin and minimum capital requirements, which should be varied according to market mood. Other tools include attending to systemic risks by ensuring that the central bank is aware of potential imbalances if, for example, too many market participants are on the same side of a particular position. Also,

3 *Financial Times*, 15 December 2009.
4 *Ibid.*

'certain derivatives, like credit default swaps, are prone to creating hidden imbalances so they must be regulated, restricted or forbidden.'[5] The implicit guarantees extended to all too-big-to-fail entities cannot now be withdrawn (since markets move in a one-directional, non-reversible manner) so they must be regulated with proprietary trading financed from their own capital, not deposits. Traders' compensation must be regulated so that risks and rewards at too-big-to-fail banks are aligned. 'This may push proprietary traders out of banks and into hedge funds, where they belong.' Although he feels that re-enactment of the separation between commercial and investment banks in the Glass-Steagall Act of 1933 is 'probably impractical' he believes that proprietary trading should be separated internally from commercial banking.

Other contributors reflect widespread sentiments e.g. John Gapper ('Goldman Sachs should be allowed to fail.') and John Kay ('Too big to fail is too dumb to keep!').

## Rebuilding a shamed subject

Lord Skidelsky's article[6] *How to Rebuild a Shamed Subject*, however, took an even more radical approach based on Queen Elizabeth's question to an economist, 'Why did no one see the crisis coming?' He points out that her question: 'accepted at face value the predictive claim of economics – a feature of economics that has distinguished it from all other social sciences. ... It is only by imagining a mechanical world of interacting robots that economics has gained its status as a hard, pre-dictive science. But how much do its mechanical constructions, with their roots in Newtonian physics, tell us about the springs of human behaviour?'

'Keynes opened the way to political economy; but economists opted for a regressive research programme, distinguished by sophisticated mathematics, that set it apart. The present crisis gives us the oppor-tunity to try again. The reconstruction of economics needs to start with the universities. First, degrees in the subject should be broadly based. They should take as their motto Keynes's dictum that 'eco-nomics is a moral and not a natural science'. They should contain not just the standard courses in elementary microeconomics and macro-economics, but economic and political history, the history of economic

5 *Financial Times, ibid.*
6 *Financial Times, ibid.*

thought, moral and political philosophy, and sociology. Though some specialisation would be allowed in the final year, the mathematical component in the weighting of the degree should be sharply reduced … The obvious aim of such a reconstruction is to protect macroeconomics from the encroachment of the method and habits of the mathematician. Only through some such broadening can we hope to provide a proper education for those whose usefulness to society will lie as much in their philosophical and political literacy as in their mathematical literacy.'

## Philosophy required…

We wholeheartedly concur with Lord Skidelsky, and insofar as including philosophy is concerned, wonder how long it will be before some diligent student of the new approach discovers the following statement[7] by Cicero (who was also a student of Plato) and asks whether it has any relevance to economics in the 21st century:

> True law is right reason in agreement with Nature; it is of universal application, unchanging and everlasting … we cannot be freed from its obligations by Senate or People, and we need not to look outside ourselves for an expounder or interpreter of it. And there will not be different laws at Rome and at Athens, or different laws now and in the future, but one eternal and unchangeable law will be valid for all nations and for all types, and there will be one master and one ruler, that is God, over us all, for he is the author of this law, it's promulgator and its enforcing judge.

Will he then perhaps consider, as we do, the law of Rent to be such a statement of natural law and of such profound significance as only to be ignored at our peril?

## …and land

Although Skidelsky does not mention it, the rebuilding of the subject would not be complete without a thorough examination of the role played by land. Brian Hodgkinson in *A New Model of the Economy*[8] not

---

7 Marcus Tullius Cicero, *De Re Publica*, Book 3, para. 22. Quoted in *Natural Law: An Introduction to Legal Philosophy* by Alessander Passerin D'Entreves, with introduction by Cary J. Nederin.
8 Hodgkinson, B., *A New Model of the Economy*, Shepheard-Walwyn, 2008.

only does this, but includes an examination of macroeconomic theory[9] showing why, with the omission of land, it never quite adds up.

## Sovereign debt crisis

The financial crisis that began in 2007 was, of course, exacerbated by the sovereign debt crisis beginning in early 2010 (sparked by the incoming Greek Government's revelations as to the wildly indebted state of the nation, which had been covered up by the previous government). The blame game was then taken to new heights after markets' concern as to the ability of other peripheral eurozone member countries to pay back loans used for what looked like unaffordable levels of welfare and overblown property speculation. Needless to say, hedge funds and the likes of Goldman Sachs took flak for their role in the drama, but what is interesting from our point of view is the fact that French and German banks had indeed bought so much of the government debt of the likes of Greece, Spain and Portugal. Whatever the justification in terms of the current system, we need to note that this was far removed from what we regard as the core function of banking; namely, providing finance and credit for production including business start-ups and infrastructure. Remember, of course, that the need for massive welfare spending is itself the result of a distorted system incapable of providing full employment for reasons which we have discussed.[10]

## Finding fixes

By mid-2013, five years down the line and many regulations and new laws later, there was still an underlying sense amongst financial experts that politicians were not about to get to the root of the problem. This is despite the fact that much of the regulation had to do with necessary addressing of excessive gearing and undercapitalisation of banks, together with distinguishing between transactional, business and commercial banking on the one hand and the higher risk taking involved in 'investment banking' on the other. This had been illustrated earlier on by John Authers in a comment from extracts prior to publication of his book:[11] 'What's more, the propensity to inflate bubbles is in the very fabric of world markets, so any reforms need to be systemic.

9 *Ibid.*, Ch. 20-26.
10 See Figures 3.5 and 3.6 in Chapter 3.
11 'The Fearful Rise of Markets: Global Bubbles, Synchronised Meltdowns, and How to Prevent Them in the Future', *Financial Times*, 22/23 May 2010.

While the absurdly complicated instruments that created the subprime bubble (such as the synthetic collateralised debt obligations that landed Goldman Sachs in trouble) should go, the roots of the problem lie far deeper. Finding fixes will involve hard choices.' While we agree with his proposals for correcting various investment industry practices, we also agree with his comments about the need for systemic reforms to prevent bubbles. This, we believe, is indeed what our proposals entail and we would be the first to accept that they require hard choices. If, however, by collecting the full rent we take away half the gas (land prices) used for the bubbles and restructure banks' incentives so as to encourage them to finance production (including start-ups and infrastructure) instead of speculation or consumption, we will have gone a very long way towards attaining this goal.

## So when can we start to collect?

The first answer is, of course, that in South Africa, the financial system (like those of many developing economies) is robust and still relatively unscathed so we are in a much better position from which to contemplate innovation. Just as in some areas of technology we can leapfrog developed countries, so may we in economic rental collection. There is no harm, however, in stress testing our ideas by looking at the global situation, if only because of the cries sure to emanate from the 'But it's never been done before!' brigade.

## Yet more capital for banks

Quite apart from the requirements of Basle 2 and 3, we should note that, although house mortgages have already been written down since 2007, there would be more to come, since a good proportion (i.e. the land value content) of the remaining value would vaporise over the implementation period of, say, 5 years. Any offers on $10 trillion? Home owners would, of course, benefit from the lower repayments required so the risks would be much lower, and hence banks' capital requirements also, with much higher loan to value ratios being acceptable.

Here, maybe a couple of analogies will help. First let us consider the analogy with slavery where, in the British Empire, owners of freed slaves were (in principle) entitled to compensation. Where were the funds supposed to have come from? We don't know, but the legislators might just have had in mind Adam Smith's economic argument against slavery quoted in P.J. O'Rourke in *On The Wealth of Nations*.[12] 'the experience of all ages and nations, I believe, demonstrates that the work done by slaves, though it appears to cost only their maintenance, is in the end the dearest of any. A person, who can acquire no property, can have no interest but to eat as much, and to labour as little as possible.' O'Rourke adds: 'This wouldn't be much of a slogan for abolitionists. But cold calculation has done more for mankind than William Wilberforce, Harriet Beecher Stowe, or John Brown.' Anyway, the fact of the matter is that the British Empire went from strength to strength after abolition in 1833. And, by the way and just as a matter of interest, what would the pre-2007 economists that Skidelsky talks about have had to say had slavery still existed? Would they have ignored it as they have the appropriation of rent? After all slavery, just like the privatisation of rent, was in contravention of natural law, and enjoyed such formidable legal protection as to be very much part of the established *status quo*.

The other analogy is that of the Weimar Republic, which, when it finally terminated the post-World War 1 hyperinflation, did so on the pretext that the currency was henceforth guaranteed 'by the land of Germany'. As it happens the trick worked; no doubt as much due to more prudent fiscal and monetary policies as well as the impressive-sounding collateral. This was despite the fact that, to our knowledge, there was no talk of collection of economic rent.

The difference here is that this is precisely what we have in mind. Consider that if, say, the US Government were to decree that the land value component of all mortgages were to be cancelled and the resultant impairment of banks' assets and diminution of capital be made good by the government it would merely be 'paying' for its 'expropriation' of rent from which it would in future derive a massive flow of income. Individual homeowners with bonds would have their assets and liabilities reduced by the same amount, while those whose houses were fully paid would be in a good position to upgrade due to the lower payments involved.

## Legacy rentiers, new banks etc.

In Chapter 10 we have already explained why the existing listed South African banks would continue to be taxed (albeit at a lower rate) in addition to paying site value rentals. Given the superabundance in

12 O'Rourke, P.J., *On the Wealth of Nations*, Atlantic Books, 2007, p.91.

developed countries of too-big-to-fail recipients of public sector bail-outs, this would apply even more so there. But while we are on the subject of a new financing model for the economy, we might as well have a closer look at how we see the principles, of paying the economic rent and incentivising production rather than consumption, applying in practice.

- Regular commercial banks – Based on the legacy principle, they would pay both site value rentals and company income tax. Consideration might in due course be given to paying only site value rentals except on income from proprietary trading, speculation, and the financing thereof.
- Investment banks
  - Proprietary trading: tax and rental plus speculation with own money only and, yes, separate from commercial banks!
  - Private equity: rental only for loans to start-ups (tax on the geared de-listing and re-listing game).
  - Advisory (corporate finance and M&A): rental only on advisory but tax on acquisition financing and trading income. Before anyone cries foul on this, we have to admit that, like many investors, we have a healthy scepticism as regards the economic value of much that passes for corporate action.[13] When Jerry Levine made a belated apology for the disastrous $164bn AOL deal in 2002 he also called for other business leaders to follow his example: 'where is the stand-up leadership that is going to take responsibility for what's happened and do something about it?'[14] In fact, we think regulators might well consider restricting finance for mega M&A deals to investors only i.e. institutions, hedge funds, individuals, and so on.
- Hedge funds – Rent and tax (except when they finance production or business start-ups).
- Venture capital – Rental only.
- Money-lending – At interest rates of <50%, they can pay tax and rental!
- Micro-finance – For consumption, rental and tax. For production à la Grameen Bank, rental only.

13 Especially when egged on by the M&A brigade – see: Gideon Haig, *Fat Cats: The Strange Cult of the CEO*, Thunder's Mouth Press, 2005.
14 *Financial Times*, 5 Jan 2010.

About the only thing approaching 'new banks' in the preceding paragraph was the Grameen Bank, while venture capital and hedge funds, of course, are not banks at all. They are, nevertheless, integral to modern finance albeit at opposite ends of the spectrum, with venture capital being investors' money in innovative production start-ups, while hedge funds usually play in secondary (securities) or commodities markets. Hedge fund operators' response to incentives and the rules of the game have been marked, not only in respect of access to massive amounts of gearing for their M&A activities, but also for speculation in commodities and currencies. With management fees between 1? and 2?%, and performance fees of around 20%, the leading individuals have been able to join the ranks of the mega-rich.

## The British problem

This is spelt out by Robert Peston in *Who Runs Britain?*,[15] which suffered the irony of having a Labour Government that swallowed the City's line that to tax the bonuses of clever investment bankers *et al* too much would be to encourage them to go elsewhere and imperil London's position as a leading global financial centre. 'Brown's pragmatism in providing a welcome for the super wealthy encouraged a City boom, which helps to sustain above-average economic growth in London and the South East – and, for all the ability of the super-rich to pay little or no tax, the prosperity of the South has generated the tax revenues that have financed public spending throughout the UK.' Peston quotes the Centre for Economics and Business Research estimates that while public spending represents a third of the economy in the South East, it amounts to more than 70% of that of the Northern Ireland economy, and 64% and 63% of the Welsh and North East England economies, respectively. What had happened, of course, was that the non-collection of the rising economic rental in London and South East England occurred while the UK tax system made minimal allowances for the lack of locational advantage elsewhere and hence retarded growth. Although there would naturally have been some redistribution to the relatively marginal regions in a natural resource rental collection regime, they would not have been actively disadvantaged and hence better off anyway. Hopefully, in due course, the British will figure out that for a balanced economy, one of their priorities should be to collect the fabulously high land rentals in London, instead of

15 Peston, R., *Who Runs Britain?*, Hodder & Stoughton, London, 2008.

letting them accrue to the likes of the Duke of Westminster.[16] As regards the mega-rich who (as Peston has pointed out) successfully avoid paying much tax, they would, to begin with, have to pay full land rentals on their business and residential properties. In addition, changing the rules of the game to favour innovation in the financing of production and trade rather than speculation in commodities, securities and derivatives should also include measures to tax, for example, the £1.2bn dividend Sir Philip Green's wife, resident in Monaco, received in 2005 from Arcadia (the retailing business he had bought in 2002 for £2m of his own cash). Much more important than this, however, is that the changed rules, while they may temper the lashings of credit that have hitherto fuelled M&A, should make it much more worthwhile to provide more direct funding for expansion in production and trade. Think about it; no tax payable!

## More new banks

This will undoubtedly require a new mindset from the financial entrepreneurs who respond to the new challenges and opportunities that will present themselves. For a start, the venture capital and private equity teams are likely to need more real nuts and bolts engineers than financial engineers, since tax complexities and incentives for massive LBOs[17] will fade away. Fortunately, however, it is not for us to anticipate how they will do so but we could, in passing, note that the principles on which the Grameen Bank was founded are likely to provide some pointers, even if Grameen has been operating at the opposite end of the spectrum, size-wise, from the mega-global banks. This is because it is first and foremost providing loans for production (albeit on a micro scale), and secondly, has succeeded over more than three decades despite intense scepticism and scorn from conventional bankers and others in the early days. Just to make the point about the new approach a little more clearly, it is worth noting some of Muhammad Yunus' principles:

- The poor (in fact all people) can be entrepreneurs;
- The poor know what to do with their loans and do not have to be trained;
- The poor pay back;

16 Cahill, K., *Who Owns Britain?*, Canongate Books, 2001, p.148.
17 Leveraged buy outs.

- 'The poor' includes women, especially where traditionally downtrodden;
- 'The poor' includes beggars (after extensive research, Grameen has lent successfully to thousands);
- We don't sit in offices, we go to the people;
- We don't hire ex-banking staff, as they cannot be retrained; and
- We are independent and not beholden to government (how Yunus achieved this, despite early assistance from the state, is a story in itself).

To those who have read *Banker to the Poor* or studied Grameen's operations, it is obvious they are worlds apart from most Western banks, let alone the global and investment banks we have been discussing. It is equally obvious to us, however, that those who succeed when rent collection replaces taxation will have found more than a little in Grameen's *modus operandi* to help them.

Note also that the 'legacy' basis for continued taxation of commercial banking profits would not apply to start-ups and it is from here that we expect much of the necessary innovation to come, as they would pay rentals only on transactional and interest income.

We believe that our proposals would lend much weight to the call by many experts for doing away with too-big-to-fail banks. This is significant, because otherwise, even after the passing of the 2007-2010 credit crisis when it should be easier to do so, central banks and governments could still duck the issue, and a good opportunity from the crisis will have been wasted.

## Southern African Grameens?

Swaziland-based entrepreneur Natie Kirsh seems to have hit upon a successful local version of Grameen with his project Inhlanyelo (Swati for 'seed') in which, together with Standard Bank Swaziland, he invested R11m which, together with repayments, had seeded 8,000 start-ups with R26m by mid-2010.[18] Some of the methods are surprisingly similar: Inhlanyelo uses established local structures with simple procedures using moral persuasion and peer pressure to ensure repayment of loans rather than legal processes. Field officers use the administrative infrastructure of Swaziland's legislative constituencies

18 *Financial Mail*, 21 May, 2010.

and the leadership structures of the chiefs' inner councils to select borrowers and monitor them. Successful applicants are visited and assessed by Inhlanyelo management and must complete a business course.

The South African state-owned Khula Enterprises is a wholesale finance institution dedicated to supporting mainly Black small businesses and counts village banks among its retail finance intermediaries.

## Private equity, venture capital

While we believe it is sensible to consider 'thinking out of the box' financial models such as Grameen's, we should not overlook the potential under the new scenario for venture capital and private equity. As noted in May 2010 in the *Financial Mail*,[19] the South African industry came through the Great Recession in good shape. One of the players[20] noted, 'But the problem is private equity has not been done properly over the past couple of years ... firms' strategies have also drifted away from original mandates. Private equity firms have opened up new lines of business, taking focus away from their investors and fund mandates. To make matters worse, the leverage on offer has proved all too seductive. As a result the core private equity principle of partnership – with investors and portfolio companies – has been distorted or neglected entirely.' As noted already, however, the elimination of the tax incentives for the listed LBO heroics will help steer the industry back to the basics where 'private equity incentive structures require fund managers to personally invest alongside portfolio executives and institutional investors'.[21] This ensures alignment of interests between the key parties and a focus on long-term value creation. In 2009 the industry association conducted its first economic impact assessment of the industry in conjunction with the DBSA,[22] which indicated that it had achieved average employment growth of 10% per annum over the three-year period from 2005/2006-2008/2009 and employed 5% of South Africa's formal sector employees. In our view, the industry is already playing a significant role and has enormous potential for nurturing growth of the new companies, which would benefit from the replacement of taxation by land rental. This would attract additional investor

---

19 'Private Equity and Venture Capital in SA: 2010 Industry Review', *Financial Mail*, May 2010.
20 *Ibid.*, Sean Dougherty, p.25.
21 *Ibid.*, Stuart Mackenzie, p.24.
22 Development Bank of South Africa.

interest as well as ensure that their investee companies received their fair share of working capital from the banks. If, however, in addition to this they still wanted to take out major listed companies and knock them into better shape privately, they would probably have to line up most of the necessary finance from investors rather than banks and, on top of that, still make it work without the tax deductibility of interest. While not impossible, it would just mean that the JSE target companies would have to have been a lot more underrated than before and the takeover players a lot smarter.

## New faces in finance

As pointed out by John Authers:[23] 'Financial innovation has a bad name, and with good reason. Precious little of it is happening in the big institutions that sparked the crash of 2008. Instead, new companies are using new technology to look at each part of the service that financial groups offer, and offer it in a new way.' He points out that payments can be made directly by mobile phone as pioneered by M-Pesa in East Africa, raising the prospect that payments systems could be separated from the bloated banks that control them. In addition, loans can be crowd sourced, even across borders, as peer-to-peer networks offer entrepreneurs the chance to raise money without needing to approach venture capitalists, or banks. The concept is springing up all over, and business models are proliferating. 'All Street, a London-based, non-profit group that aims to support alternative finance, lists separate peer-to-peer finance groups for equity, rewards, donations, trade finance, and personal and company loans... The aim is to democratise finance, using the same technology that allows social networks to grow.' One possible drawback is that 'relying on the wisdom of crowds to raise finance runs the risk that the critical elements of trust and judgement will again be missing (as they have been with securitised loans) and borrowers never meet their creditors face to face'.

All these developments sound promising and governments will no doubt watch closely but allow them to develop, safe in the knowledge that these experiments, if they fail, are unlikely to be too big not to be allowed to do so.

---

23 'We should pay heed to the new faces in finance', *Financial Times*, 1 June 2013.

## Cycles

The phenomenon of cycles is the subject of much economic debate[24] into which we need not enter, other than to suggest that taking full account of rent will throw much-needed light on the topic. Certainly there are those who argue strongly that house prices have moved in 18-year cycles for centuries[25] and we believe that, had Messrs Greenspan and Bernanke taken cognisance of these arguments, they would not so blithely have reiterated their belief that house prices do not seriously fall. Consequently, they would have been better equipped to tackle the bubble early on. Please note that under a natural resources rental collection system, rising house prices would lead to the Treasury skimming off the excess automatically as it arose; thus rendering bubbles less likely. It would make central banking a lot easier, even at the risk of reducing the awesome mystique surrounding the ritual of their open market and monetary policy meetings.

It is usually the case that recessions are ascribed to varying (and always different) causes but never to unrealistic land prices. This particular recession was foreseen by Fred Harrison in 2005[26] and Fred Foldvary in 2007[27] Harrison had earlier explored the theory of the 18-year cycle in his book *The Power in the Land*[28] in which he also foresaw the problems looming for Japan from its property bubble which burst in 1989.

While these booms and their resulting busts may be ascribed to varying causes, they are always in the end due to uncollected resource rents being allowed to accumulate in the price of the underlying resources, especially land. In other words, to paraphrase the Bill Clinton election slogan, one could say of the whole house-price crisis, 'It's land prices, stupid!' If these resource rents are not collected, government revenues have to be levied on income, expenditure or capital in a variety of taxes that generally fall with the harshest intensity on the poor.

---

24 For a comprehensive discussion on this and other topics in this chapter, see Professor Mason Gaffney, *After the Crash – Designing a Depression-Free Economy*, Wiley-Blackwell, 2009, in particular Ch.3.
25 Harrison, F., *Boom Bust, House Prices, Banking and the Depression of 2010*, Shepheard-Walwyn, London, 2005.
26 *Ibid.*
27 Foldvary, F., *The Depression of 2008*, The Gutenberg Press, Berkley, California, 2007.
28 Harrison, F, Shepheard-Walwyn, London, 1983

## So, yes let's trust people to produce!

In *A New Model for the Economy*,[29] the author points to the debilitating effect that non-collection of rent has on new business start-ups. Absent this 'oversight' and with incentives turned back towards financing production, we, therefore, look forward to the rising of a new generation of banks and other funders of production, from the village level to massive modern industries.

Polonius' warning to his son regarding loans not only included a prescient observation on the profligacy that could result, but could be taken as advice to leave them to specialists in the granting of credit, to which we would add: especially for production!

29 Hodgkinson, B., *A New Model for the Economy*, Shepheard-Walwyn, 2008.

## CHAPTER 17

# WHY SOUTH AFRICA?

*'Ex Africa aliquid semper novi.'*[1]
Pliny the Elder (CE 29-73)

## Why South Africa?

SOUTH AFRICA CAN fairly claim to have been a world leader in reconciliation and establishing constitutional democracy between oppressors and the oppressed. It has not been afraid to punch above its weight – and controversially at that – in foreign affairs. So it would by no means be out of character for the country to jettison its failed Eurocentric tax model and take a lead instead in global tax reform if it wanted to. As Pliny indicated, the Romans, at any rate, would not have been surprised at something new from Africa. More-over, South Africa has, since 1994, recognised the communal 'owner-ship' of some resources (for example, minerals and water), and is probably in a better position than almost any other country in the world to explore a different and empowering fiscal system.

This recognition, together with the statement from the preamble to the constitution quoted on p.54, is itself deeply rooted in the African tradition of communal land tenure that would have precluded the amassing of wealth by individuals purely from control of natural resources. Although there is some evidence to show that the Anglo-Saxon system of land tenure might have developed more equitably from its communal tendencies, which were not unlike some African systems, William the Conqueror put paid to that in 1066 and firmly rooted English land ownership in conquest *'vi et armis'* (by force of arms)! Land title was passed by the feudal overlords (the vassals of the

---

1 'Out of Africa always something new'.

king) to a favoured few, and this system was later transmitted to Anglo-Saxon countries overseas. In Latin America, the latifundia model had a similar effect. South Africa is probably unique with its Roman-Dutch heritage of a clear-cut system of registration providing security of individual land tenure, together with its African heritage that will naturally enable it to appreciate the need to collect community-created natural resource rentals.

In addition, the fiscal, monetary and financial systems of most developed countries are so complex and deeply entrenched as to deter contemplating such innovations. Relative to worse-managed economies elsewhere, they have seemed, until the global credit crisis, well-enough off to indulge in the delusion that their economic management was as good as it gets. Economic dissatisfaction continues, however, to lurk beneath the surface and manifests in loud protests when times are tough. In addition, many developed countries (e.g. France and Hungary) enjoy an agricultural resource that is largely arable so that the glaring inconsistency of taxing marginal locations is less evident than in South Africa, where only 15% of the land is arable. Moreover, developing countries whose economic systems are as sophisticated as South Africa's are often hampered by powerful vested interests that resist economic changes that do not suit them. South Africa's democracy is still young and eager enough to want to succeed, and, more to the point, its natural resource rentals are not (yet) monopolised by such vested and politically dominant interests.

Despite their established systems and relative wealth, the economies of the United States, the UK and many other Western countries experienced a massive credit crisis in 2007 that led to recession. South Africa, with its mixture of first- and third-world economy, healthy banking sector, and its abundance of mineral resources that could protect it in part from major recessions, is in the perfect position to explore an empowering economic path that may guide other economies out of the 18-year 'boom-bust' prison. To do this, however, it needs to become an investor-friendly destination, which means an end to the ongoing confusion regarding mining titles and nationalisation. Needless to say, we believe that a shift to resource rental collection will do the job quickly and efficiently.

## What about the others?

Despite what we have said about the developed countries, it is not as though there is no trace of these principles within living memory. The renascent Liberal Democrats in Britain can trace their ancestry to the Liberal Party, which had the temerity to include a land tax in its Budget of 1909 and which was vetoed by the House of Lords despite many rousing speeches by Winston Churchill denouncing 'the oldest monopoly.'[2] Not long before that, in the late 19th century, the Americans had their Henry George whose *Progress and Poverty* was a worldwide bestseller but who antagonised the Economics profession and then died while running for mayor of New York in 1897. An account of how his ideas were subsequently buried is given by Professor Mason Gaffney and Fred Harrison.[3] Prior to Adam Smith the French had their Physiocrats with their proposed '*l'impôt unique*' (single tax on land), while the Japanese surge into industrialisation following the Meiji Restoration in the 1870s relied heavily on a land reform and land tax programme. The same applied in Taiwan when the Nationalist Chinese fled there in 1949 and put into practice some of the principles of their guiding light, Sun Yat Sen, who had read Henry George.[4] Throughout much of its successful history Hong Kong has relied on regular land lease auctions, thus facilitating its famously low levels of taxation, despite there being recent indications that the full rental is by no means being collected.[5]

## European Union

It is, nevertheless, tempting to wonder when the long-suffering European consumer will give the heave-ho to agricultural subsidies, which fatten land prices (to the detriment of tenant farmers and benefit of land owners) more than livestock and rob developing countries of export opportunities. Moreover, while they are about it, what about beginning with a land tax (on urban as well as rural land) instead of sales or value-added tax? Now that would make a big difference to their lives as well as incentivising more production! Come to think of it, after Greece's financial woes, shouldn't governments be looking at a better source of revenue as well? The eurozone crisis stemmed largely from putting monetary union way ahead of fiscal and banking integration. Should this ever be fully achieved, the eurozone would have the opportunity for real economic revitalisation by collection of the high land rentals in the more highly developed industrial and

2 Churchill, W., *The People's Rights*, Jonathan Cape, London, Republished 1970.
3 Gaffney, M. and Harrison, F., *The Corruption of Economics*, Shepheard-Walwyn, London, 1994.
4 Li, K.T., *Economic Transformation of Taiwan* (R.O.C.), 1988, p.83.
5 'Hong Kong's Land System that Time Forgot', *Financial Times*, 10 March 2011.

financial centres of the core countries as well as much lower rentals in the peripheral countries. Whilst the mere thought at this stage would probably elicit a vociferous chorus of 'neins', there is little doubt that for the eurozone to survive intact, the core countries will have to give one way or another – bearing in mind the huge advantages that accrued to Germany, for one, from what was (for it) a relatively undervalued currency. Eventually, they would have to get used to it, in the same way that the peripheral countries would need to eliminate all other barriers to economic efficiency. The United States, which, along with many other countries, was applying massive stimulus programmes in the Great Recession, was subsequently forced by sovereign debt fears in the capital markets to look at curbing budget deficits. The US, which has not yet gone down the road of value-added tax, might in desperation go there, but would be much better advised to take the advice of its own Henry George and start collecting some land rentals instead. The Alaska Permanent Fund is also a useful American model for collection of natural resource rents.[6]

## Developing Countries
### Africa
In our own neighbourhood we have seen attempts by Zambia and others to impose windfall taxes when commodity prices spiked. Needless to say, the ensuing controversy and uncertainty that discourages foreign investment could be avoided by something like the gold mining tax formula (GMF) discussed in Chapter 8 as an acceptable proxy for collecting the natural rent. Given the lack of a developed land market in the Western sense, the introduction of this system as regards mining would be a good place to start. In Mozambique, where land belongs to the state, transparency and security of tenure needs to be established regarding the allocation and market-based payment for long-term leases. Botswana has benefited from the arrangement with De Beers including the 15% share in Debswana – just imagine how few diamonds the state would have seen if 10,000 artisanal miners were digging up Jwaneng instead! It would also benefit from introducing the GMF, provided the Minister of Finance emulated Joseph ahead of the seven lean years![7]

6 Hartzog, A., *The Alaska Permanent Fund: A Model of Resource Rents for Public Investment and Citizens Dividends*, www.earthrights.net/docs/alaska.html.
7 Sovereign Wealth or Stabilisation Funds can be useful in this regard.

## Zimbabwe

The proposals for 51% indigenisation of mining and other businesses in Zimbabwe are merely a *reductio ad absurdum* of the 26% target in the South African mining charter. As we have explained at length in this book, if we wish capital to be risked in new ventures it must be granted the full fruits of its endeavour at the same time as paying the full rent. The state on the other hand, needs to recognise that the more stable and transparent an environment it creates, the higher that rent will be. In principle, therefore, there is no need for state shareholdings in private companies, and any minor shareholdings (perhaps to establish 'skin in the game') should be fully paid for.

The ultimate absurdity, to which the Zimbabwean version of black economic empowerment (BEE) is driving, is related to the fact that for it to work in the first place, the state must not be collecting the full rent. Only then can the existing shareholders afford the dilution (for this is what BEE entails, albeit dressed, disguised and delayed in complex deals dreamt up by clever bankers and lawyers). In other words, in the unlikely event of the Zimbabwean 51% indigenisation working, it would only be because the returns on capital of the remaining 49% of shareholders of, say, one of the platinum mines, were still attractive. For this to be the case, booming platinum group metals prices and low company tax rates would be necessary. But then the return to the state (or people) would be far less than it should be where it simply collected the rent via, say, GMF. In most cases, such returns would simply not be available, thereby forcing the original owners out of business. Thus indigenisation (which requires exceptionally high returns to be viable) would rule out of the game similar mines on less favourable ground. This would be the opposite of rental collection, which facilitates all business including those on marginal sites.

## Nigeria

In terms of the 2012 Nigerian Petroleum Industry Bill, companies in the oil and gas sector are regulated by separate tax laws. Tax rates are different for resident companies in the upstream sector of the oil and gas industry. The rates range from 50% for some of the new production-sharing contracts to 65.75% for others in the first five years, during which all pre-operation expenses are expected to be fully amortised, and 85% of their chargeable profits thereafter. Each upstream petroleum company has to remit on a monthly basis 10% of the net profit (adjusted profit less Nigerian Hydrocarbon Tax (NHT) and Companies Income Tax (CIT)) to the host community fund. Any act of vandalism or sabotage that occurs in a community will lead to a forfeiture of the community's portion of the Fund up to the amount sufficient to repair and remediate the damage caused. Contributions made to the Fund will be available as credit against fiscal rent obligations being royalty, NHT and CIT. These rates, which apply to onshore and shallow areas of not more than 200 metres depth, reduce to 25% for bitumen, frontier acreages or deep water areas. Although oil revenues comprised 64% of the total Nigerian Budget in 2012, we do not know to what extent these taxes constituted over- or under-collection of natural resource rental[8] because there may well be oil fields that are not being exploited due to these taxes rendering them unprofitable. Lower taxes for offshore fields would, however, constitute at least partial recognition of the need to take into account locational advantage. Another commendable feature is the allocation of 10% of profits to host communities. Equitably administered, this could go a long way towards defusing the longstanding complaints (which have led to years of violent mayhem) that the richest oil-bearing areas suffer the most due to pollution and lack of infrastructure. In any event, it is common cause in the meantime that the very considerable revenues that are received are inadequately applied, and for this to be remedied, the democratic accountability of Nigeria's federal, state and local government institutions needs to be raised to new levels.[9]

In South Africa, the provinces receive 'equitable allocations' in terms of the constitution, while the Mining Charter obliges miners to undertake community developments in the immediate vicinity of operations. In principle, such activities belong to the realm of government, but given the lack of capacity of many local authorities, the expertise employed by the miners in this regard could be more effective. It could also be regarded as a payment in kind of resource rental. The problem with this, however, is that it discriminates against more marginal projects because it conflicts with the principle that no attempt be made to collect rent where there is no locational advantage.

The World Bank has expressed some concerns as regards the discovery of oil in Ghana and Uganda including Dutch disease 'in which oil crowds out other sectors of the economy, pushing up costs – prices,

---

8 Nigerian oil rents, described as the difference between the value of crude production at world prices and total costs of production were estimated at 29.5% of GDP in 2008-2012. The estimates were based on sources and methods described in *The Changing Wealth of Nations: Measuring Sustainable Development in the New Millenium*, World Bank, 2011.

9 www.pwc.com/nigeriataxblog, accessed 23 March 2013.

wages and exchange rates – for all other businesses and making them less competitive.'[10] We believe resource – including land – rental collection and the ensuing lower taxation would alleviate such situations.

## Asia

Like China, most Western nations, when they were experiencing the heady growth phase of industrialisation, were by no means fully democratic. Thus rural folk could be moved off the land without too many constitutional niceties such as proper compensation. Non-collection of the rents arising from new urban developments enabled landowners to accumulate wealth rapidly 'paid for' in both cases by the state providing little or no social welfare. In this way, the labouring classes were kept with noses to the grindstone despite their protests, which, in the case of China, seem to run into thousands each year. Collection of these rents now would allow the Chinese government to put in place the social welfare net needed to wean the people from their traditional high level of savings, boost sales of consumer goods in China and, by reducing the excessive dependence of the economy upon exports, help temper the massive global imbalances that arose from over-spending America and over-saving China. In 2013, the new leadership took action to curb the excessive credit granted (mainly by the 'shadow banking system'), and most of this, in turn, for property speculation – underlying which, of course, are the rising land values. Initially, at any rate, it focused on administrative measures in an attempt to divert funds from speculation to new private enterprises, which it sees as the key to renewed real growth. It remains to be seen whether, instead of relying purely on the indiscriminate effect of higher interest rates, it would take the speculative gas out of the system via land rental collection, which would not detract from new business start-ups. Moreover, in order to extend the China miracle from the Maritime Provinces to the interior, it needs to continue with its massive infrastructure programme in order to render it accessible across the inhospitable terrain with which China (in contrast to most of Western Europe and the US) has to contend. Collection of the rents that arise there will be necessary both to recoup this expenditure as well as for further development. Essentially it's the same story: rent must go to the people, not party apparatchiks.

India, like South Africa, has the 'disadvantage' in terms of rapid growth in that it is democratic but not yet fully industrialised, and

10 *Time Magazine*, 5 May 2010, p.35

let no-one pretend the situation is simple as indicated by this excerpt from a Land Research Action Network[11] posting of 21 January 2003 describing the situation after over 50 years of attempts at land reform:

> Even in states that have attempted reforms, the process has often halted midway with the co-option of the beneficiaries by the status quoits [*sic*] to resist any further reforms. For instance, with the abolition of inter-mediary interests, the erstwhile superior tenants belonging mostly to the upper and middle classes have acquired a higher social status. Hence problems related to land such as concentration, tenancy rights, access to the landless etc. still continue to challenge India. The criticality of the issue, in fact, may be gauged from the fact that notwithstanding the decline in the share of agriculture to the GDP, nearly 50% of India's population is still dependent on agriculture for livelihood. More than half of this percentage (nearly 63%), however, owns smallholdings of less than 1 ha while the large parcels of 10 ha of land or more are in the hands of less than 2%. The absolute landless and the near landless (those owning up to 0.2 ha of land) account for as much of as 43% of the total peasant households.

Quite apart from confusion regarding land tenure systems, there is still controversy as regards the economic and ecological effects of the Green Revolution and much else besides. Needless to say, we suspect that a missing key to development in all this would be a programme to collect both rural and urban rentals, beginning with appropriate size thresholds. Collection of the full market rental will eliminate land-lordism, with its multi-tiered layers of tenants, by incentivising the owners to do the work themselves or sell. To the extent that this also eliminates agricultural inefficiencies, there should be plenty of jobs awaiting displaced tenants in nearby low land rent paying industries.

## Brazil

Not much has changed from the '*latifundia*' heritage since the post-1985 constitution, one of the architects of which was President Lula Da Silva, and in which were enshrined some principles of land reform, albeit heavily hedged. For the last 20 years, the highly organised land-less workers movement, MST, has used activist tactics in terms of the constitution to chip away at the situation where less than 2% of the population controlled half the arable land but, although it succeeded in getting public opinion behind it, its successes were limited in terms

11 www.landaction.org

of the big picture. Ironically enough, the ex-Workers Party leader Lula Da Silva (who the MST thought would be more sympathetic) turned Brazil into a global investor destination with his relatively orthodox economic policies. He also favoured agri-business with its links to the large landowners and somewhat questionable ecological practices. MST's decision to step up its activism backfired and swung public opinion against it. We believe the MST would be better advised to campaign for far more effective application of existing rural land taxes as a means of collecting land rents, as well as a catalyst to trigger not only land reform, but more efficient use of the resource. It should also team up with urban allies to suggest something similar in the cities.

## Russia

Russia had a golden opportunity in the early 1990s of extracting full market rents from the exploitation of its natural resources,[12] but was thrown away when the former state-owned enterprises and other properties were given to the 'oilygarchs' for a song. This enabled them to accumulate vast wealth and, in some cases, harbour political ambitions, which in turn made them a target for Putin's wrath. The mechanisms for collecting natural rent throughout this vast country would have to cope with the fact that, until 20 years ago, there weren't even the beginnings of a land market. We suspect, however, that, given their egalitarian heritage, the concept of natural resource rental collection would find ready acceptance with the Russian people once properly understood.

## Why South Africa indeed?

To apply the principles proposed here, South Africa will have to make a clear break from the Eurocentric, nay global, fiscal model followed since transition. So it will require from us a global leadership. But as we have said before, this has already been displayed in a far more important arena. The Rainbow Nation born in 1994 looked a little frayed at the edges before and after the 2010 Soccer World Cup, but given clear-cut common goals, the New South Africa worked in relative harmony to pull it off and the country continued to be an inspiration and example to the rest of the world. Many other regions, alas, remain mired in bloody conflict. The current frustrations and

12 Harrison, F., *The Silver Bullet*, The International Union for Land Value Taxation, UK, London, 2008, especially p.22-29.

disappointments in our country indicate clearly to the writers that, once again, we have to take a lead in climbing out of the poverty trap. In particular, these measures are urgently required to clean up and stabilise our mining jurisdiction, revitalise our manufacturing industry and provide a win-win approach for the stability and inclusive development of agriculture. What is more, we have on hand the necessary proven financial expertise in government and private sector – including hundreds of competent economists – to investigate these proposals, improve on them and put them into practice. Some of them may seem a little complex (and we have no doubt better ideas will be forthcoming) but the basic principles are astoundingly simple, rooted as they are in the fundamental laws governing humanity and its surrounding universe. As such, they are eminently capable of being understood by all South Africans, close as they are to the African tradition of completely equitable access to natural resources. The independence of mind required for this task has been amply demonstrated at various times in their history by all the strands that make up the Rainbow Nation. Moreover, if we but half succeed, our example is sure to be followed by others, including the leading investment destination BRIC[13] countries all of whom, as we have indicated, need a better model than the one they have now.

So why South Africa? Because we can![14] But more important than that: we understand land. This, in turn, will make it easier to collect rent. Then the jobs will follow!

13  Brazil, Russia, India and China.
14  With acknowledgements to President Obama.

# FARM LAND VALUES
# 2005-2006

Data taken from various property for sale advertisements:

| | Area (ha) | Price (Rm) | R/Ha | Date | Description |
|---|---|---|---|---|---|
| **NORTHERN CAPE** | | | | | |
| Barkly West | | | | 06-May-05 | |
| Riverbend | 198 | 3.3 | 16 667 | | |
| Farm 143 | 1 714 | 1.5 | 875 | | |
| Prieska | | | | | |
| Blinkfontein (portion) | 32 | 0.2 | 6 250 | | |
| | | | | | |
| **WESTERN CAPE** | | | | | |
| Barrydale | 663 | 0.96 | 1 448 | 09-Feb-07 | Fresh water, river runs through |
| | 314 | 1.6 | 5 096 | 01-Aug-06 | Fynbos, 2 freshwater fountains, Karoo view |
| Baviaans | 932 | 0.78 | 837 | 05-Jan-07 | Jackal-proof fencing |
| | 3 200 | 2.4 | 750 | 06-Jan-07 | Jackal-proof fencing |
| Calitzdorp | | | | 06-May-05 | |
| Huisrivier | 98 | 0.4 | 4 082 | | |
| Ceres | 1 540 | 1.25 | 812 | 30-Dec-05 | Frischgewaagd |
| | 1 384 | 0.62 | 448 | | Bovenlangkloof |
| Elgin/Grabouw | | | | | |
| Wine farm | 32.5 | 6.5 | 200 000 | 31-Mar-06 | 8 ha chardonnay, 3 ha pinot noir, 13 ha fallow |
| Baardskeerdersbos | 43 | 2.95 | 68 605 | | 35 ha conservation area, 7 ha agric. Indigenous forest, 2/BR cottage |

| | Area (ha) | Price (Rm) | R/Ha | Date | Description |
|---|---|---|---|---|---|
| Laingsburg | 6 172 | 1.73 | 280 | | Kraggasdrift |
| | 3 187 | 0.29 | 91 | | Farm 274 |
| Langeberg Mtns. | 90 | 2.2 | 24 444 | 01-Aug-06 | Farm 274 first user mountain water |
| Langkloof | 85 | 1.1 | 12 941 | 05-Jan-07 | 6 labourers' cottages |
| Malmesbury | | | | | |
| Farm 820 | 58 | 0.69 | 11 828 | 05/01/2007 | |
| Goedehoop(p) | 22 | 1.25 | 56 818 | | |
| Riversdale | | | | 06-May-05 | |
| Derustplek | 422 | 2.7 | 6 398 | | |
| Farm 388 | 430 | 1.39 | 3 233 | | |
| Groenrug | 414 | 1.2 | 2 899 | | |
| Spiegelrivier | 210 | 1.21 | 5 762 | | |
| Caledon | 245 | 2.95 | 12 041 | 06-May-05 | Eliasgat |
| Oudtshoorn | 1 473 | 1.48 | 1 005 | | Buffeldrift |
| | 150 | 4.5 | 30 000 | | 2 large dams, 1 old farmhouse |
| Swellendam | 478 | 7.3 | 15 272 | | Farm 625 |
| | 90 | 2.2 | 24 444 | 01-May-06 | Near Marloth Nature Reserve |
| | 90 | 2.6 | 28 889 | 01-Dec-06 | On Breede River, 1.2km frontage |
| Stellenbosch | 3 | 5.71 | 900 000 | 09-Feb-07 | |
| Uniondale | 1 320 | 2.28 | 1 727 | | Misgund |
| | 457 | 0.85 | 1 860 | | Smaldeel |
| | 4 956 | 3.2 | 646 | | Strydomskloof etc. |
| Worcester | | | | 06-May-05 | |
| Eikehof | 203 | 1.7 | 8 374 | | |
| Osplaats | 180 | 2.42 | 13 444 | | |
| Farm 794 | 59 | 0.21 | 3 559 | | |

**SOUTHERN CAPE**

| | Area (ha) | Price (Rm) | R/Ha | Date | Description |
|---|---|---|---|---|---|
| Hartenbos | 1 224 | 0.55 | 449 | 05-Jan-07 | Seemeeupark |

**EASTERN CAPE**

| | Area (ha) | Price (Rm) | R/Ha | Date | Description |
|---|---|---|---|---|---|
| Bathurst | 314 | 0.355 | 1 131 | 06-May-05 | Farm 91 & Farm 94 |
| | 58 | 0.32 | 5 517 | | Farms 55/56 & Lanpeter |
| Graaff Reinet | 1 900 | 3.75 | 1 974 | 09-Feb-07 | Seeff Graaff Reinet |
| | 2 090 | 3.75 | 1 794 | 01-Oct-06 | |
| Maclear | 838 | 0.365 | 436 | | Snowyside |

| | Area (ha) | Price (Rm) | R/Ha | Date | Description |
|---|---|---|---|---|---|
| Stutterheim | 36 | 0.082 | 2 278 | 06-May-05 | Callistemon |
| Uitenhage | | | | 06-May-05 | |
| | 20 | 1 | 50 000 | | Selborne |
| | 517 | 2.11 | 4 081 | | Tzoetgeneugh etc. |
| | 40 | 0.43 | 10 750 | | Stratsomers Estate |
| | 1 078 | 1.2 | 1 113 | | Olifantskop |
| | 20 | 0.55 | 27 500 | | Kruisrivier |
| | 24 | 0.491 | 20 458 | | Commandantskraal Estate |
| | 300 | 0.45 | 1 500 | | Scheepersvlakte |
| | 104 | 0.15 | 1 442 | 30-Dec-05 | Elandsfontein |
| | 434 | 0.85 | 1 959 | | Coegasrivier |
| | 344 | 1.5 | 4 360 | | Kentish Plains West |
| | 70 | 4.1 | 58 571 | | |
| | 335 | 0.805 | 2 403 | | Prenticekraal |
| East London | 218 | 1.5 | 6 881 | | Farm 1016 |
| Tarkastad | 5 200 | 18.5 | 3 558 | 31-Mar-06 | 3 quality homesteads; pvt. game res. |
| | 2 190 | 2.9 | 1 324 | 30-Dec-05 | 7 farms |
| Bedford | 715 | 1.2 | 1 678 | 30-Dec-05 | Boschfontein |

## FREE STATE

| | Area (ha) | Price (Rm) | R/Ha | Date | Description |
|---|---|---|---|---|---|
| Bloemfontein | | | | | |
| Fortuna | 10 | 0.25 | 25 000 | 06-May-05 | |
| Rodenbeck(p) | 34 | 0.17 | 5 000 | | |
| Kwaggafontein | 47 | 2.35 | 50 000 | | |
| Wilhelmshohe | 16 | 0.5 | 31 250 | | |
| | 11 | 0.28 | 25 455 | 05-Jan-07 | |
| Phillopolis | 3 334 | 5.8 | 1 740 | 31-Mar-06 | Orange R .game farm; 11km frontage |
| | | | 1 550 | 04-Apr-06 | Same area w/o river frontage |
| | | | 1 275 | 04-Apr-06 | Ave. good ordinary stock farm |
| | | | 780 | 04-Apr | Farm close to town w/o improvemts. 3ha:1 small stock unit; 8ha:1 large stock unit in Colesberg |
| Fouriesburg | 59 | 0.35 | 5 932 | 06-May-05 | Tweekop etc. |
| Bothaville | 605 | 2 | 3 306 | 06-May-05 | Hartebeestkuil |
| | 138 | 0.622 | 4 507 | | Zoetvlakte |

| | Area (ha) | Price (Rm) | R/Ha | Date | Description |
|---|---|---|---|---|---|
| Bothaville | 844 | 2.75 | 3 258 | | Beestkraal Noord |
| | 377 | 3.01 | 7 984 | | Korenhof |
| | 601 | 3.8 | 6 323 | | Twistniet etc. |
| Vrede | 290 | 0.649 | 2 238 | | Heeltevreden |
| | 494 | 0.65 | 1 316 | | Vaalklip |
| | 350 | 1.17 | 3 343 | | Lourentia etc. |
| | 349 | 0.376 | 1 077 | | Bloemhof etc. |
| | 892 | 0.63 | 706 | | Kalabasfontein etc. |
| | 900 | 0.912 | 1 013 | | Coenradina etc. |
| | 226 | 0.125 | 553 | | Zoetbron |
| | 866 | 1.39 | 1 605 | 30-Dec-05 | Saulshoek etc. |
| | 1 427 | 2.19 | 1 535 | | Elizabeth etc. |
| | 428 | 0.9 | 2 103 | | Geluk |
| | 858 | 1.14 | 1 329 | | Driefontein etc. |
| | 485 | 1.62 | 3 340 | | Grootfontein |
| Reitz | 143 | 0.2 | 1 399 | 06-May-05 | Elgin |
| Bethlehem | 215 | 0.3 | 1 395 | | Matinusdal |
| | 126 | 0.44 | 3 492 | 05-Jan-07 | |
| | 390 | 1.65 | 4 231 | | Windhoek etc. |
| Theunissen | 308 | 0.446 | 1 448 | 06-May-05 | Kalkleegte |
| | 178 | 0.65 | 3 652 | | Uitkomst |
| Fauresmith | 482 | 0.58 | 1 203 | 06-May-05 | Welverdiend etc. |
| | 1 265 | 1.1 | 870 | | Sandymount Park |
| Boshoff-Dealesville | 396 | 0.346 | 874 | 06-May-05 | Elandsfontein |
| | 1 370 | 0.66 | 482 | | Kareelaagte etc. |
| | 816 | 1.1 | 1 348 | | Braklaagte |
| | 1 052 | 1.42 | 1 350 | | Leeuwfontein |
| | 852 | 1.58 | 1 854 | | Damplaats |
| Odendaalsrust | 122 | 0.11 | 902 | | Uitkyk to HDSA |

**MPUMALANGA**

| | Area (ha) | Price (Rm) | R/Ha | Date | Description |
|---|---|---|---|---|---|
| Komatipoort | 577 | 13 | 22 530 | 06-May-05 | Outeniqua |
| Kruger Natl. Park | | | 20 000 | | R15 to R25k nr KNP p8 |
| Lydenburg | 555 | 0.53 | 955 | 30-Dec-05 | Enkeldoorns (non-commercial) |
| | 480 | 0.3 | 625 | | Brakspruit257 |
| | 257 | 1 | 3 891 | | Kaalbooi |
| | 340 | 1 | 2 941 | | Voetpad |
| Ohrigstad | 1 597 | 0.25 | 157 | | Riversdale (HDSA x 2) |
| | 268 | 0.539 | 2 011 | | Krugerspost |

| | Area (ha) | Price (Rm) | R/Ha | Date | Description |
|---|---|---|---|---|---|
| White River | 428 | 3.255 | 7 605 | 09-Feb-07 | Crocodile R. 50 ha of water rights |
| Witbank | 584 | 1.6 | 2 740 | 06-May-05 | Rietfontein |
| | 100 | 1 | 10 000 | | Elandsdrift |
| | | | | | |
| **LIMPOPO** | | | | | |
| Waterberg | 2 000 | 5.7 | 2 850 | 31-Mar-06 | Pure unspoiled Bushveld; 21000 ha portions w/i 5 000 ha managed farm. |
| Tzaneen | 3 000 | 12 | 4 000 | 23-Dec-05 | Game, cattle, 18 camps, 5 boreholes 2 homesteads |
| Thabazimbi | 3 000 | 9.5 | 3 167 | 23-Dec-05 | Game R1m, big trees, big water |
| | 1 500 | 5.35 | 3 567 | | Excl. game, thatch house, pool, good o/blds, elect. fence, 8km boundary river |
| Dwaalboom | 550 | 1.95 | 3 545 | | 3 game farms at same price |
| | 180 | 0.85 | 4 722 | | No detail |
| Mabula | 1 895 | 6.7 | 3 536 | 23-Dec-05 | Game farm, excludes game R2.3m and improvements R6m |
| Vaalwater | 500 | 5.5 | 11 000 | 23-Dec-05 | Excellent game fence, 4 chalets, bush camp, game R600 K |
| | 535 | 2.75 | 5 140 | | Opposite Douw Steyn. Game fenced. |
| Rooiberg | 530 | 3.2 | 6 038 | | Excludes game R400 k. Near thatch Camp. 20% mountain. |
| | 900 | 14 | 15 556 | | Excl. R1m game. Lodge, chalet, conf. facility, accomodates 120. River. |
| | 1 000 | 10 | 10 000 | | Game farm. Excl. R550 k game. |
| Naboomspruit | 410 | 1.95 | 4 756 | | Game farm. 15 boreholes. Water rights for 70ha. House and outbuildings. |
| Potgietersrus | 130 | 1.35 | 10 385 | | Quaint house. Excellent position. Beautiful scenery. |

| | Area (ha) | Price (Rm) | R/Ha | Date | Description |
|---|---|---|---|---|---|
| **KWA-ZULU NATAL** | | | | | |
| Dundee-Weenen | 122 | 0.1 | 820 | 06-May-05 | Belleck |
| | 534 | 0.534 | 1 000 | | Spetskop |
| | 721 | 0.578 | 802 | | Uithoek |
| Midlands | 108 | 2.9 | 26 852 | | UmGeni River boundary, Berg views. |
| Mooi River | 1 240 | 2.5 | 2 016 | | Beef ranch, 40 ha irrigated, 3km river, house, sheds |
| PMB | 242 | 61 | 252 066 | 06-May-05 | Langefontein |
| | 70 | 3.2 | 45 714 | | Bredasfontein |
| | 255 | 2.78 | 10 902 | | Hopevalley |
| Kokstad | 3 000 | 12 | 4 000 | 23-Dec-05 | 4 farms, 163 ha irrigated mainly pivot, |

# Abbreviations

| | |
|---|---|
| ACSA | Airports Company of South Africa |
| bn | billion |
| BEE | Black Economic Empowerment |
| Capex | capital expenditure |
| CBD | Central Business District |
| CDS | credit default swap |
| DBSA | Development Bank of South Africa |
| DEAT | Department of Environmental Affairs and Tourism |
| DLA | Department of Land Affairs, which subsequently became Department of Rural Development and Land Affairs |
| DME | Department of Minerals and Energy |
| DWAF | Department of Water Affairs and Forestry |
| EMS | electromagnetic spectrum |
| EBIT | Earnings before Interest and Tax |
| EBITDA | Earnings before Interest Tax and Depreciation |
| ETS | Emissions Trading Schemes |
| GDP | Gross Domestic Product |
| GMF | gold mines (tax) formula |
| GST | General Sales Tax |
| Ha | hectare |
| ICASA | The Independent Communications Authority of South Africa |
| JSE | Johannesburg Stock Exchange |
| KZN | KwaZulu-Natal |
| LBO | leveraged buy out |
| LSU | large stock unit e.g. mature cow or horse |
| M&A | mergers and acquisitions |
| MLRA | Marine Living Resources Act 18 of 1998 |
| MPRDA | Mineral and Petroleum Resources Development Act |
| MRRT | Mineral Resources Rent Tax |
| MST | Movimento dos Trabalhadores Rurais Sem Terra (Landless Worker's Movement) |
| Mtpa | million tonnes per annum |
| NDP | National Development Plan |

NGO        Non-governmental Organisation
OECD       Organisation for Economic Cooperation and Development
PAYE       Pay As You Earn taxation
PRRT       Petroleum Resources Rental Tax – enacted by Australian
           Government instead of RSPT.
PWD        Public Works Department
RDP        Reconstruction and Development Plan
RR         Resource rentals
RSPT       Resources Super Profits Tax – mooted then discarded by
           Australian Government in mid-2010
SAA        South African Airways
SABC       South African Broadcasting Corporation
SARS       South African Revenue Services
SMME       Small, Medium and Micro-sized Enterprises
STC        Secondary Tax on Companies
TAC        Total Allowable Catch
TAE        Total Applied Effort
3G         3rd Generation
UIF        Unemployment Insurance Fund
VAT        Value-added Tax

# Bibliography

Bishop, M. (2000). *Pocket Economist.* The Economist in association with Profile Books, London.

Bosquet, B. (2002). *The Role of Natural Resources in Fundamental Tax Reform in the Russian Federation*: policy working paper # WPS 2807.*www-wds.worldbank.org. (accessed 5 March 2011).*

Cahill, K. (2001). *Who Owns Britain?* Edinburgh: Canongate Books.

Churchill, W. (1957). *A History of the English-Speaking Peoples.* London: Cassell & Co.

Churchill, W. (1970). *The People's Rights.* London: Jonathan Cape.

d'Entrèves, A.P. (1970). *Natural Law: An Introduction to Legal Philosophy.* Introduction by Cary J. Nederin. London: Hutchinson.

Dunkley, G.R.A. (1990). *That All May Live.* Johannesburg: A. Whyte Publishers.

Foldvary, F. (2007). *The Depression of 2008.* Berkley California: The Gutenberg Press.

Gaffney, M. (2009). *After the Crash – Designing a Depression-Free Economy.* Wiley-Blackwell.

Gaffney, M. and Harrison, F. (1994). *The Corruption of Economics.* London: Shepheard-Walwyn.

Haigh, G. (2005). *Fat Cats: The Strange Cult of the CEO.* New York: Thunder's Mouth Press (an imprint of Avalon Publishing Group, Inc.).

Harrison, F. (2010). *Boom Bust, House Prices, Banking and the Depression of 2010.* London: Shepheard-Walwyn.

Harrison, F. (2008). *The Silver Bullet.* London: The International Union for Land Value Taxation.

Hodgkinson, B. (2008). *A New Model of the Economy.* London: Shepheard-Walwyn.

Jupp, Sir Kenneth. (1997). *Stealing Our Land: Law, Rent, and Taxation.* London: Othila Press.

Letsoalo, E. (1987). *Land Reform in South Africa.* Johannesburg: Skotaville Publishers.

Li, K.T. (1988). *Economic Transformation of Taiwan (R.O.C.)* London: Shepheard-Walwyn.

O'Rourke, P.J. (2007). *P.J. O'Rourke on The Wealth of Nations.* London: Atlantic Books.

Peston, R. (2008). *Who Runs Britain?* London: Hodder & Stoughton.

Ricardo, D. (1969). *The Principles of Political Economy and Taxation.* London: Dent.

Riley, D. (2001). *Taken for a Ride.* London: Centre for Land Policy Studies.

Smith, A. (1994). *An Inquiry into the Nature and Causes of the Wealth of Nations.* New York: Modern Library.

*Technical Committee on Mining Taxation, Report of the.* (1988). Chairman: Dr G. Marais, Deputy Minister of Finance, Department of Finance. Established in terms of the recommendations of the Margo Commission by the Minister of Finance on 20 November 1986.

# Glossary of Terms Used

## Auction mechanism

In a situation where the full rent is collected annually land prices tend to zero, which means that the relative value matrix in the form currently provided by land prices will not be available. Land pricing will be on the basis of annual resource rentals payable. It may be necessary, especially in the case of large transactions, to auction sites – including mineral rights, landing slots and the electromagnetic spectrum – to establish current market values. As regards the improvements, their value would have to be agreed or established up front, with bidders at the auction having to provide the ability to pay so as to prevent frivolous or mischievous bids.

## Margin

When we talk about the 'the margin' in this book, we use it in two senses. First, we mean the least favourable site or location on which a specific economic activity is still viable. For example, a retailer of cheap imported clothing may be viable in a small rural town; a retailer of better quality clothing may not go beyond a large provincial town, and a high-fashion retailer beyond a metropolitan area. Those would be the 'margin' for these specific business enterprises.

The second sense is that where an entire region is 'beyond the margin' for most commerce and industry, the region as such (including rural towns) could be described as sub-marginal, and where typically the quantum of housing and population is not supported by any meaningful economic activity, but mainly by erratic economic activity (subsistence agriculture, seasonal work, hawking, etc.) and/or social grants.

## Natural law

Cicero's definition is quoted in Chapter 16 while the following is attributed to Edmund Burke: 'the principles that guide us in public and in private, as they are not of our devising, but moulded into the nature and essence of things, will endure with the sun and moon – long, very long after Whig and Tory, Stuart and Brunswick, and all such miserable baubles and playthings of the hour, are banished from existence and from memory.'[1]

In general terms natural law refers to reason as applied to discover the ideal and just laws which should govern human society: it is therefore distinct from the study of laws as they are (positive Law) and seeks to provide an objective standard against which the latter can be judged.

For a concept relatively unknown to the modern person in the street, there is a surprising amount of literature; including, from a more positive standpoint, *Natural Law* by Alessandro d'Entrèves.

The authors' standpoint is unambiguously in favour, while acknowledging that much controversy has arisen in the past due to specious claiming of natural law status for countless imposters.

## Natural rent/economic rent/rent/locational advantage

These terms have been used interchangeably with resource rentals. See also Chapter 3 (last para. 'Discussion of a progressive formula tax') for a discussion on various concepts relating to, and definitions of, economic rent. Our preferred definition of rent is the 'difference between what can be produced on the least productive site in use and all others assuming equal inputs of labour and capital.'

## Natural resources

These include attributes of a particular area that pre-exist human occupation, but are necessary for humans' continued occupation of that area, or at least would contribute to the health and well-being of people living there. Land is obviously the most important resource, but is not sufficient in itself; rainfall, fertile soil and a reasonable climate are also necessary but are not considered to be natural resources for the purposes of this book, as they cannot be privatised by individuals. Other natural resources considered are: minerals, water (riparian rights), coastal waters, air space and the electromagnetic spectrum.

## OPR/ERF

Operating Profit: Revenue/EBIT: Revenue Formula. These are similar, although one needs to remember that, with the gold mines, capital

---

1 Stanliss, 333Peter J. in Edmund Burke's Legal Erudition and Practical Politics: Ireland and the American Revolution. *Political Science Reviewer*, Fall 2006 edition.

expenditure needs to be recouped before becoming liable for tax. With EBIT, the operating profit takes into account regular depreciation. In both cases, costs extraneous to production, such as finance, are ignored.

## Resource rentals

This refers to the rental that arises on the relative value (e.g. the locational value in the case of land) of any unit of natural resource, excluding improvements effected by the owner of that resource (i.e. the unimproved value). The capitalised value of this return before commencement of natural resource rental collection (e.g. land price), in the hands of a private owner would decrease with increases in resource rent, theoretically becoming zero with the highest rental an owner would be willing to pay. In many cases these rentals could be – and increasingly are – determined by public auction or tender, e.g. where portions of the electromagnetic spectrum are made available to media and telecommunication companies as well as rights to exploit oil or natural gas deposits.

## Site value rating

In South Africa this is the term used to describe the municipal rating system used by Gauteng and other municipalities up to the early 'noughties', whereby residents paid according to the unimproved value of the land only that they owned – regardless of whether they were using it efficiently or at all. In a small way, therefore, it was a way of capturing some of the natural rent and worked very well. Whereas some jurisdictions rate on improvements only, rating on both land and improvements is more common.

## Taxable capacity

In modern tax parlance, taxes are predicated mainly on the basis of certain cash flows. For example, if an entity such as a corporation or an individual receives income and/or has expenditure, they are considered to have taxable capacity. Obvious exceptions are local property taxes, estate duties and customs and excise duties. At a superficial level, the cash-flow basis appears to be completely fair and equitable; customs and excise duties are paid by importers and manufacturers and built into the cost of goods (and therefore are unseen and ignored), while property taxes and estate duties are considered to be inequitable because there is no related cash flow.

This, however, is indeed a very superficial view. In a country like

South Africa where vast numbers of people live on what we have described as 'the margin', their meagre income (from state grants, subsistence agriculture, hawking, etc.) is taxed when this is spent, either by way of VAT or on increased prices caused by fuel levies, customs and excise duties and a myriad of other taxes that are built into the cost of goods and services.

For the purposes of this book, 'taxable capacity' refers to the relative advantage conferred by the value of a site. Thus prime sites with high values have the greatest taxable capacity, whereas sites at or below the margin have little or no taxable capacity. In due course the term 'rentable capacity' might come to be preferred.

## Unimproved site value

This relates to the value of a unit of a natural resource before any improvements have been made. It is a relative value that is derived from the perceived value of that unit to a prospective user. Thus, land near Clifton Beach may be 'worth' $R25,000/m^2$, but in a small rural town only $R100/m^2$. This relative value can be due to a number of factors such as: local amenities (infrastructure, schools, hospitals, administrative services, levels of law and order, etc.), aesthetic beauty, soil fertility, proximity to markets and suppliers, potential size of the market, perceived value of mineral wealth, etc. None of these factors can be changed or controlled by the owner of a unit of a natural resource. As with any unit of fixed property, such perceived values can be used to determine their resource rental, which may, of course, change over time with changing perceptions and surrounding local conditions.

# Index

# The Authors

## Stephen Meintjes

Stephen Meintjes studied law at Stellenbosch, and at Oxford where he was a Rhodes Scholar. He was active in student and opposition politics until the late Eighties when he became increasingly concerned with what would happen to the economy after political transition. This led to the publication of a precursor to the present book, *The Trial of Chaka Dlamini – an Economic Scenario for the New South Africa*, co-authored with Michael Jacques (Amagi Books, Johannesburg, 1990). Stephen has spent most of his career in investment research and management and is frequently quoted in the media, including radio and television. He is currently Head of Research for Imara S.P. Reid.

## Michael Jacques (Late)

Michael was a chartered accountant with Peat, Marwick and Mitchell, before lecturing at the Faculty of Commerce at the University of the Witwatersrand. Together with Stephen Meintjes, he co-authored *The Trial of Chaka Dlamini – an Economic Scenario for the New South Africa*. He worked with Stephen on natural resources rental collection, this book, and proposals to the Treasury on windfall taxes, royalties and general tax reform, until his death in January, 2009.